Getting Started

With Microsoft

Access 2.0

For Windows

Getting Started With Microsoft Access 2.0 For Windows

Henry Gaylord
Pace Computer Learning Center
School of Computer Science and Information Systems
Pace University

Babette Kronstadt
David Sachs
Series Editors
Pace Computer Learning Center
School of Computer Science and Information Systems
Pace University

JOHN WILEY & SONS, INC.
New York / Chichester / Brisbane / Toronto / Singapore

Trademark Acknowledgments:

Microsoft is a registered trademark of Microsoft Corporation
Excel for Windows is a trademark of Microsoft Corporation
Windows is a trademark of Microsoft Corporation
Word for Windows is a trademark of Microsoft Corporation
Microsoft Access is a registered trademark of Microsoft Corporation
1-2-3 is a registered trademark of Lotus Development Corporation
WordPerfect is a registered trademark of WordPerfect Corporation
IBM is a registered trademark of International Business Machines Corporation
Paradox is a registered trademark of Borland International, Inc.

Portions of this text were adapted from other texts in this series and from Pace University Computer Learning Center manuals.

ISBN 0-471-12056-1

Printed in the United States of America

10 9 8 7 6 5 4

Preface

Getting Started with Microsoft Access 2.0 for Windows provides a step-by-step, hands-on introduction to *Microsoft Access*. It is designed for students with basic PC and Windows skills who have little or no experience with *Microsoft Access*. Basic skills are taught in short, focused activities which build to create actual applications.

Key Elements

Each lesson in *Getting Started with Microsoft Access 2.0 for Windows* uses eight key elements to help students master specific database concepts and skills and develop the ability to apply them in the future.

- **Learning objectives**, located at the beginning of each lesson, focus students on the skills to be learned.
- **Project orientation** allows the students to meet the objectives while creating a real-world application. Skills are developed as they are needed to complete projects, not to follow menus or other artificial organization.
- **Motivation** for each activity is supplied so that students learn *why* and *when* to perform an activity, rather than how to follow a series of instructions by rote.
- **Bulleted lists of step-by-step general procedures** introduce the tasks and provide a handy, quick reference.
- **Activities with step-by-step instructions** guide students as they apply the general procedures to solve the problems presented by the projects.
- **Screen displays** provide visual aids for learning and illustrate major steps.
- **Independent projects** provide opportunities to practice newly acquired skills with decreasing level of support.
- **Feature reference** at the end of the book allows students to have a single place to look for commands to carry out the activities learned in the book.

Stop and Go

The steps for completing each *Microsoft Access* feature introduced in this book are covered in two ways. First they are described clearly in a bulleted list, which can also be used for reference. Then the steps are used in a hands-on Activity. Be sure to wait until the Activity to practice each feature on the computer.

Taking Advantage of Windows

Getting Started with Microsoft Access 2.0 for Windows provides a balanced approach to using a Windows application. The use of the mouse and buttons for carrying out commands is emphasized. However, familiarity with the menus is developed so that students can take advantage of the wider range of options available in menu commands.

Shortcut keys are introduced when appropriate. The convenient **Feature Reference** at the end of the book summarizes menu commands and mouse and keyboard shortcuts for each of the features covered in the lessons. Students can use this both to review procedures or learn alternate ways of carrying out commands.

Flexible Use

Getting Started with Microsoft Access 2.0 for Windows is designed for use in an introductory computer course. As a "getting started" book, it does not attempt to cover all of the features of the software. However, the topics included in later lessons allow instructors to provide opportunities for individualized or extra credit assignments or use the book in short courses focused specifically on *Microsoft Access*. While designed to be used in conjunction with lectures or other instructor supervision, basic concepts are explained so that students can use the book in independent learning settings. Students should be able to follow specific instructions with minimal instructor assistance.

Data Disk

Data disks are provided to the instructors for distribution to the students. A few of the projects use files from the data disk so that the focus of the lesson is on the new skills being learned in each project. Initial projects require that students develop applications from the beginning, and later projects build on those applications. Enough explanation is always included so that students understand the full application that they are building.

Acknowledgments

While the author has written the words, this book represents the work and effort of many individuals and organizations. Babette Kronstadt provided energetic leadership and orchestrated the production of not only this book but all of Pace's books in the *Getting Started* series. Nancy Treuer, Sally Sobolewski, and Matthew Poli worked miracles with the layout and text formatting. Katherine Sherer patiently and exhaustingly examined the text and activities, locating many of my errors and offering innumerable suggestions.

I received enormous institutional support from Pace University and the School of Computer Science and Information Systems (CSIS). In particular, much personal support and personal leadership for the work has come from the Dean, Dr. Susan Merritt.

From another perspective, this book is also a product of the Pace Computer Learning Center which is a loose affiliation of approximately 15 faculty and staff who have provided more than 7,000 days of instruction to over 60,000 individuals in corporate settings throughout the United States and around the world during the past nine years. My shared experiences in the development and teaching of these non-credit workshops, as well as credit bearing courses through the Pace University School of Computer Science and Information Systems, was an ideal preparation for writing this book. In addition, none of the books for Wiley would have been possible without the continuing support of Dr. David Sachs, the director of the Computer Learning Center.

The *Getting Started* series has received many invaluable comments and suggestions from instructors at other schools who were kind enough to review our earlier books and offer their suggestions for the current books. My thanks go to Jack D. Cundiff, Horry-Georgetown Technical College; Pat Fenton, West Valley College; Sharon Ann Hill, University of Maryland; E. Gladys Norman, Linn-Benton Community College; and Barbara Jean Silvia, University of Rhode Island.

My thanks also go to the many people at Wiley who provided needed support and assistance. The editor, Beth Lang Golub, and editorial program assistant, David Kear, have been very responsive to concerns, and supportive of all of the Pace Computer Learning Center's writing projects. Andrea Bryant was invaluable in her management of all aspects of the production of this book.

Henry Gaylord

February, 1995
White Plains, New York

Contents

INTRODUCTION 1

Objectives ... 1
Purpose of the Introduction ... 1
What is Microsoft Access? ... 1
Getting Started ... 1
The Access Welcome Screen ... 2
The Access Screen ... 4
The Mouse Pointer ... 6
Using the Menu ... 7
Dialog Boxes ... 8
Using the Toolbar Buttons ... 12
Terms ... 14
The Help System ... 15
Exiting from Access ... 20
Conventions Followed in this Book ... 21
Summary ... 22
Key Terms ... 22
Independent Projects ... 22
Independent Project I.1: The Cue Cards ... 22

1 CREATING DATABASES AND TABLES 25

Objectives ... 25
Project Description ... 25
The Database ... 26
Creating Objects ... 27
Filling in the Table Grid ... 27
Data Types ... 28
Saving the Design ... 31
Entering Data in a Table ... 33
Modifying a Table ... 35
Primary Key Fields ... 36
Printing a Table ... 38
Summary ... 39
Key Terms ... 39
Independent Projects ... 39
Independent Project 1.1: The School Newspaper ... 39
Independent Project 1.2: The Book Store ... 41
Independent Project 1.3: The Real Estate Office ... 43
Independent Project 1.4: The Veterinarian ... 45

2 WORKING WITH A TABLE'S DATA 47

Objectives ... 47
Project Description ... 47
Opening a Database ... 48
Moving About Within a Table ... 48
Sizing Fields ... 50
Moving Fields ... 52
Editing a Table's Data ... 54
Searching for Records ... 56

Deleting Records ... 60
Summary ... 61
Key Terms ... 62
Independent Projects ... 62
Independent Project 2.1: The School Newspaper ... 62
Independent Project 2.2: The Book Store ... 63
Independent Project 2.3: The Real Estate Office ... 65
Independent Project 2.4: The Veterinarian ... 66

3 MULTIPLE TABLES 67

Objectives ... 67
Project Description ... 67
Importing a Table from Another Access Database ... 68
Importing Additional Tables ... 70
Attaching a Table from Another Access Database ... 71
Renaming a Table ... 73
A Relational System of Tables ... 74
Creating a Form ... 76
Using a Form ... 79
A Multi-Table Form ... 81
Summary ... 85
Key Terms ... 86
Independent Projects ... 86
Independent Project 3.1: The School Newspaper ... 86
Independent Project 3.2: The Book Store ... 88
Independent Project 3.3: The Real Estate Office ... 90
Independent Project 3.4: The Veterinarian ... 92

4 QUERIES 95

Objectives ... 95
Project Description ... 95
Querying a Table ... 96
A Single Table Query ... 96
Selecting the Fields ... 99
Sorting the Dynaset ... 101
Removing a Field from the QBE Grid ... 103
Sorting by Two Fields That are not in Left to Right Order ... 104
Saving a Query Design ... 106
Selecting Matching Records with a Query ... 106
The Inequality Symbols in Queries ... 108
Print Previewing a Query Result ... 110
Text Criteria in a Query ... 111
Date Criteria in a Query ... 112
Summary ... 114
Key Terms ... 114
Independent Projects ... 114
Independent Project 4.1: The School Newspaper ... 114
Independent Project 4.2: The Book Store ... 116
Independent Project 4.3: The Real Estate Office ... 118
Independent Project 4.4: The Veterinarian ... 120

5 MULTIPLE CRITERIA AND MULTI-TABLE QUERIES 121

Objectives ... 121
Project Description ... 121

Multiple Criteria 121
Including Every Field in the QBE Grid 125
Additional Query Operators 126
The Between Operator 127
The Not Operator 128
The Null Operator 129
Wild Cards 130
Multiple Table Queries 133
Altering a Query 139
Summary 140
Key Terms 140
Independent Projects 141
Independent Project 5.1: The School Newspaper 141
Independent Project 5.2: The Book Store 143
Independent Project 5.3: The Real Estate Office 144
Independent Project 5.4: The Veterinarian 146

6 REPORTS 147

Objectives 147
Project Description 147
Designing a Report 148
The Report Wizard 149
Changing a Report Design 155
Designing a Groups/Totals Report 158
Changing the Formatting of Controls 163
Designing Mailing Labels 166
Summary 171
Key Terms 171
Independent Projects 171
Independent Project 6.1: The School Newspaper 171
Independent Project 6.2: The Book Store 173
Independent Project 6.3: The Real Estate Office 176
Independent Project 6.4: The Veterinarian 177

7 CALCULATIONS AND ACTION QUERIES 179

Objectives 179
Project Description 179
Calculation in Queries 179
Summary Calculations in Queries 183
Querying a Query 185
Grouping in Calculations 186
The Update Query 189
The Delete Query 192
Summary 194
Key Terms 195
Independent Projects 195
Independent Project 7.1: The School Newspaper 195
Independent Project 7.2: The Book Store 197
Independent Project 7.3: The Real Estate Office 200
Independent Project 7.4: The Veterinarian 202

Appendix: Features Reference 203

Index 207

Students and Instructors

Before Getting Started Please Note:

WINDOWS INTRODUCTION

Getting Started with Microsoft Access 2.0 for Windows assumes that students are familiar with basic Windows concepts and can use a mouse. If not, instructors may consider using the companion book, *Getting Started with Windows 3.1*, also published by Wiley. Windows has a tutorial which can also help students learn or review basic mouse and Windows skills. To use the Windows Tutorial: 1) turn on the computer; 2) type: **win** or select Windows from the menu or ask your instructor how to start Windows on your system; 3) press the **ALT** key; 4) press the **H** key; 5) when the **Help** menu opens, type a **W**; and 6) follow the tutorial instructions, beginning with the mouse lesson if you do not already know how to use the mouse, or going directly to the Windows Basic lesson if you are a skilled mouse user.

STUDENT DATA DISKS

Most of the projects in this book require the use of a Data Disk. Instructors who have adopted this text are granted the right to distribute the files on the Data Disk to any student who has purchased a copy of the text. Instructors are free to post the files to standalone workstations or a network or provide individual copies of the disk to students. This book assumes that students who use their own disk know the name of the drive that will contain it. When using a network, students must know the name(s) of the drives and directories which will be used to open and save files.

SETUP OF WINDOWS AND ACCESS

One of the strengths of Windows and *Access* is the ease with which the screens can be customized. This, however, can cause problems for students trying to learn how to use the programs. This book assumes that Windows and *Access* have been installed using the default settings and that they have not been changed by those using the programs. Some hints are given about where to look if the computer responds differently from the way it would under standard settings. If your screen looks different from those in the book, ask your instructor or laboratory assistant to check that the defaults have not been changed.

VERSION OF THE SOFTWARE

All of the screenshots in this book have been taken using Version 2.0 of *Microsoft Access*. If you are using a different version, the appearance of your screen and the effect of some commands may vary slightly from those used in this book.

Microsoft Access

Introduction

Objectives

In this lesson you will learn:

- What a database is
- How to start Microsoft *Access*
- The parts of the screen
- How to use the menus and dialog boxes in *Access*
- How to use the toolbar in *Access*
- Database terminology
- How to use the Help System
- How to exit from *Access*
- The typographical conventions used in this book

PURPOSE OF THE INTRODUCTION

Unlike the other lessons in this book which contain specific steps to complete database projects, this introduction will discuss databases and Microsoft *Access* in general. It will start with how to get *Access* running, review the Windows aspects of *Access*, point out the features that are different from other Windows programs you may have used, and examine the Help system. It will also explain several terms that are used in database work. The final section describes the typographical conventions used by this book.

WHAT IS MICROSOFT *ACCESS*?

Every business and institution needs to keep lists of facts. A customer list, an inventory list, a sales invoice list, and a list of course enrollments would be but four examples. Such lists are called *databases*, and the facts and figures they contain are called *data*. To work with these databases on the computer, businesses and institutions, as well as individuals, use database programs. One such program is Microsoft *Access*.

Access is a powerful, yet remarkably straightforward, database tool. It is a *RDBMS*, or Relational Database Management System, which means it handles multiple lists of data simultaneously. It allows you to organize, edit, search for, report on, and perform calculations on your data. Since most people dislike keeping and working on long lists of data on paper, using *Access* on a computer makes an otherwise tedious job quick and painless; many would say fun.

One goal of a database program is the simple creation, maintenance, and organization of data. *Access* will streamline such routine tasks. The ultimate goal of databases is deriving summary information. Examples would include the total of all invoices, a list of customers by state, or the average price for each category of products. *Access* is equally adept at these tasks. This book will explore both the necessary rudimentary jobs, as well as many of the summary tasks.

GETTING STARTED

Access is a Windows program. That is good news, because if you know how to start and work with any other Windows program, you already know a portion of how to work with *Access*. This book assumes you have previously used a mouse, and that you know how to run Windows on the computer you are using, as well as the fundamentals of operating Windows. Any basic procedures that are unique to *Access* will be discussed in this introduction.

Because *Access* is a Windows program, and both *Access* and Windows can be customized in various ways, there might be small differences between the appearance of your screen and the illustrations in this book. For example, the thickness of the frames around the windows can be changed in Windows from the normal 3 dots wide to any number desired. If someone made the frames 20 dots thick, the frame lines would look peculiar in every Windows program, including *Access*. They would still work the same way, however. By simply setting the frame width back to 3, all would appear normal again.

Like any Windows program, there are ways to perform operations with the mouse and with the keyboard. While *Access* was designed for a mouse, occasionally a key combination is easier. This book will favor whichever method is easier, although both ways will be described.

To start *Access*:

- Turn on the computer and start Windows.
- Locate the *Access* icon that represents the program.
- Double-click on the *Access* icon or name. Alternatively, click once to highlight the icon's name, then press the **ENTER** key.

Activity I.1: Starting Access

1. Turn on the computer and start Windows.

Microsoft Access

2. Locate the *Access* icon. In order to find the icon you may need to open the program group that contains the icon by double-clicking on the group icon, or clicking once on the group icon and choosing **Restore** from the control menu that appears.

   The Access icon could be in almost any program group, but the likely candidates would be groups named ***Microsoft Office, Access,*** *or* ***Windows Apps****. If none of those groups contains Access, consult your instructor or lab assistant.*

3. Run *Access* by double-clicking on the *Access* icon or clicking once to highlight the name and pressing the **ENTER** key.

THE *ACCESS* WELCOME SCREEN

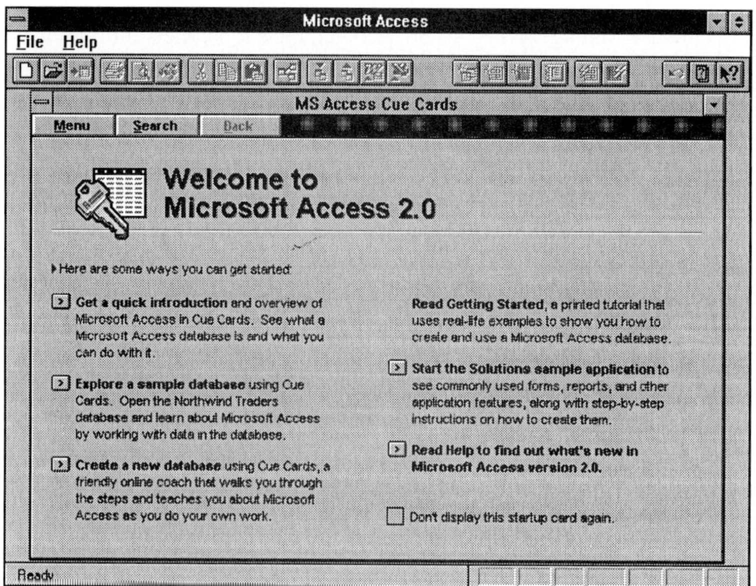

Figure I - 1

When *Access* first begins, you **may** see a "Welcome to Microsoft Access" window like Figure I - 1. While you might want to explore the introductory topics presented on that screen on your own sometime, once you have worked with *Access* for a while you will already know most of the information that screen offers.

At the bottom middle of that window (see Figure I - 1) is a box that can be checked so the screen will not be displayed the next time *Access* is run. If anyone who previously used the computer you are now using checked that box when they used *Access*, this window will not appear. Do not worry if it didn't appear as you do not need the Welcome window; we do not do anything with it. In fact, the next thing we will do is close that window if it is showing.

Closing the Welcome window:

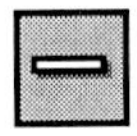

- If the "Welcome to Microsoft Access" screen is displayed, click on the Control Menu at the left end of the line that says "MS Access Cue Cards" and pick **Close** (see Figure I - 2). Be very careful not to pick Close in the Control Menu on the very top line that says "Microsoft Access," as that would close the program instead of the Welcome window. Also, do not press the **ALT+F4** key combination, which is mentioned on the line with Close; that often closes *Access* along with the Cue Card window.

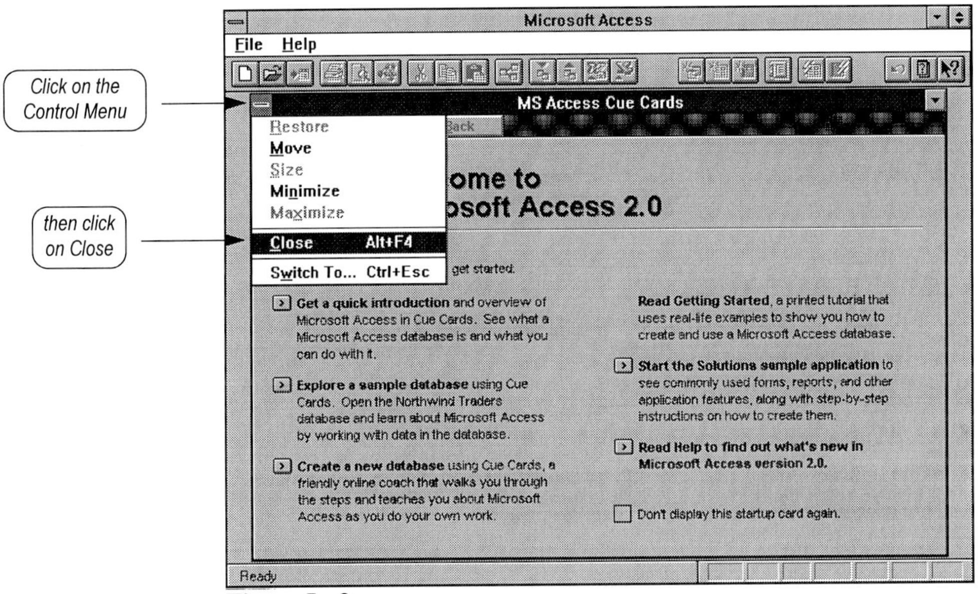

Figure I - 2

Activity I.2: Closing the Welcome window

1. If the "Welcome to Microsoft Access" screen is not displayed, skip directly to step 4.

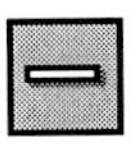

2. Click the left mouse button once on the **Control Menu** on the left end of the line that says "MS Access Cue Cards."

   Be careful ***not*** *to accidentally use the Control Menu on the Microsoft Access line. If you do, Access itself will close, you will return to the Windows Program Manager, and you will need to run Access all over again.*

   If you did accidentally click the wrong Control Menu, click on that dash again to close the menu and try step 2 again.

3. Click the left mouse button once on **Close**.

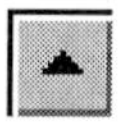

4. If the window that contains *Access* is not covering the entire screen, click the **Maximize** button to make the *Access* workspace as large as possible.

   *The **Maximize** button is the button with the upward pointing triangle at the extreme right end of the line that says Microsoft Access. If the window is already maximized (covering the entire screen), however, the maximize button is replaced by the **Restore** button, a button showing a pair of triangles, one pointing up, the other pointing down. The **Restore** button puts the program back into a less-than-full-screen window.*

THE *ACCESS* SCREEN

Once the Welcome screen is out of the way, you will see the *Access desktop* (see Figure I - 3). Very little is on the desktop until you choose the data you want to work on. It should resemble a typical Windows screen with a *Title Bar* at the top, the *menu bar* on the second line, the *toolbar* (probably) on the third line, and the *Status Bar* at the bottom. (If your screen resembles, but doesn't look exactly like Figure I - 3, we will adjust it in the next section so it matches.)

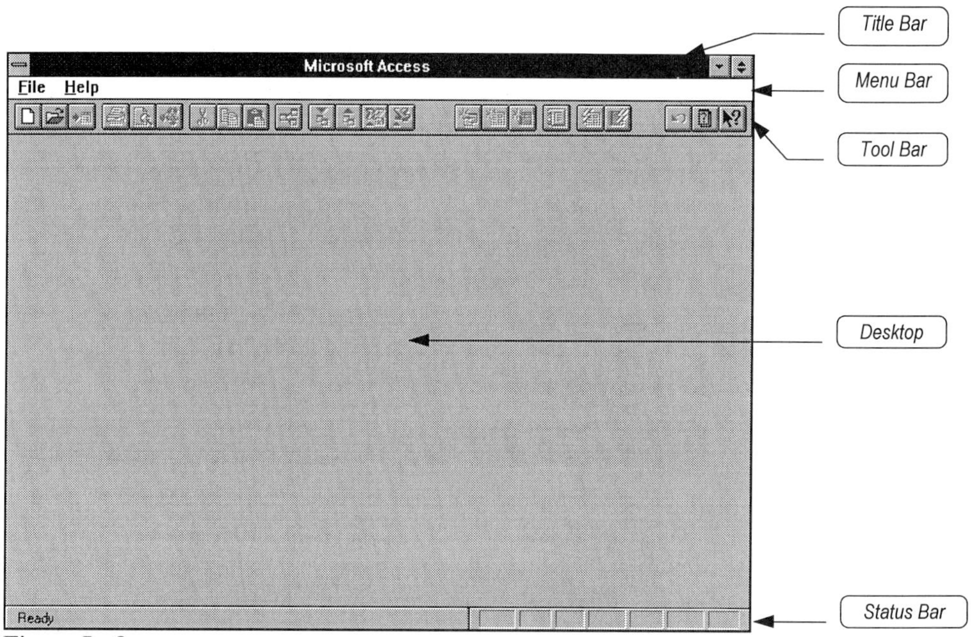

Figure I - 3

The Title Bar

The *Title Bar* is the colored bar at the very top of *Access*' window. It contains the name of the program in the center, the *Application Control Menu* at the left end, and the **Minimize** button and **Restore** button at the right end (see Figure I - 3). These are all common to every Windows program.

The Menu Bar

The second line contains the *Menu Bar* (see Figure I - 3). There are different menu bars for working on different items. *Access* automatically displays the appropriate menu bar. Since no data has been opened on the desktop there is nothing to work on, and *Access* is currently displaying a minimal menu bar. The menu bar is common to all major Windows programs.

The Status Bar

The bottom line of the window is the *Status Bar* (see Figure I - 3). Its left section displays various messages about the current operation. Some of the more useful messages describe the currently highlighted menu selection or the toolbar button that the mouse pointer is on top of. In the indented boxes on its right end *Access* names the toggle keys like Caps Lock and Num Lock, which are currently turned on. It is important to read the status bar during operations in *Access* to obtain its information.

The Scroll Bars

When the length of the listings in any *Access* list extends beyond the size of the window that displays those listings, *Scroll Bars* will automatically appear at the right side of the list, the bottom of the list, or both (see Figure I - 4, Figure I - 9, and Figure I - 19 for examples). To operate the scroll bars, click the mouse on the arrow that points in the desired direction of movement at one end or the other of the scroll bar. The listings in the window will scroll. Continue clicking until the desired rows or columns scroll into view. The box within the scroll bar will travel along it to indicate the position of the listings that currently show relative to the entire set of listings.

The Toolbar

The third line at the top of the window is the *toolbar* (see Figure I - 3). It contains buttons that provide shortcuts to the most frequently used activities in *Access*. The toolbar will automatically switch among the 18 built-in toolbars to supply the appropriate tools for the item you are currently working on.

The last person to use this copy of *Access* might have turned off the option to see the toolbar; if so, you will see in the next section how to make it reappear. Similarly, the last user may have displayed additional toolbars. Normally, only one toolbar should be showing at a time and *Access* automatically selects the appropriate one. Thus, we will remove any extra toolbars in the next section, as well.

The toolbar is normally displayed on the third line at the top of the window. However, some *Access* users prefer other locations on the desktop. It can be moved to any position within the program window by moving the mouse pointer on top of a gap between two buttons or onto the border area next to a button, holding down the left mouse button, and dragging the toolbar someplace else.

To display the default toolbar on the third line of the window:

- With no database on the workspace, open the **FILE** menu and pick **Toolbars**. (Were there a database on the workspace, then **Toolbars** would be in the **VIEW** menu.)
- In the list of toolbars that is displayed (see Figure I - 4), click on the name **Database** to highlight it, and click the **Show** button. (If the toolbar is already showing, that button will say **Hide**.)

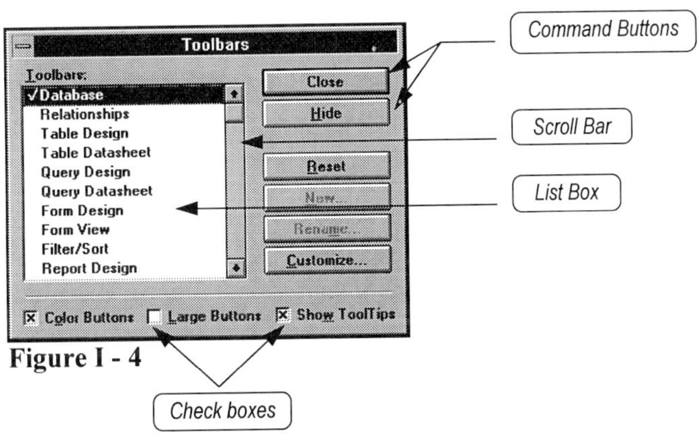

Figure I - 4

- If any other toolbar names have check marks in front of them, click on their names and click the **Hide** button, one at a time. There are more names than can show at one time in the list, so you may need to use the scroll bar to scroll down to look for additional checks.
- Close the list of toolbars by clicking the **Close** button.
- If the toolbar is not on the third line of the window, move the mouse pointer onto the border area beside any button, hold down the left mouse button, and drag the toolbar toward the top of the window. When the mouse pointer is just below the menu bar and about 1/3 of the way across the screen, the dotted line frame that represents the shape the toolbar will take will become a wide rectangle just one button tall. Release the mouse button and the toolbar should be positioned on the third line of the window (see Figure I - 3).

Activity I.3: Displaying the default toolbar

We will verify that only the appropriate toolbar is displayed and make sure it is on the third line at the top of the desktop.

1. Move the mouse pointer on top of the **FILE** menu and click the left mouse button once to open that menu.
2. Within the open menu, move the mouse pointer on top of **Toolbars** and click the left mouse button once to open the list of toolbars.
3. If the top name, **Database**, already has a check to the left of its name, leave it alone and skip to step 6.
4. Click on the top name, **Database**, to highlight it.
5. Click on the button that says **Show**.

   A check mark will appear next to the name in the list and the toolbar will appear on the screen, probably on the third line.
6. If any other name besides **Database** has a check mark, click on that other name and click the **Hide** button. Repeat this step until only **Database** is checked.
7. Close the list by clicking on the **Close** button.

   Only the toolbar shown in Figure I - 3 should be showing.
8. If the toolbar is not on the third line of the window, move the mouse pointer onto the border area beside any button and hold down the left mouse button. Don't release the mouse button until the end of step 9.
9. Drag the toolbar toward the top of the window by moving the mouse with the button still held down. When the mouse pointer is just below the menu bar and about 1/3 of the way across the screen, the dotted line frame that represents the shape the toolbar will take will become a wide rectangle just one button tall. Release the mouse button.

   Your screen should now match Figure I - 3. This is the normal starting configuration for Access.

THE MOUSE POINTER

There are several different shapes for the mouse pointer, depending on what tool or item the mouse pointer is on top of. First, you must not confuse the mouse pointer with the text cursor. The text cursor is a blinking vertical bar that will only be seen within text while you are typing or ready to type. Clicking the mouse button while the mouse pointer is on top of some text will cause the text cursor to move to that spot. Otherwise, there is no relationship between the two.

The various mouse pointer shapes include the regular diagonal arrow ( ) for choosing items on the screen like a menu, various hollow double-headed arrows (for example) for sizing items, a solid black arrow ( ) for picking an entire column or row, a solid black double-headed arrow with a bar between the arrows ( ) for sizing columns, various hands (for example) for moving items on designs like a report design, a diagonal arrow with a question mark ( ) for clicking on an item about which you need to see help, and the hourglass ( ) for those occurrences when an operation will take a little time. These mouse pointers will be described at each place in the book when they are encountered. For the moment, simply be ready to see many different shapes.

USING THE MENU

The menu in Access works exactly the same way any other Windows program's menu operates. That is, you push the mouse until the mouse pointer is on top of the desired choice on the menu bar and click the left mouse button once to open that menu. You then click on the particular choice within the menu to initiate an action. The choices within the menus are commands.

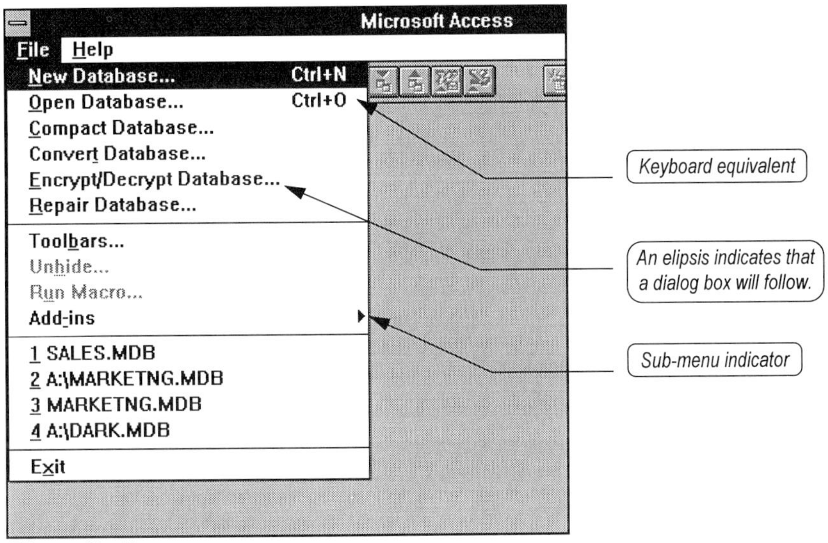

Figure I - 5

Three things can happen when you click on a command. If the choice within the menu has a triangle to the right of its name (see Figure I - 5), a submenu will open (see Figure I - 6) and you may pick from its choices. If the command name ends with an elipsis (...) like most of the commands in the **FILE** menu that is shown in Figure I - 5, a *dialog box* will appear for the selection of options pertaining to that command. Dialog boxes will be fully described in the next section. If just the command name appears on the line within the menu, the command will be carried out directly. If the command is displayed in pale letters, it is currently unavailable; it will become available when the proper items are open on the desktop. Clicking on a pale command will accomplish nothing.

Occasionally you will see a check mark to the left of a menu choice. The check means that command option has been activated. It will remain active as long as the check remains. Clicking a command that is checked would deactivate that action and remove the check mark. Of course, you can click that command yet again to reactivate it.

Also, there are some key combinations that will initiate certain menu commands. Those keys are named at the right of any command that has a keyboard equivalent, like the two shown in the **FILE** menu in Figure I - 5.

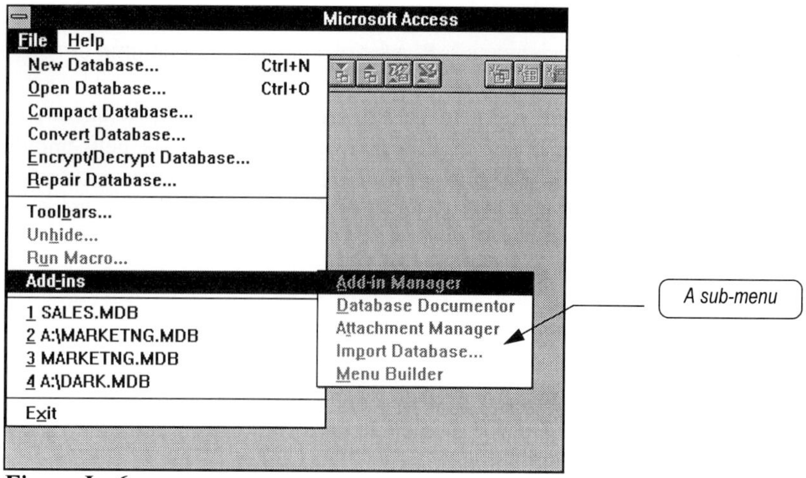

Figure I - 6

To initiate any menu command:

- Push the mouse until the mouse pointer is on top of the desired menu.
- Click the left mouse button once to open that menu.
- In the open menu, move the mouse on top of the desired choice.
- Click the left mouse button once to initiate that command.
- If a submenu opens, choose from it by clicking on the desired command.
- If a dialog box opens, fill out the various items as described in the next section.

KEYBOARD ALTERNATIVE: Press the **ALT** key to activate the menu bar, then tap the underlined letter in the desired menu name to open that menu. Within the menu, tap the underlined letter or digit in the desired command name. Note that in both cases the underlined letter is not necessarily the first letter of the menu or command name.

To close a menu without selecting a command:

- Click the left mouse button again on the menu name. The quickest keyboard method is to press the **ALT** key.

DIALOG BOXES

A dialog box is the Windows tool you use to select options for a command. For example, if the menu command you pick is to open a database, which database do you want, on which disk drive is it recorded, and in which directory?

There are five different active elements that can appear in a dialog box in *Access*. Table I - 1 describes each item, and Figure I - 4 and Figure I - 7 show examples.

Often a text box and a list box will be associated so that clicking on a name in the list automatically types that entry into the text box. When this happens, the list box will be directly underneath the text box and will not have a title of its own, like the **File Name** combination in Figure I - 8.

Element	How it Works	Figure Showing an Example
Text Box	Click within the box and type the desired entry. You may need to remove the default entry that is already in the text box.	Figure I - 7
List Box	Click on the desired item within the ordered list. Sometimes the list will be longer than the allowed space, in which case there will be a scroll bar (see Figure I - 4). To consume less space within the dialog box, the list is often a drop-down list with an arrow you can click to open the list (see Print Quality in Figure I - 7).	Figure I - 4
Check Box	A square box that if turned on will have an X in the box. To switch the setting, click on either the box or the name of the option. You may activate any, all, or none of the check box choices.	Figure I - 4 and Figure I - 7
Option Button (or Radio Button)	A round button that always comes in groups. One option within the group must be selected and only one can be selected. The black dot within the circle denotes the chosen option. Click the mouse on the circle or name of the desired option.	Figure I - 7
Command Button	These are the action buttons. Click the mouse on top of the desired action. The two most common command buttons are OK and Cancel. The OK button carries out the options selected in the dialog box. The Cancel button closes the dialog box without making any of the changes you selected.	Figure I - 4 and Figure I - 7

Table I - 1

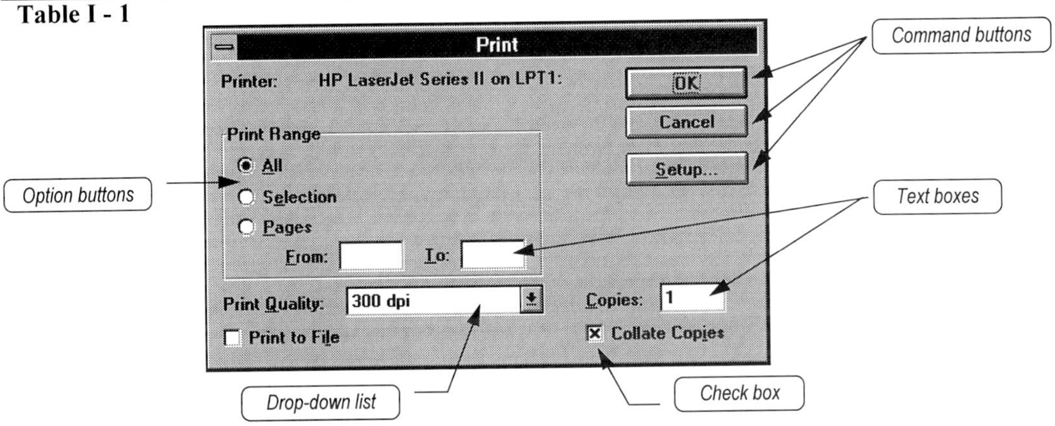

Figure I - 7

Activity I.4: Using the menus and dialog boxes

We will work with a menu and a dialog box to see how their components function. Our task is to open the **marketng.mdb** database that is supplied on the Student Diskette. We will not do anything with the database at this time, except to open and close it.

1. Insert your copy of the Student Exercise Diskette into the A: drive.

   If the disk drive you will be using is some other drive, substitute its name into the instructions in this book each time you see A:.

2. Move the mouse pointer on top of the **FILE** menu and click the left mouse button once to open that menu.

3. Move the mouse pointer on top of **Open Database** within that menu.

   Notice the elipsis (...) that follows the command name, indicating that a dialog box will open so you can pick the various options that accompany opening a database. There is a quick key, ***CTRL+O****, but using the menu is probably easier than trying to remember that key combination.*

4. Click the left mouse button once to choose **Open Database.**

   The Open Database dialog box appears on the desktop (see Figure I - 8).

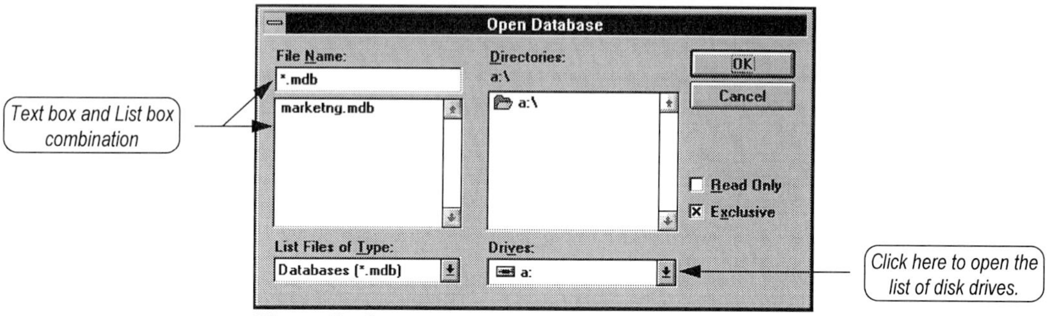

Figure I - 8

5. The currently selected drive is probably not A:. To switch to the A: drive, click the left mouse button once on top of the **drop-down arrow** at the right end of the box titled **Drives:** to open the list of the drives that are available to you (see Figure I - 9).

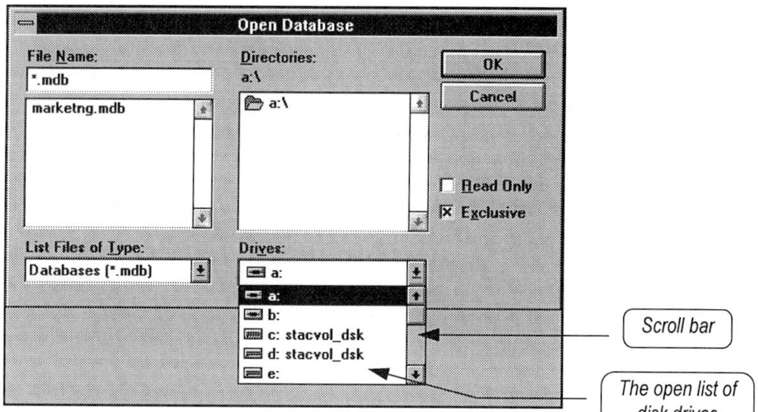

Figure I - 9

The names of some of the drives that will be in your list will probably differ from the names in Figure I - 9. If you use the A: drive, the other names do not matter.

You may need to scroll upward to see the A: name in the list. Click the mouse button one or more times while the mouse pointer is on top of the upward pointing arrow at the top of the scroll bar (see Figure I - 9) to scroll the list until you can see A:. The list will always be in alphabetical order.

6. Click the mouse button once while the mouse pointer is on top of **A:**.

   If you get a ***Cannot read drive a:.*** *message, make sure you have put a diskette in drive A: properly, then click the mouse pointer on the* ***Retry*** *button. If you are not going to use drive A:, click on the* ***Cancel*** *button and select the drive that you will be using.*

*The name **marketng.mdb** should be showing in the File Name list box (see Figure I - 8). Other file names may show as well.*

7. Click the left mouse button once on the name **marketng.mdb** in the list box under File Name.

   The name will be highlighted to show it has been selected and the File Name text box should contain a copy of that name (see Figure I - 10).

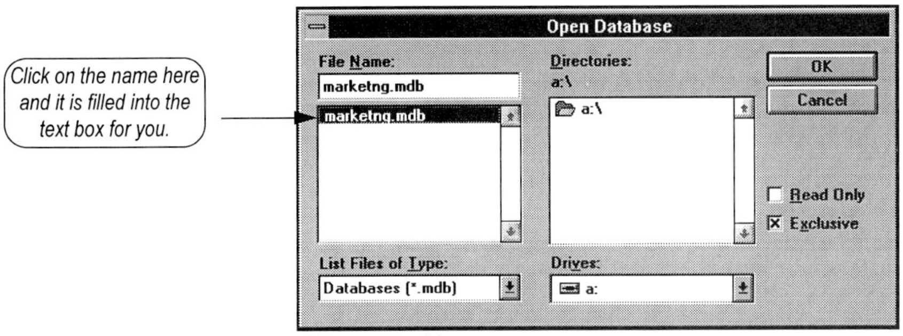

Figure I - 10

8. Click on the **OK** command button to complete the operation.

   Several things happen when the MARKETNG database opens onto the desktop (see Figure I - 11). First, the database appears in a database window. Second, since there is now an object on the desktop, the menu changes to offer the appropriate choices for that object. Third, the toolbar buttons become active. (Had a different object been placed on the desktop, the toolbar would have changed to match the object.)

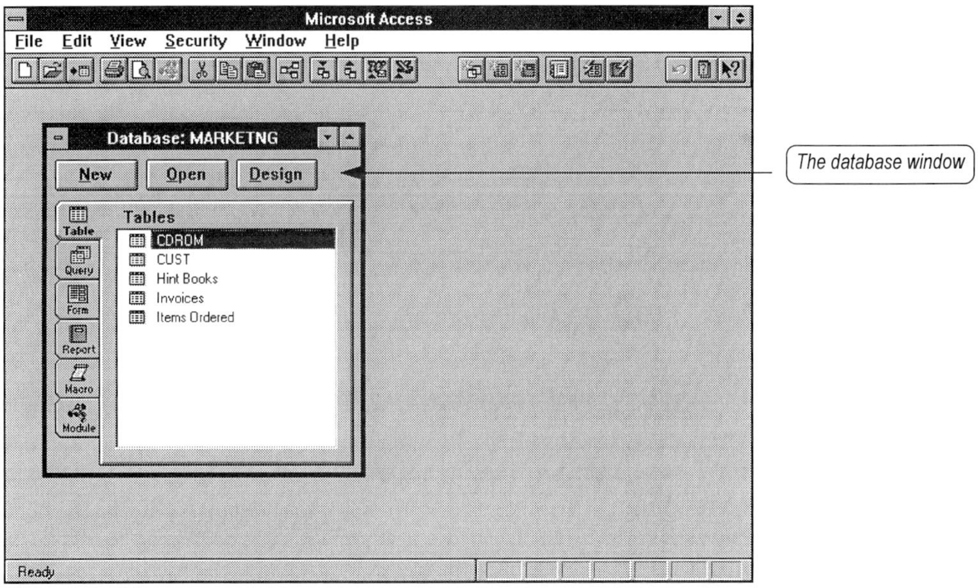

Figure I - 11

9. Move the mouse pointer on top of the **FILE** menu and click the left mouse button once to open that menu.

10. Move the mouse pointer on top of **Close Database** within that menu.

There is no elipsis following the command name, so no dialog box will appear. This command is carried out immediately with no options. Also, there is no quick key listed.

11. Click the left mouse button once to choose **Close Database**.

    The database window disappears and the database is closed. The menu bar reverts to its minimal form. Most of the toolbar buttons become pale, indicating they are inactive. The desktop should again resemble Figure I - 3.

USING THE TOOLBAR BUTTONS

As mentioned previously, the *toolbar buttons*, which are sometimes called tools, are shortcuts to the most common operations in *Access*. There is nothing the toolbar buttons can do that cannot be accomplished through the menus or with a key combination; it's just much quicker with the toolbar buttons. For example, the second button on the toolbar is the **Open Database** tool. Therefore, to initiate opening a database, you could either click on the **FILE** menu and then click on **Open Database** in that menu, or you could make a single click on the toolbar button. Clearly, one click is quicker than two. Often the difference is even greater. For example, making text bold requires four clicks with the menu, but only one with the toolbar.

While the picture on each button is usually easy to associate with the button's purpose, to see a description of any tool on the toolbar, move the mouse pointer on top of the tool without pressing any mouse buttons, and read the Status Bar message. Additionally, the name of the tool will appear in a colored box immediately below the button when the mouse pointer pauses on top of a tool for a second or two. Those names are called "Tool Tips."

To use a toolbar tool:

- Click the left mouse button once while the mouse pointer is on top of the tool.
- If a dialog box opens, fill out the dialog box.

Activity I.5: Using the toolbar tools

To practice with the toolbar tools, we will open the **marketng.mdb** database again, and make some changes to the appearance of one of the tables of data within it.

1. Move the mouse pointer on top of the first button on the toolbar. Do **not** press the mouse button.

   What is the name of this first tool and what does it do? Read the Tool Tips name and the Status Bar description to find out.

2. Move the mouse pointer on top of the second button on the toolbar. Note its name, **Open Database**, and its description, then press the left mouse button once on top of it to activate it.

   *The Open Database dialog box opens, just as it did in the last activity when we chose **FILE/Open Database**. Access should have remembered that we want the A: drivc, but if not, change the drive to A: by repeating steps 5-6 from Activity I.4. If the Student Exercise Diskette is not in the disk drive, you will need to put it in again.*

3. Click the mouse button on top of the name **marketng.mdb** in the list under File Name to have *Access* type in the database name for you.

4. With **marketng.mdb** in the text box under File Name (see Figure I - 10), click the **OK** button.

   The database window appears on the desktop (see Figure I - 11*).*

5. Within the **Database: MARKETNG** window, click the mouse once on top of the name **Hint Books** to highlight that name (see Figure I - 12).

Figure I - 12

6. At the top of the **Database: MARKETNG** window, click the mouse button once on the **Open** button to open the table of data onto the desktop (see Figure I - 13).

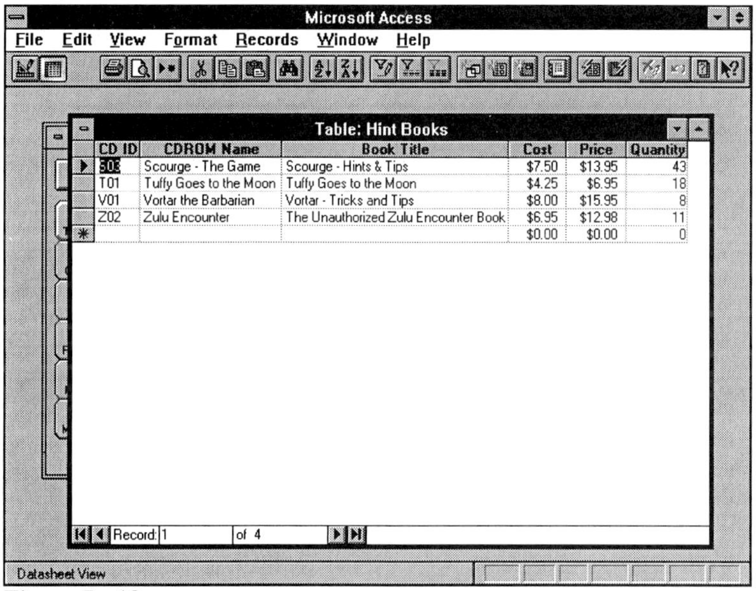

Figure I - 13

You may notice that the menu bar and toolbar have changed to reflect that you are now working on a table rather than the database. This is not important at the moment, so do not be concerned about it.

7. Press the **TAB** key four times to move the highlight from the CD ID column to the **Price** column.

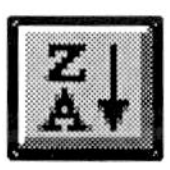

8. On the toolbar, move the mouse pointer on top of the eleventh button, the **Sort Descending** button, and click the mouse button once to activate it.

The listings should be reordered so that they are from highest price to lowest (Figure I - 14). To accomplish this sorting through the menu would have required clicking on the ***RECORDS*** *menu, then* ***Quick Sort*** *within that menu, and finally on* ***Descending*** *in the submenu.*

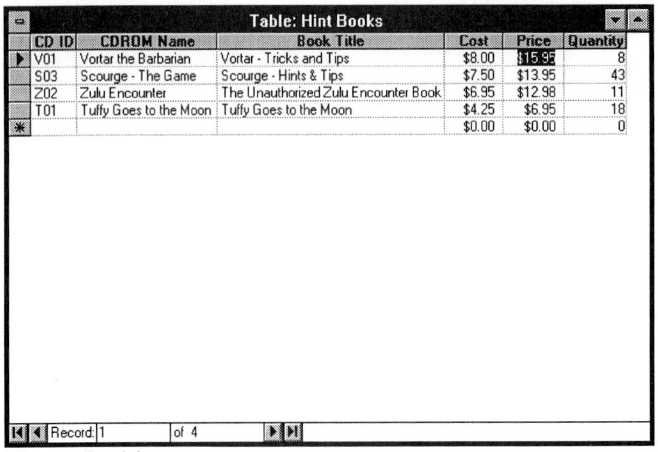

CD ID	CDROM Name	Book Title	Cost	Price	Quantity
V01	Vortar the Barbarian	Vortar - Tricks and Tips	$8.00	$15.95	8
S03	Scourge - The Game	Scourge - Hints & Tips	$7.50	$13.95	43
Z02	Zulu Encounter	The Unauthorized Zulu Encounter Book	$6.95	$12.98	11
T01	Tuffy Goes to the Moon	Tuffy Goes to the Moon	$4.25	$6.95	18
			$0.00	$0.00	0

Figure I - 14

9. Move the mouse pointer on top of the remaining toolbar buttons to see what their names and descriptions are. Do **not** press the mouse button.
10. Click the mouse button on **FILE** to open that menu.
11. Click on **Close** within that menu to close the Hint Books table.
12. Click the mouse button on **FILE** to open that menu again.
13. Click on **Close Database** within that menu to close the **MARKETNG** database.

    The desktop is again empty.

TERMS

There is a set of terms that you will encounter again and again within this or any book that discusses databases. Since it is important to understand what those terms mean, we will describe them here.

- *Data* are the facts and figures that are stored by *Access*. Names, addresses, telephone numbers, and prices, are typical data elements.
- A *table* is a single set of data. It might be a list of customers, a list of sales, or an inventory list.
- A *database* in *Access* (but not necessarily other database products) is a grouping of one or more tables of data, report designs, forms, queries, macros, and modules, comprising an entire accumulation of data and the tools to work with that data.
- A *record* is a single listing within the table of data. Thus, a table with 25 listings has 25 records.
- A *field* is a column of similar data. For example, in Figure I - 13 the Hint Books table has six fields: CD ID, CDROM Name, Book Title, Cost, Price, and Quantity.
- The *field name* is the title or heading given to a field.

THE HELP SYSTEM

As with all major Windows programs, there is an extensive help system available any time you get stuck or need more information about any *Access* topic. Either the Help menu, the F1 key, or the **Help** button on the toolbar will run the Microsoft *Access 2.0* Help program. The Help system is a separate program from *Access*, and, thus, runs in its own window with its own menu bar and buttons. Since the Help system is a part of Windows, if you have used Help in any other Windows program, you already know most of how the Help system works.

Each of the three different methods you can use to run the Help program enters Help in a different place. Additionally, the Help menu contains four choices for different parts of the Help system. (The Help menu's fifth choice, About Microsoft *Access*, opens a dialog box with information about your particular version and copy of *Access*.) Table I - 2 outlines each different method of entering Help.

Method of Starting the Help System	**What You Get**
HELP/Contents	Runs the Help program and displays the Contents page.
HELP/Search	Runs the Help system, displays the Contents page, and opens the Search dialog box.
HELP/Cue Cards	Runs the MS *Access* Cue Cards, a separate part of the Help System that displays on the desktop.
HELP/Technical Support	Runs Microsoft *Access* 2.0 Product Support, a separate section of the Help system
F1	Runs the Help system and displays the page with the topic closest to whatever you were working on in *Access*. This is called context-sensitive help.
Help button on the toolbar	Displays a question mark and arrow mouse pointer. When you click that pointer on any item on the desktop or on a menu choice, it runs the Help system and displays the page explaining whatever item you clicked on.
SHIFT-F1	Displays the question mark and arrow mouse cursor and then behaves the same as the Help button on the toolbar.

Table I - 2

Once in the Help system, a screen can contain three types of items. The information to be read will be displayed as text. A word or phrase that is underlined with a solid line (and will be green on a color screen) is a *jump term.* A *jump term* is the name of another topic that you might want to jump to in order to see the information on its screen. A dotted underlined phrase (which will also be green on a color screen) will pop open a box of information without changing topics. To activate either kind of underlined item, move the mouse pointer on top of the phrase and click the left mouse button once. When you move the mouse on top of an underlined term, the mouse pointer will change to a hand with a pointing index finger ().

In *Access,* the pop-up box from a dotted underlined phrase could contain two different types of information. If the dotted underlined item is part of a sentence, you will get a definition of the word or phrase in a pop-up box. Those terms are called *glossary terms.* When finished reading the definition, click again anywhere on the screen to close the definition box. If the item stands alone on its line, it represents a list of additional topics that are related to the current screen. Since all of the related topics in the pop-up box will be jump terms (underlined with a solid line), you may click on one to jump to that new topic.

The row of buttons immediately below the menu bar includes buttons to jump to the **Contents** screen, open the **Search** dialog box, move **Back** to any previous topic one screen at a time, see the complete **History** of the topics you have viewed in case you want to jump back to one, see the complete **Glossary**, and move to the next (>>) or previous (<<) topic in the current sequence. Additionally, the **FILE** menu contains the choice Print Topic to print the current screen's information.

To use the Help system:

- Click on **HELP** in the menu bar.
- Click on **Contents** in the HELP menu to open the Help system to the Contents page, or **Search** to access the Contents page and open the **Search** dialog box.
- Starting on the Contents page, choose each successive jump term until you arrive at the desired topic.
- In the **Search** dialog box, choose a topic from the list in the upper section and click the **Show Topics** button, and then pick the individual page name in the lower section of the dialog box and click the **Go To** button to jump to that screen of help.

Activity I.6: Using the Help system

To experience the Help system, we will look for information about the Database Window and the HELP button on the toolbar.

1. Click the mouse on the **HELP** menu to open that menu.
2. In the **HELP** menu, click on **Contents**.

   The Help Contents screen appears in its own window (see Figure I - 15).
3. If the help window is not covering the entire screen, click on the **Maximize** button.

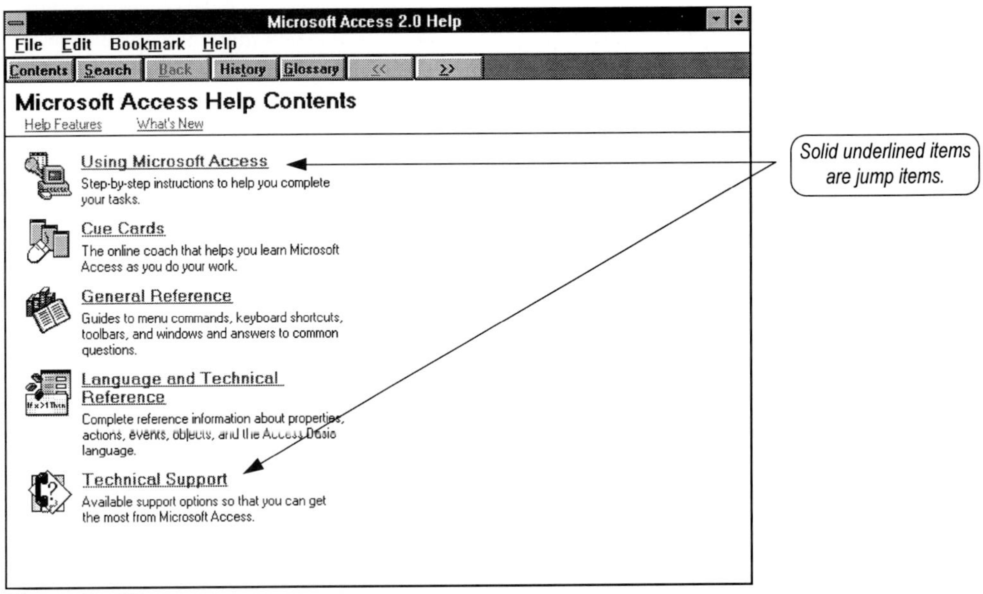

Figure I - 15

4. Move the mouse pointer on top of the **Using Microsoft Access** jump term.

The mouse pointer becomes a hand with a pointing index finger.

5. Click the mouse button on **Using Microsoft Access** to jump to that topic.

   More jump terms appear on the ***Using Microsoft Access*** *screen (see Figure I - 16).*

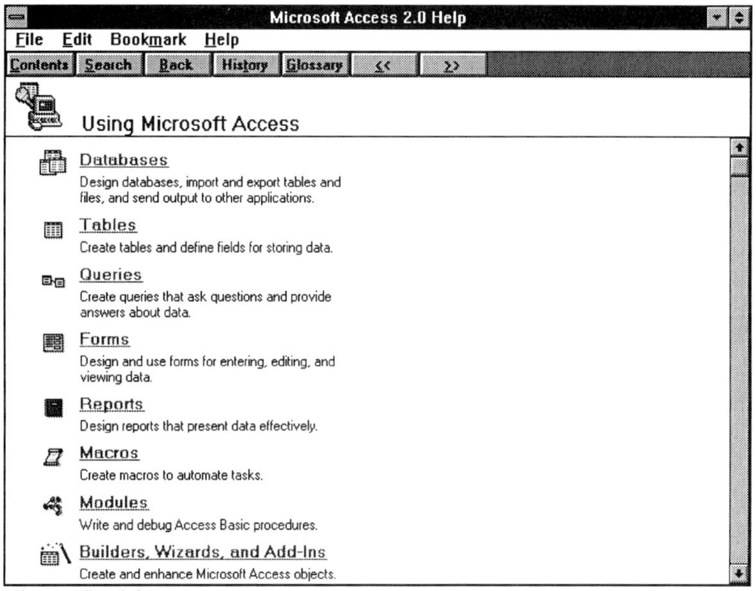

Figure I - 16

6. Click the mouse on **Databases** to jump to that topic.

   The dotted underlined terms in the ***How To's*** *section (see Figure I - 17) will open lists of related topics.*

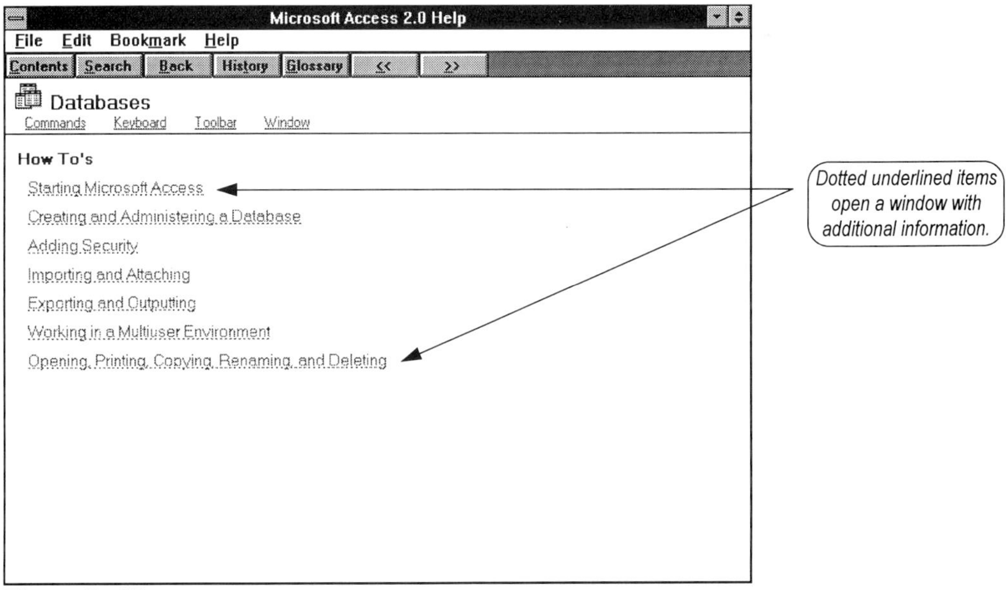

Figure I - 17

7. Click once on **Opening, Printing, Copying, Renaming and Deleting** to see the list of related topics (see Figure I - 18).

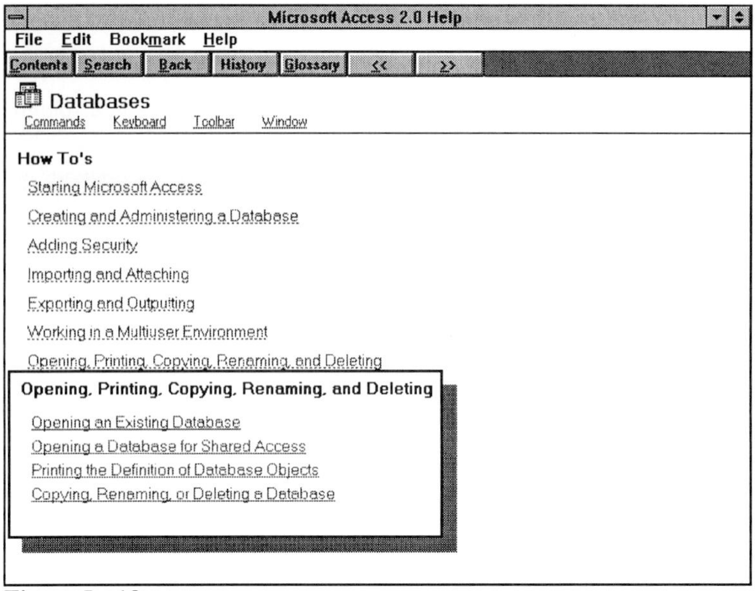

Figure I - 18

8. Click the mouse once outside of the Opening, Printing, Copying, Renaming and Deleting box to close the box without choosing any of its topics.
9. In the upper section of the Databases screen, click on the **Window** jump term.
10. On the Database Window screen (see Figure I - 19), click on the dotted underlined term **database objects**.

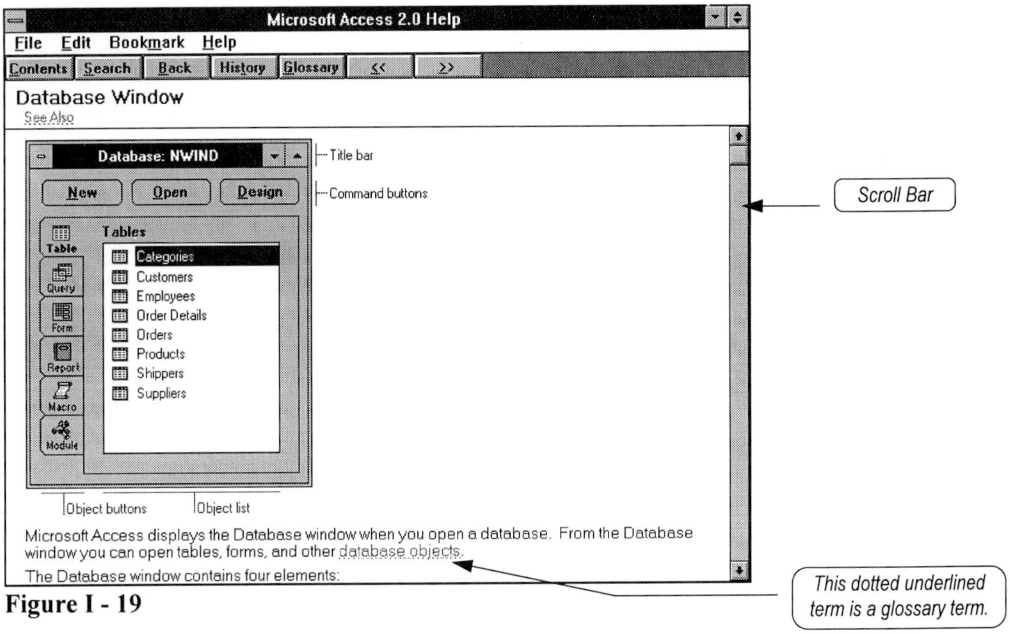

Figure I - 19

The glossary definition of that term appears (see Figure I - 20).

11. Once you have examined its definition, click the mouse one more time to close the box.
12. Click on the **Back** button to return to the previous screen.

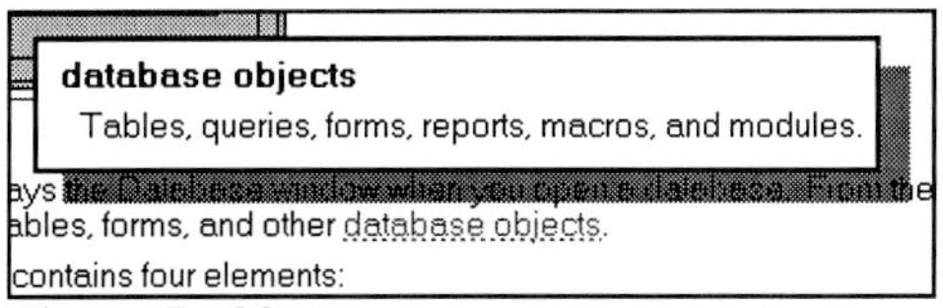

Figure I - 20

13. Click on **Back** again to return to the **Using Microsoft Access** screen.
14. Click on the **Search** button near the top of the window.

    The Search dialog box opens (see Figure I - 21). It has an upper section where you type in the text box or pick from the list the category from which you want to choose a particular topic.

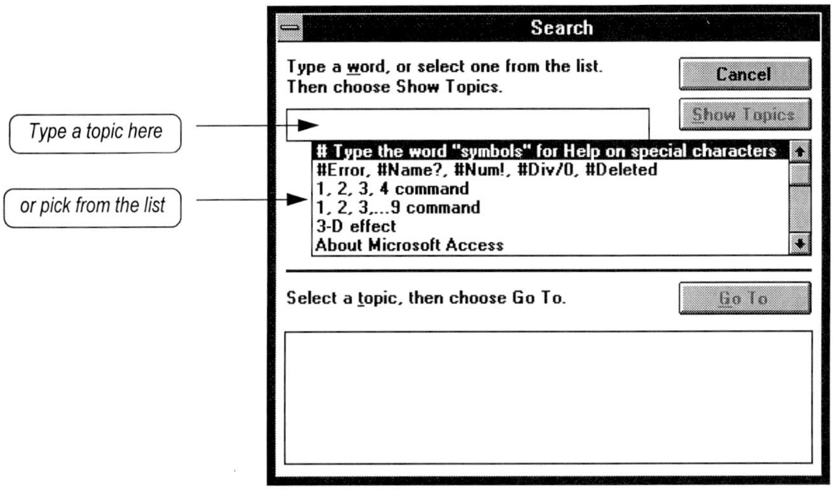

Figure I - 21

15. Type: **help button**
16. Click on the **Show Topics** button.

    The name of only one topic appears in the lower section of the dialog box, ***Miscellaneous Toolbar Buttons*** *(see Figure I - 22).*

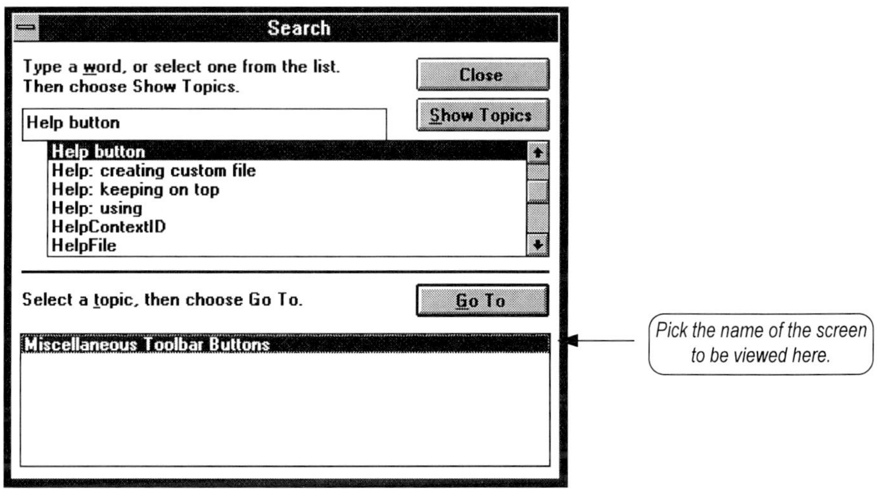

Figure I - 22

17. Since the highlight is already on **Miscellaneous Toolbar Buttons**, click the **Go To** button.

    The Help system jumps to the ***Miscellaneous Toolbar Buttons*** *screen (see Figure I - 23).*

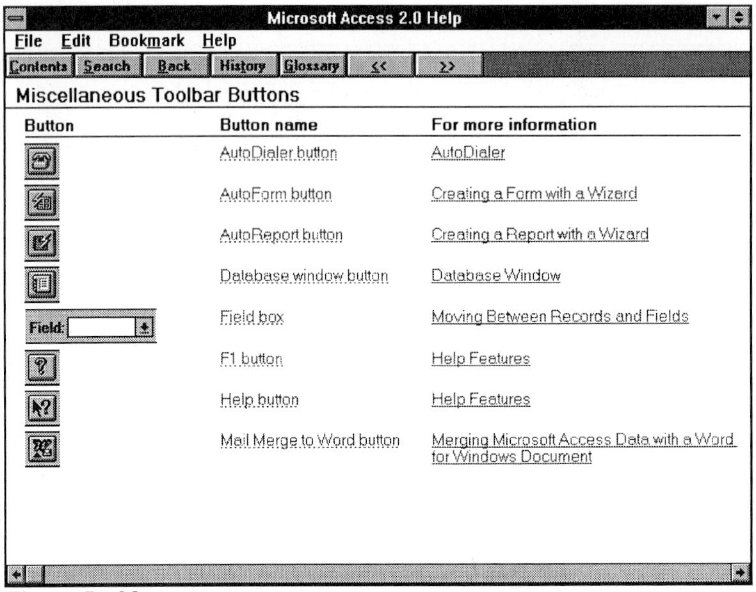

Figure I - 23

18. Click on the glossary term **Help button.**
19. After looking at the definition, click the left mouse button again to close the pop-up box.
20. Click the mouse on the **FILE** menu to open it, and pick **Exit** to close the Help system and return to *Access.*

EXITING FROM ACCESS

Although *Access* automatically saves the data you type, there is no guarantee it has saved yet. Thus, you must **never** turn the computer off without properly exiting from *Access*. There is nothing you can do to prevent the electricity from going off occasionally, and that may cause some problems and force you to have to repair a database once in a while (Repair Database is in the **FILE** menu), but do not do it to yourself by turning the computer off prematurely.

Also, if you are using a floppy diskette for your data, **never** switch floppy diskettes while a database is open in *Access*, even if you switch programs first. *Access* is expecting that same diskette to be there at all times, and will complain if it cannot locate it, and may even overwrite the second diskette.

It is also a good idea to properly exit from Windows as it saves the screen arrangement and cleans up temporary files when you exit properly.

To exit from *Access*:

- Click on **Exit** in the **FILE** menu.
- If there are design changes that have not been saved yet, *Access* will ask in an alert box (see Figure I - 24 for a typical example) whether to save them or not before exiting.
- If you get an *alert box*, click **Yes** to save and exit, **No** to exit without saving, **Cancel** to cancel the request to exit and return to where you were in *Access*, and **Help** if you do not understand the question in the alert box. An *alert box* is like a dialog box with only command buttons, and operates the same way.

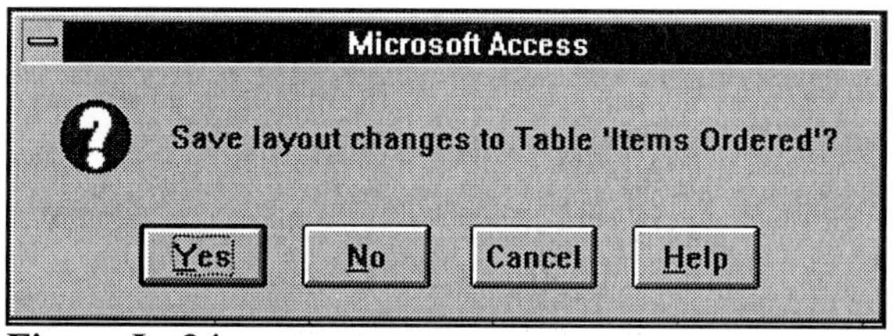

Figure I - 24

To exit from Windows:

- Click on **Exit** in the Program Manager **FILE** menu.
- Click **OK** in the **This will end your Windows session.** alert box.

Activity I.7: Exiting from Access

If you will be stopping rather than moving on to Lesson 1 or the Independent Project, you should exit from *Access*.

1. Click on the **FILE** menu.
2. Click on **Exit**.

CONVENTIONS FOLLOWED IN THIS BOOK

Table I - 3 explains the conventions used in this book when giving instructions.

Task	Notation in the Book	What To Do
Highlighting a choice or activating a button with the mouse	click on, click the mouse button	Move the mouse pointer on top of the menu name, button, or choice in a list and press the left mouse button once.
Selecting from a list with the mouse	double-click on	Move the mouse pointer on top of the choice in a list and click the left mouse button two times rapidly without moving the mouse.
Moving or sizing an object with the mouse	drag the mouse	Move the mouse on top of the item to be moved or sized, hold down the left mouse button, move the mouse with the button still held down until the position or size of the object is as desired, and release the mouse button.
Choosing a menu command	Pick **MENU/Command** Choose **MENU/Command**, then **Submenu Command**	(1) Move the mouse pointer on top of the **MENU** name and click the left mouse button once. (2) Within the menu that opens, move the mouse pointer on top of the desired **Command** name and click the left mouse button once. (3) If a submenu appears, move the mouse pointer on top of the desired **Submenu Command** name in the submenu and click the left mouse button once.
Pressing a key	Press **ENTER**	Press the **ENTER** key on the keyboard.
Using a key combination	Press **SHIFT+TAB**	Hold down the first key (**SHIFT**) and, while it is down, tap the second key (**TAB**).

Table I - 3

SUMMARY

In this introduction you have run *Access*, explored its screen components, used its basic tools (the menu, dialog boxes, and the toolbar, among others), and run the Help program. The major terms were also defined. You opened a supplied database, opened a table within that database, and made some alterations to the table. You closed the table, closed the database, and exited from *Access*. As these are the fundamentals that you will use throughout the lessons in this book, feel free to come back to review some procedures or terms. Keep in mind that the Help system is an enormous source of information about *Access* and should be utilized.

KEY TERMS

Alert Box
Application Control Menu
Check Box
Command Button
Control Menu
Data
Database
Desktop
Dialog Box
Field
Drop-down List
Field Name
Glossary Term
Jump Term
List Box
Maximize Button
Menu Bar
Minimize Button
Option Button
RDBMS
Record
Restore Button
Scroll Bar
Status Bar
Table
Text Box
Title Bar
Tool Tips
Toolbar
Toolbar Button

INDEPENDENT PROJECTS

Independent Project I.1: The Cue Cards

Cue Cards are a section of the Help system that gives general information about basic processes in *Access* and lists step-by-step instructions for performing those operations. They are sometimes called the "online coach" as they remain on top of the right third of the desktop while you work in *Access*.

This project will begin exploring the Cue Cards by examining the information in its **Build a database with tables** topic.

1. Run *Access*.
2. Maximize the *Access* window if it does not already cover the entire screen.
3. Click on the **HELP** menu.
4. Click on **Cue Cards** in that menu to open the Cue Cards (see Figure I - 25).
5. Click the mouse on the tiny button with an arrow head on it that is immediately to the left of **Build a database with tables**.

   A new list of topics appears.
6. Click on the arrow head button for **See what databases and tables are**.
7. Examine this screen for definitions, and click the **Next** button when finished.
8. Repeat step 7 two more times for the remaining two screens.

   *The Cue Cards return to the **Build a database** with tables screen. You could explore other topics on your own, or click the **Menu** button to return to the beginning set of choices and select a new major topic.*

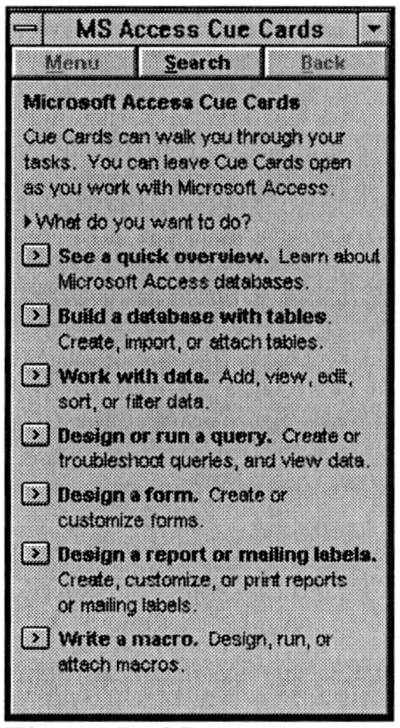

Figure I - 25

9. Click on the **Control Menu** at the upper left corner of the **Cue Cards** window (not *Access*' window), and click on **Close**.
10. Exit from *Access* with **FILE/Exit**.
11. If you are finished with Windows, exit from Windows with **FILE/Exit Windows** and a click on the **OK** button in the **This will end your Windows session.** alert box.

Lesson

1 Creating Databases and Tables

Objectives

In this lesson you will learn how to:

- Create a new database
- Design and create a data table
- Distinguish between the data types in *Access*
- Enter data into a table
- Modify the structure of a table
- Create a primary key

PROJECT DESCRIPTION

The project that we will pursue through these lessons is that of a small retailer of CDROMs for computers. This lesson will begin by creating the employee file, which will contain the employees' names, identification numbers, date of hire, salary, phone extension, and any important notes. Subsequent lessons will build other components using tables of invoices, products, and customers. All of these tables of data will fit together by the final lesson into a system of related tables, in what is called a Relational Database Management System or RDBMS.

At the end of this first lesson you will have created the table of data shown in Figure 1 - 1.

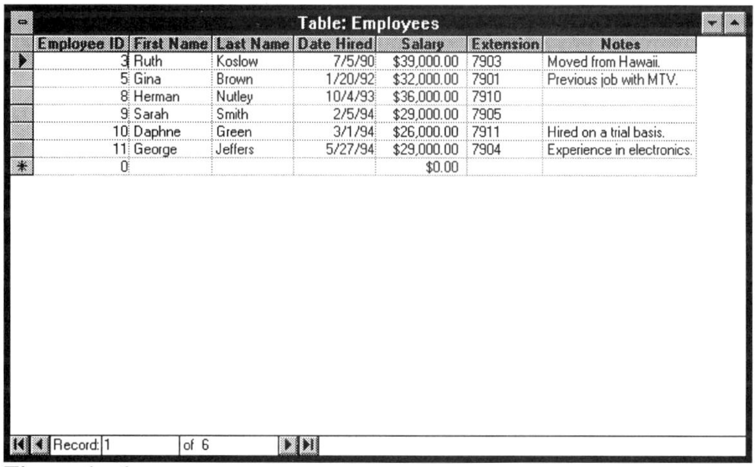

Table: Employees

Employee ID	First Name	Last Name	Date Hired	Salary	Extension	Notes
3	Ruth	Koslow	7/5/90	$39,000.00	7903	Moved from Hawaii.
5	Gina	Brown	1/20/92	$32,000.00	7901	Previous job with MTV.
8	Herman	Nutley	10/4/93	$36,000.00	7910	
9	Sarah	Smith	2/5/94	$29,000.00	7905	
10	Daphne	Green	3/1/94	$26,000.00	7911	Hired on a trial basis.
11	George	Jeffers	5/27/94	$29,000.00	7904	Experience in electronics.
0				$0.00		

Figure 1 - 1

THE DATABASE

A database in *Access* is a container that can hold tables of data, report and label designs, screen designs called forms, queries for selecting subsets of listings, and both recorded and designed programming. Since the tables, reports, forms, queries, macros, and modules that you create to put together a system for obtaining information are called *objects*, the database contains all of the objects for one system of data.

The employee table that we will create in this lesson must be contained within such a database, so we must create the database first.

Since the database contains all other objects, it is the only item that is saved onto a disk from *Access*, and, thus, has the only name that must abide by the DOS file naming rules. Objects follow the more liberal *Access* naming rules, which are outlined below in the section on creating objects.

To create a database:

- Choose **FILE/New Database** in the menu, or click the **New Database** button on the toolbar.
- In the **New Database** dialog box, pick the desired drive and directory. The type of file should be **Databases (*.mdb)**.
- In the **File Name:** text box, replace **db1.mdb** with the name by which the database will be recorded, and click the **OK** command button. Since this is a DOS name, you may use at most 8 characters and the name may not contain any spaces.

Activity 1.1: Creating the Database

1. Click the mouse on the **FILE** menu to open it, then pick **New Database** within that menu by clicking on that choice.

   The ***New Database*** *dialog box will open (see* Figure 1 - 2*).*

2. In the **File Name:** text box of the **New Database** dialog box, type: **SALES** as in Figure 1 - 2.

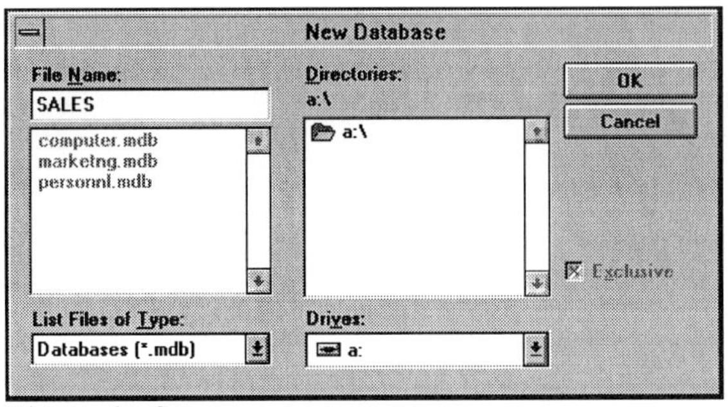

Figure 1 - 2

The extension on the filename, which is normally .mdb for Microsoft database, will be added automatically by Access provided you do not type any other extension. It is probably not wise to use a different extension since Access normally lists only files with the standard .mdb.

3. Check to make certain that the currently selected drive and directory are correct, and that List Files of Type: says Databases (*.mdb).
4. Click the **OK** button and the database will be created and opened on the workspace (see Figure 1 - 3).

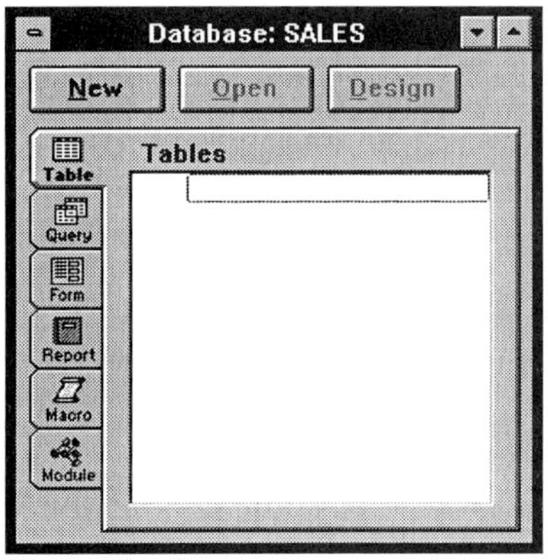

Figure 1 - 3

Creating Objects

Now that the database exists, we are ready to create the table to hold the employee data. The most direct way to create an object like a table is to click on the tab for the design category at the left edge of the **Database** window (table, report, etc.), and click the **New** button at the top of the window.

Since the objects within the database are not recorded separately on the disk, their names need only conform to the *Access* rules for names. Those rules allow the length of a name to be up to 64 characters. Any characters except the exclamation point, period, accent mark, or square brackets (! . ` [ ]) are legal; thus, spaces are allowed.

The names of tables and other objects should fully describe their function. As there are hardly any restrictions, you should not name a table **EMPL** when it could be **Employees**. Similarly, **Equipment In Use** is better than **EQPINUSE**, and **Accounts Receivable** fully describes a table whereas **AR** or **ACCTRECV** is potentially confusing.

To create a table:

- Click the **Table** tab at the left edge of the **Database** window.
- Click the **New** button at the top of the **Database** window.
- Select the **New Table** button to design a data table from scratch, or pick **Table Wizard** to use one of the supplied designs to get started.
- Assuming you selected **New Table**, fill in the grid with the names for the columns, data types, and descriptions.

Filling in the Table Grid

The window for designing tables has three columns in the top section and a group of *Field Properties* in the lower section. To fill in the three columns, type the desired *Field Name* for a field in your table following the same rules as for the names of objects (see Creating Objects above), select a *Data Type* (see the next section), and optionally enter a description of the field. The description will not only remind you or another person of the purpose for the field, but also will be displayed on the Status Bar during data entry. Thus, the description is an excellent place to include instructions that will be automatically displayed during data entry.

The *Field Properties* in the lower section of the window control the details and options for each field. Only one field's properties show at a time, and, as you move from field to field in the upper portion of the window, the Field Properties for that current field are shown. Such options as the length of a text field and the specific variety of a numeric field are set with Field Properties.

Data Types

There are eight types of data that can be stored in an *Access* table. Additionally, the numeric type has five varieties. When designing a table, you must plan carefully and select the proper type for each column of data. The details of each type and variety are listed in Table 1 - 1 below. Pay particular attention to the limitations, as that often dictates what type cannot be used for a specific purpose.

Data Type	Subtype	Size Limitation	Special Characteristics
Text		1-255 characters	most common field type
Memo		0-64,000 characters	may have not only text, but tabs, carriage returns, font changes, etc.
Number			
	Byte	an integer from 0 to 255	requires 1 character of storage
	Integer	an integer from -32,768 to 32,767	requires 2 characters of storage
	Long Integer	an integer from -2,147,483,648 to 2,147,483,647	requires 4 characters of storage
	Single	a decimal with up to 7 decimal places from $-3.4*10^{38}$ to $3.4*10^{38}$	requires 4 characters of storage
	Double	a decimal with up to 15 decimal places from $-1.797*10^{308}$ to $1.797*10^{308}$	requires 8 characters of storage
Date/Time		a date or a time or both	from the year 100 to 9999
Currency		up to $999 trillion with 4 decimal places	2 decimal places is the default
Counter			automatically numbers each record when the record is entered; the number assigned cannot be changed
Yes/No		only Yes or No	
OLE Object		up to 1 gigabyte	a picture or other binary file

Table 1 - 1

Activity 1.2: Creating a Table

In this activity you will create the fields that are needed in the Employees table. The business will need the name, an identification number, the hired date, the salary, the phone extension, and a place for important notes.

1. Click the **Table** tab at the left edge of the **Database** window.
2. Click the **New** button at the top of the **Database** window.
3. Select the **New Table** button in the **New Table** dialog box (see Figure 1 - 4).

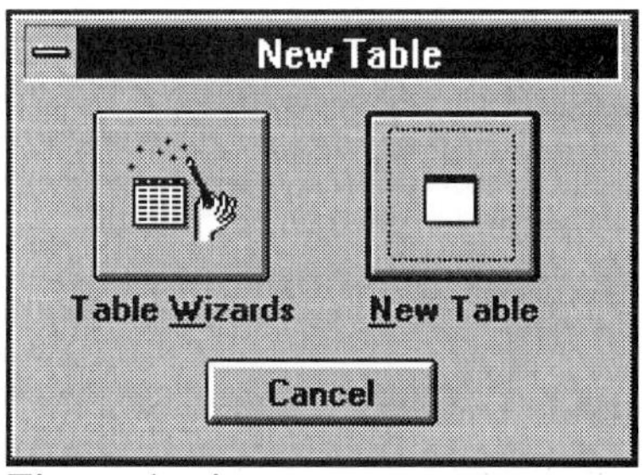

Figure 1 - 4

*The **Table** window that opens is where you define the fields for the new table (* Figure 1 - 5*).*

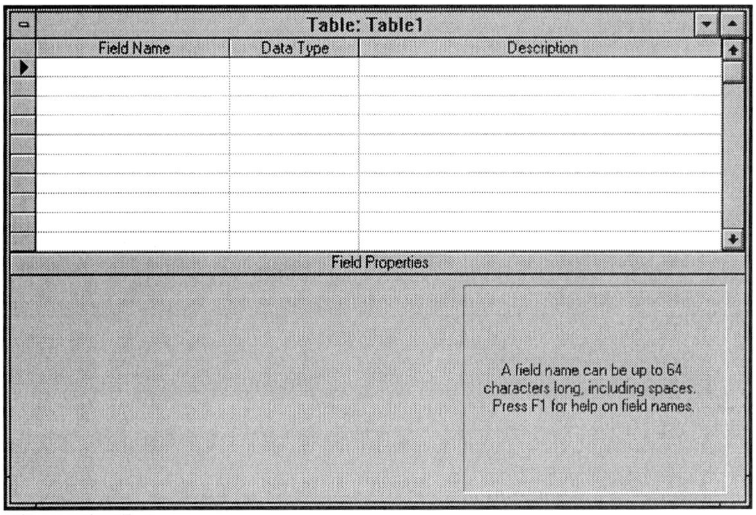

Figure 1 - 5

4. On the first row in the **Field Name** column, type the name of the first field: **Employee ID**
5. Press the **TAB** key to move to the **Data Type** column.
6. **Text** is the default data type, but we want the Employee IDs to be numbers. Therefore, we must change the **Data Type**. Click the drop-down list arrow to open the list of data types and select **Number** (see *Figure 1 - 6*).

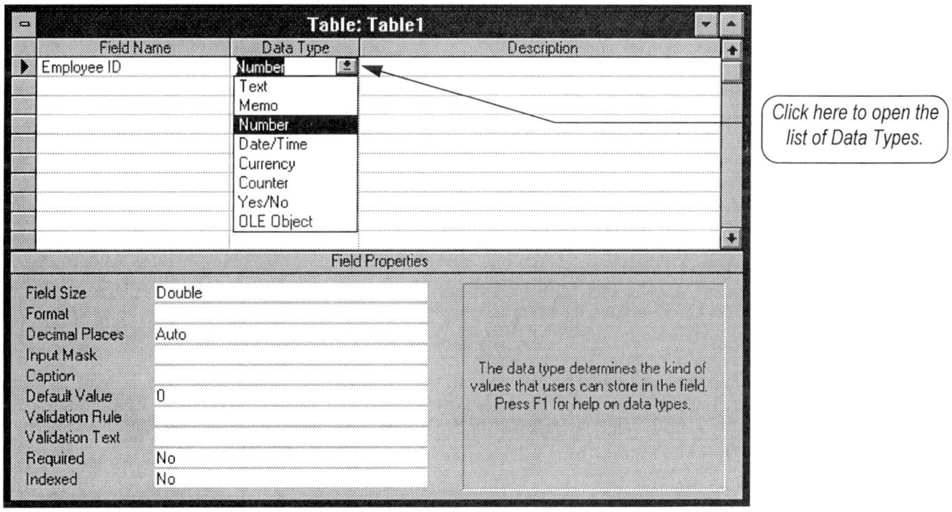

Figure 1 - 6

*The **Field Properties** list in the lower section of the **Table** window contains the options for the current field. Notice that the **Field Size** of the Employee ID field is set to **Double** (see* Figure 1 - 6*). That would allow much larger numbers than are needed. Since the company is small, we will need only two digits. Also, the Employee ID numbers will not need decimal places, so we can use **Integer** as the **Field Size**.*

*The Status Bar mentions that the **F6** key will switch panes from the upper section to the lower and vice versa. Alternatively, clicking the mouse within the lower section or the upper section will move to that section.*

7. Press the **F6** key to switch to the lower pane.
8. Click on the arrow to open the drop-down list and select **Integer** (see Figure 1 - 7).

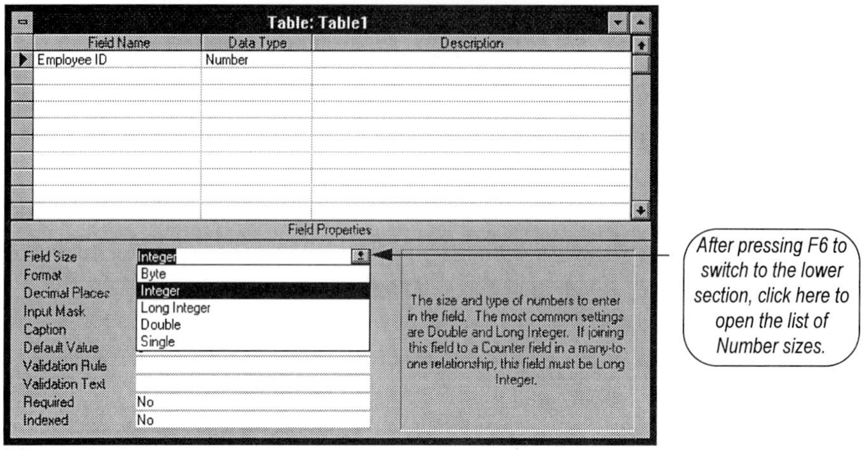

Figure 1 - 7

9. Press **F6** to return to the upper pane.
10. Press **TAB** to move to the **Description** column.
11. Enter the description: **Consecutive numbers assigned upon hiring**
12. Press **TAB** to move to the second line.
13. On the second row in the **Field Name** column, type the field name: **First Name**
14. Press the **TAB** key to move to the **Data Type** column.
15. Since **Text**, the default data type, is correct, merely press **TAB** to move to the **Description** column.

    *The **Field Properties** list in the lower section of the **Table** dialog box shows the size of the First Name field as 50 characters wide. That is wider than needed.*

16. Press the **F6** key to switch to the lower pane.
17. Replace the 50 on the **Field Size** line with **15** as shown in Figure 1 - 8.

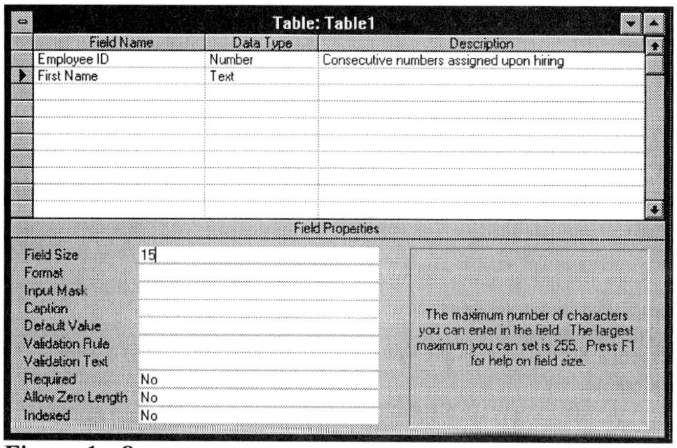

Figure 1 - 8

18. Press **F6** to return to the upper pane.
19. As it is obvious what a first name is, we do not need a description, so press **TAB** to move to the third line.
20. Enter the remaining five fields as displayed in the last five lines of Table 1 - 2. When finished, the grid should look like Figure 1 - 9.

Field Name	Data Type	Size (in lower pane)	Description
Employee ID	Number	Integer	Consecutive numbers...
First Name	Text	15	
Last Name	Text	20	
Date Hired	Date/Time	(size is automatic)	
Salary	Currency	(size is automatic)	
Extension	Text	4	
Notes	Memo	(size is automatic)	

Table 1 - 2

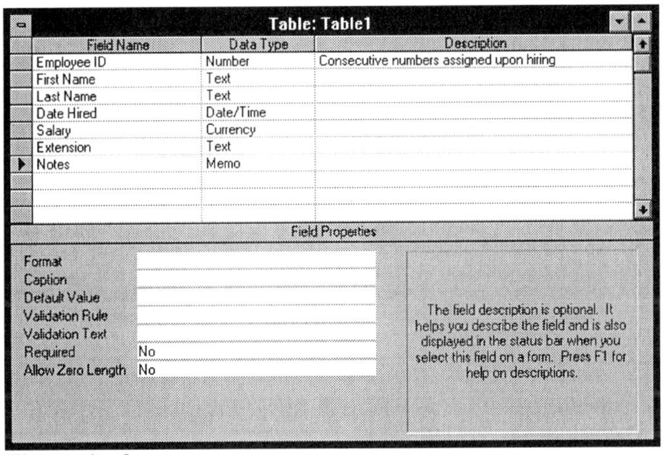

Figure 1 - 9

Notice that the ***Extension*** *was created as a Text field even though a phone extension contains only digits and looks like a number. When a field will contain only digits, but they are never involved in calculations, it is usually more efficient to make them text fields. Zip codes and area codes are two more examples.*

SAVING THE DESIGN

With the design completed, you need to save the table structure into the database. Here you decide on a descriptive name. Since this table contains data on the employees, you will name it **Employees**.

Should you try to close the table without saving, *Access* will ask whether you want to save the design. You may save it by choosing **Yes** and entering a name for the table, or discard the design with **No** if you really don't want it.

To save a table design:

- Choose **Save As** menu.
- Type the desired name for the table.
- Click on the **OK** button.

Activity 1.3: Saving the Table Design

We will save the table with the name **Employees**.

1. Select **FILE/Save As**.
2. In the **Save As** dialog box, type the name for this table: **Employees** and click the **OK** button (see Figure 1 - 10).

Figure 1 - 10

3. When *Access* asks **There is no primary key defined. Create a primary key?** click the **No** button (see Figure 1 - 11).

   We will discuss primary keys in a few pages and assign one at that time.

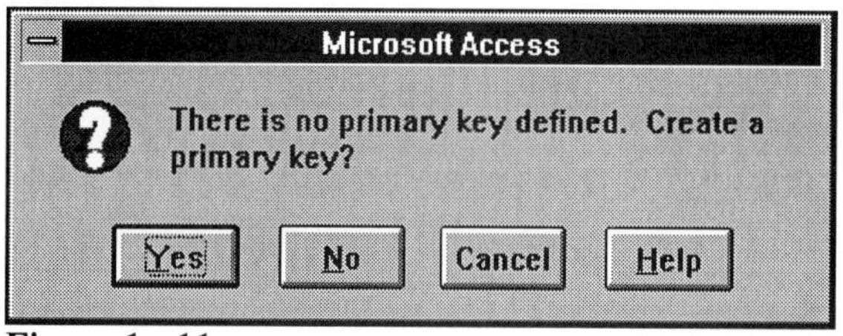

Figure 1 - 11

Access will record the table design in the Sales database.

4. Since we are finished with the design, close the **Table: Employees** window with **FILE/Close**.

   The new table Employees will be listed in the Table section of the Sales database (Figure 1 - 12).

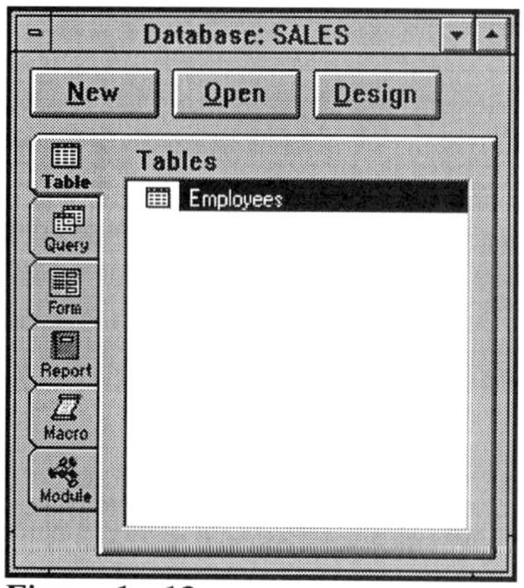

Figure 1 - 12

ENTERING DATA IN A TABLE

The next step is to enter the data into the new Employee table. To type new data into a table, open the table, move to the desired place in the table, and type each item of data. Unless you uncheck the **RECORDS/Allow Editing** menu selection, the table will always accept new records.

When you first move onto a line, a rightward pointing triangle at the left edge of the table indicates the current record. As soon as you begin typing, that triangle changes to a pencil. The pencil means data has been typed on that line, but not yet saved. Saving data is automatic; you do not need to make any menu choices or click any buttons to tell *Access* to save the data you have typed. The moment you change lines, the previous line of typing is saved. Thus, there is never more than a single line of unsaved data. Even if you close the table without telling *Access* to save the active record, *Access* saves the line automatically. When saved, the pencil icon disappears and the triangle marks the new line.

To move to the proper field while entering data into an *Access* table:

- The **TAB** key, the **ENTER** key, or the **RIGHT ARROW** key will move to the next field.
- Should you need to back up to a previous field, press either the **SHIFT+TAB** key combination or the **LEFT ARROW**.
- You may click the mouse in any field to move the cursor there.
- If you are in the last field, the same movement keys wrap around to the first field on the next line so that you are ready to type another record.

Keep the following points in mind while entering data in an *Access* table:

- If you move back to a field that already contains data, the entire set of characters in that field will be selected. Should you begin typing when the whole field is highlighted, the first character you type will replace the entire previous set of characters! While this is handy when replacing outdated data, it might happen accidentally. Either the **Undo** button on the toolbar, or the **EDIT/Undo Typing** command in the menu will restore the field contents.
- To substitute a cursor for the highlighting, press the **F2** key to switch out of Replace mode and into Edit mode. Alternatively, click the mouse in the field. When you click the mouse on a field, it places the cursor within that field in Edit mode rather than Replace mode.

To fix typing errors while entering data:

- If you notice a typing error before moving to a new field, press the **BACKSPACE** key to remove the error, and then retype.
- Should you notice an error in a previous field, either move to the field and retype the entire entry, or click the mouse cursor next to the mistaken character(s), press the **BACKSPACE** key to remove characters to the left of the cursor or press the **DELETE** key to erase characters to the right of the cursor, and retype the required characters.

Activity 1.4: Entering Data into the Table

In this activity you will enter the data for the six employees of the company.

1. Click on the **Table** tab at the left edge of the **Database** window if it is not already selected.
2. Select the table name **Employees**.
3. Click the **Open** button at the top of the **Database** window. Alternatively, you may double-click the table name to automatically open it.

*The triangle at the left edge of the table (see Figure 1 - 13) should mark the current line and the cursor should be blinking in the **Employee ID** field. Notice the description for the Employee ID field on the left end of the Status Bar.*

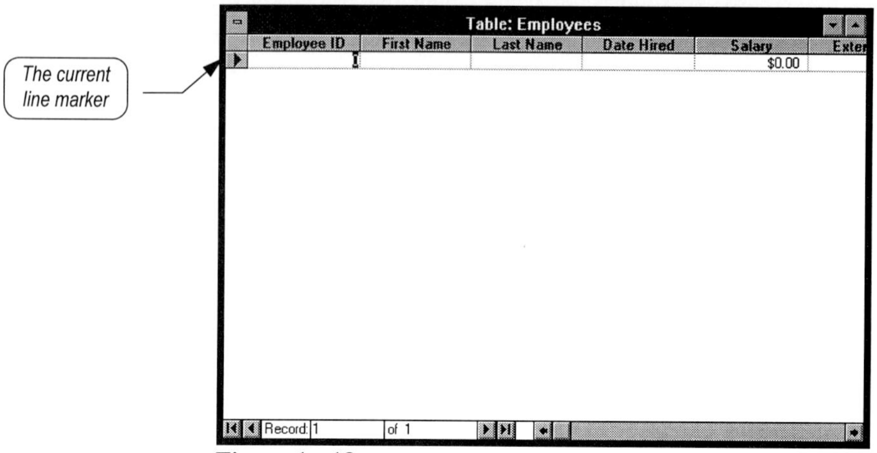

Figure 1 - 13

4. Type **3** for the first employee's ID number and press the **TAB** key to move to the next field.

   The pencil icon should show at the left edge of the table indicating that this record is now being typed (see Figure 1 - 14).

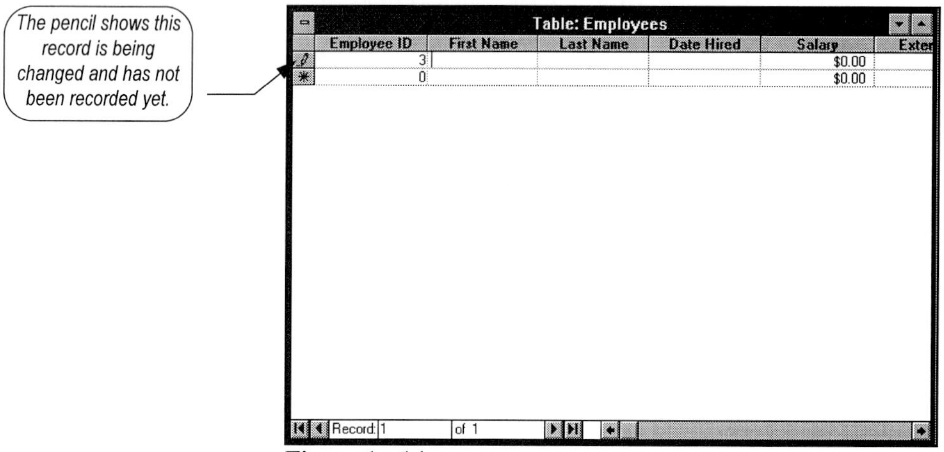

Figure 1 - 14

5. In the **First Name** field, type: **Ruth** and press **TAB**.
6. For **Last Name** enter: **Koslow** and move to the next field.
7. In **Date Hired** type: **7/5/90** and move to the next field.
8. Enter: **39,000** for **Salary**.

   Although you may type them, you do not need to type a dollar sign or comma. Nor is it necessary to enter the decimal point and two zeros any time the decimal places are .00. Those will be added automatically when you leave the field.

9. Move to **Extension** and type: **7903**.

   If the table scrolls within the window, that is normal when the fields cannot all fit within the width of the current window frame. As you move within the table, Access will automatically scroll the table so that you can see the field on which you are working. To scroll the table yourself, use the scroll bars.

10. Press **TAB** to move to the **Notes** field and type: **Moved from Hawaii.**

    If the contents of a field are too long for the displayed width of the field, the characters will scroll. We will see later how to adjust the width of a column.

11. Press **TAB** to finish this record and move to the next line.

    The pencil icon disappears, the previous record is saved to disk, and the triangle marks the next line.

12. Type the five additional records as shown in **Table 1 - 3**.

Employee ID	First Name	Last Name	Date Hired	Salary	Extension	Notes
5	Gina	Brown	1/20/92	32,000	7901	Previous job with MTV.
8	Herman	Nutley	10/4/93	36,000	7910	
9	Sarah	Smith	2/5/94	29,000	7905	
10	Daphne	Green	3/1/94	26,000	7911	Hired on a trial basis.
11	George	Jeffers	5/27/94	29,000	7904	Experience in electronics.

Table 1 - 3

13. As we are finished with data entry, close the table with **FILE/Close**.

    The current record is automatically saved and the table window is closed.

MODIFYING A TABLE

After working with a table of data for a while, it usually becomes evident that some alterations need to be made. Perhaps new requirements demand changes, or you might see a better way of accomplishing your objectives.

The company decides that placing the sales staff on a base salary plus commissions will spur sales. Non-sales staff will continue with a full salary. Thus, the employee table needs to record who is on commission by adding a new field.

To modify a table's structure:

- While the table name is highlighted in the **Database** window, click the **Design** button.
- Move to any field that needs to be altered and type any changes or select any different options.
- To insert a new field, move to the field that currently occupies the position where you want the new field to be and choose **EDIT/Insert Row**. On the new blank line, type the new name, data type, and description.
- To add a new field at the end of the current group of fields, click on the blank line just below the last field and type the new name, data type, and description.
- To remove a field, click on the gray block just to the left of the field name. The entire line will be highlighted. Press the **DELETE** key and confirm the deletion.

Activity 1.5: Modifying the Table Structure

You decide to insert the new Commissioned field between Salary and Extension.

1. With the highlight on the table **Employees**, click the **Design** button at the top of the database window.
2. Click the mouse pointer on the field name **Extension** to move onto that line.
3. Choose **EDIT/Insert Row** to insert a new line, which will push Extension and Notes down a row (see Figure 1 - 15).

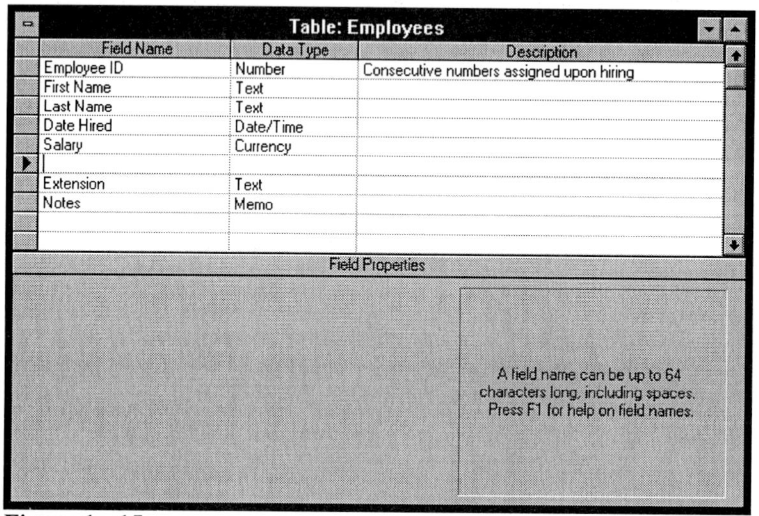

Figure 1 - 15

4. Type the new field name: **Commissioned** and press **TAB.**
5. Select a **Yes/No** field type by typing the letter **Y** and pressing **TAB.**

   *Each data type except Counter begins with a unique letter; thus, to select the type, merely type the first letter and press **TAB**. To select Counter, type the first two letters.*

6. For the **Description** type: **Yes means base salary plus commissions; No means full salary.**

   The size of a Yes/No field is automatic, so you do not need to change the Field Properties.

7. Save this alteration with **FILE/Save.**

   If you are continuing on to the next section now, do not close the table design.

PRIMARY KEY FIELDS

If the data in a table is kept in order, finding a particular listing is much quicker. For example, since the telephone book is in alphabetical name order, to locate the name Quinn, one could open the book in the exact middle and look at the first name on the page to see whether Quinn was further along in the book or in the first half of the book. Supposing Quinn is further along than the middle, you can ignore the first half of the book, for you know Quinn cannot be there. If you then divided the second half in half again and looked to see which of those quarters Quinn was in, you would have narrowed the search down to only one fourth of all listings in just two tries. Continuing in similar fashion, you could search thousands of listings in about a dozen tries.

If, however, the names in the telephone book were not in order, you would need to read every name to locate a particular listing, a process that could take thousands of tries to search thousands of records. *Access* reaps the same benefit from having the records in order, and, thus, has what is called a *primary key* to keep the records in order.

A *primary key* can consist of one or more fields in the table design. Normally you designate which field or fields will make up the primary key, although *Access* will ask whether it should establish the primary key the first time you save a table design that does not have one. If allowed, *Access* will select a counter type of field; if there is no counter field, *Access* will insert one and designate it the primary key.

You should select as a primary key a single field that will have unique values in it, like an ID field, or a combination of fields that taken together will be unique. Uniqueness is a requirement of a primary key. Once established, *Access* will not accept either duplicate entries in a primary key field (or the combination of fields), or a blank primary key field.

Primary key fields are often a requirement for multiple table operations. For example, when a relational system uses several tables simultaneously, editing across multiple tables is not allowed without primary keys. Thus, you often must designate primary keys.

To designate a primary key field:

- Select the field in the table design window.
- Either choose **EDIT/Set Primary Key** or click the **Set Primary Key** button on the toolbar.
- A key symbol will appear on the gray block at the left edge of the line for that field.

Activity 1.6: Assigning a Primary Key

We will select the Employee ID field as the primary key since it contains a unique value for each employee.

1. If you are not still in the **Table: Employees** design window (see Figure 1 - 16), select the table name **Employees** and click the **Design** button.
2. Click anywhere on the line for the **Employee ID** field.

   The triangle icon will appear on the left end of the Employee ID line.
3. Click the **Set Primary Key** button on the toolbar or choose **EDIT/Set Primary Key**.

   A key icon will appear to the left of the field name (see Figure 1 - 16).

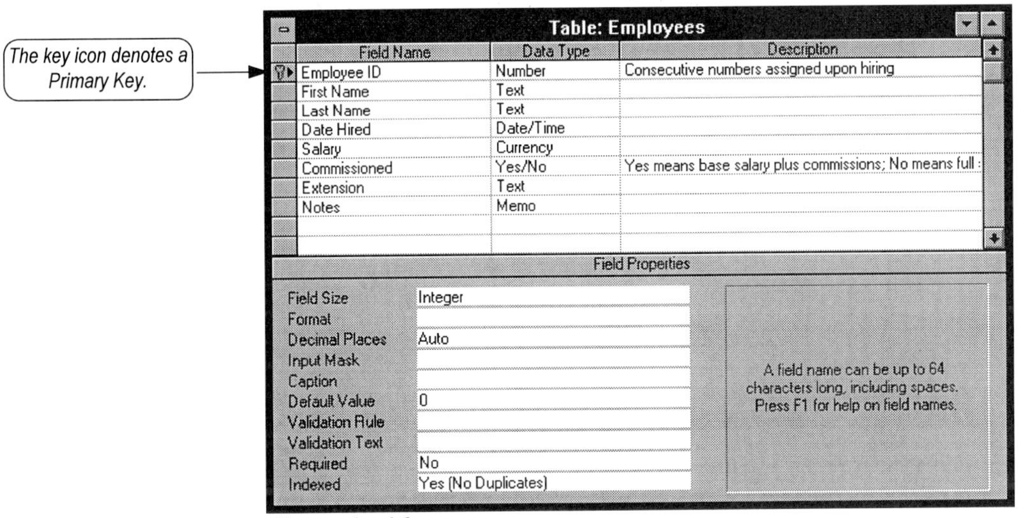

Figure 1 - 16

4. Select **FILE/Save** to save the design.

   This altered design is saved over the previous version of Employees, so the table design has been updated.

5. Select **FILE/Close.**

   We will update the data by filling in whether the employees are on commission or not in the next lesson.

PRINTING A TABLE

When you need a paper copy of the data in a table, the table can be printed. This is a quick printout, not a designed report. On a table printout all fields are included. Also, no calculations, font changes, titles, or other frills are included. It is a dump of the data onto paper. In a later lesson we will explore designed reports.

To print a table:

- Either open the table or move the highlight onto the table name in the database window.
- Choose **FILE/Print** in the menu, or click the **Print** button on the toolbar.
- In the **Print** dialog box, set any options.
- Click the **OK** command button.

Activity 1.7: Printing a Table

1. The highlight should still be on **Employees.**
2. Click the mouse on the **FILE** menu to open it, then pick **Print** within that menu by clicking on that choice.

   *Alternatively, you could click the **Print** toolbar button or press **Ctrl-P**.*

3. In the Print dialog box (see Figure 1 - 17), **All** should be the option for Print Range and Copies should have a 1 in the text box.

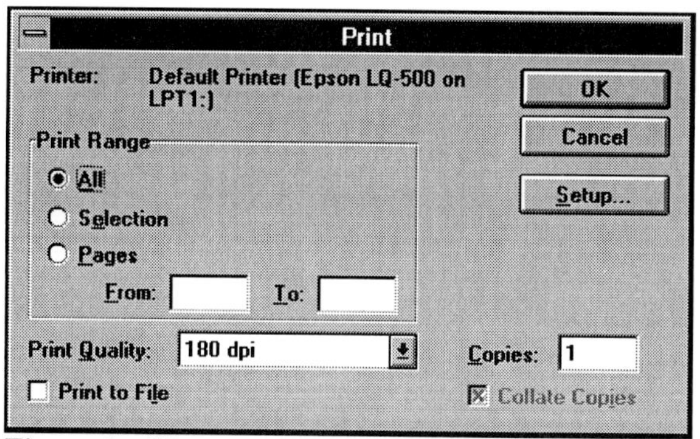

Figure 1 - 17

   Your computer will probably have a different printer listed at the top of the dialog box and a different value for Print Quality.

4. Click the **OK** button.
5. Select **FILE/Close Database** to close the **SALES** database.

SUMMARY

In this project you created a database to hold the various designed objects that we will need and built the first table for that database. You entered records into the table, modified the structure of the table, and established a primary key. In Lesson 2 you will further develop your editing and searching capabilities. Lesson 3 will then add additional tables to Sales by importing the data from other sources.

KEY TERMS

Data type
Database
Field Name
Field Properties
Object
Primary key
Table

INDEPENDENT PROJECTS

The following four independent projects give you a chance to work with *Access* in creating databases and tables. The first two projects give explicit directions to complete the steps. The third leaves more of the decisions and details to you. The fourth project merely outlines the project and leaves most of the planning to you.

Independent Project 1.1: The School Newspaper

The school newspaper needs your help. They are currently recording the advertisements they solicit in composition books. However, they are going to need summary statistics and the thought of performing them by hand is not appealing.

They ask you to design a table for recording the ads. The paper records they show you have six columns of data: Ad Number, Purchased By, Size, Price, Date Paid, and Salesperson ID. Ad Number is a unique number that is pre-printed on each sheet the sales force uses to write up a sale. Since it is unique, Ad Number will be the primary key. Size is a two letter code representing the size of the ad. (See the Description column for the meanings of the four possible codes.) Salesperson ID is the letter plus two digit code for the sales person. The structure of the table is outlined in Table 1 - 4.

Figure 1 - 18 shows the data you will need to get started.

Field Name	Data Type	Size (in lower pane)	Description
Ad Number	Number	Integer	Number on Solicitation sheet
Purchased By	Text	30	
Size	Text	2	FP=Full page, HP=Half page, QP =Quarter page, EP=Eighth page
Price	Currency	(Size is automatic)	
Date Paid	Date/Time	(Size is automatic)	
Salesperson ID	Text	3	Letter plus 2 digits for salesperson.

Table 1 - 4

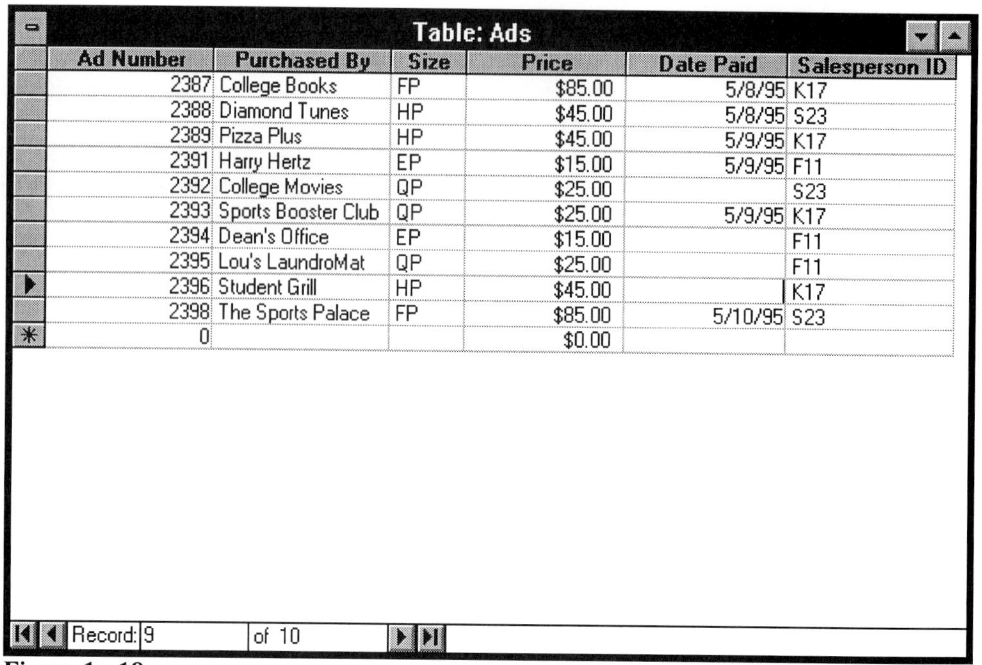

Table: Ads

Ad Number	Purchased By	Size	Price	Date Paid	Salesperson ID
2387	College Books	FP	$85.00	5/8/95	K17
2388	Diamond Tunes	HP	$45.00	5/8/95	S23
2389	Pizza Plus	HP	$45.00	5/9/95	K17
2391	Harry Hertz	EP	$15.00	5/9/95	F11
2392	College Movies	QP	$25.00		S23
2393	Sports Booster Club	QP	$25.00	5/9/95	K17
2394	Dean's Office	EP	$15.00		F11
2395	Lou's LaundroMat	QP	$25.00		F11
2396	Student Grill	HP	$45.00		K17
2398	The Sports Palace	FP	$85.00	5/10/95	S23
0			$0.00		

Record: 9 of 10

Figure 1 - 18

1. Run *Access*.
2. Maximize the *Access* window if it does not already cover the entire screen.
3. Begin creating a new database to hold the newspaper ads (and any other data they may eventually need to record) by picking **FILE/New Database** or clicking the **New Database** button on the toolbar.
4. Make certain the drive and directory are correct in the dialog box. For example, if you will be using the A: drive and that is not currently selected, click on the drop-down arrow for the **Drives:** list and click on **A:**.
5. Type the name for the new database, **XERCISE1**, in the File Name box of the New Database dialog box and click the **OK** button.
6. Make sure the **Table** tab is selected and click the **New** button to begin a new table.
7. Click the **New Table** button in the **New Table** dialog box.
8. Fill in the six fields as shown in Table 1 - 4. Remember to set the Size for each field (except the automatic ones) in the lower section of the window.
9. Make **Ad Number** the Primary Key by clicking anywhere on the line for Ad Number and clicking the **Primary Key** button on the toolbar. The key icon will appear on the record selector.
10. Save the table by picking **FILE/Save As**, entering the name: **Ads**, and clicking the **OK** button.
11. Close the Table Window with **FILE/Close**.
12. With the highlight on **Ads**, click the **Open** button to open the table for data entry.
13. Enter the ten records shown in Figure 1 - 18. Be careful to match the upper or lower case characters for each entry. Some of the entries will scroll and be partially hidden since they are longer than the width that is currently showing for the column. That is perfectly all right. We will correct the situation in the next lesson.
14. When finished, close the table with **FILE/Close**.

The newspaper had previously kept the ads for different issues of the paper on separate sheets in the ad book. That will not work in a database table, so you realize after working with the data a while that the table will need an additional column to record the issue of the newspaper. Rather than the issue number which would not mean much by itself, you decide to add the date of issue to the table structure.

15. With the highlight on **Ads**, click the **Design** button to open the design of the table.
16. Click on the next available line, line 7.
17. Type the field name: **Issue Date** and press **TAB** to move to the Data Type column.
18. It will be a **Date/Time** field, so type a **D** and press **TAB**. The size will be automatic. No description is necessary.
19. Save the altered design with **FILE/Save**.
20. Close the table with **FILE/Close**.
21. Click the **Open** button to open Ads.
22. Move to the **Issue Date** column and enter: **5/20/95** for all ten records. (As a shortcut, type 5/20/95 in the first record, move down with the **DOWN ARROW**, and press the Ditto key for each of the remaining records. The Ditto key is **CTRL+'** , that is hold down CTRL and tap the apostrophe. Continue until all ten are done. The Ditto key copies whatever is in the field immediately above into the current field.)
23. Print the table with **FILE/Print** or the **Print** button on the toolbar. Click the **OK** button in the Print dialog box.
24. Close the table with **FILE/Close**.
25. Close the database with **FILE/Close Database**.
26. If you are finished with *Access*, exit from *Access* with **FILE/Exit**.
27. If you are finished with Windows, exit from Windows with **FILE/Exit Windows**.

Independent Project 1.2: The Book Store

The local bookstore has asked you to create a database to keep track of the books that it stocks and their publishers. The owner has written out the items that need to be recorded. That list names Title, Author, Year of Publication, Publisher Code, Price, and Quantity in Stock.

After reviewing the owner's plans, you spot one problem with the list. You want to include a Primary Key, but nothing in the list is sure to be unique. Therefore, you decide to add to the six suggested fields a Book Code as the first field in the design. The resulting table structure is displayed in Table 1 - 5. The data you are given to get started and test the table is shown in Figure 1 - 19.

Field Name	**Data Type**	**Size (in lower pane)**	**Description**
Book Code	Text	6	Unique code of 3 letters and 2 digits
Title	Text	40	
Author	Text	40	
Year of Publication	Text	4	4 digit year
Publisher Code	Text	4	2 letters plus 2 digits
Price	Currency	(Size is automatic)	
Quantity in Stock	Number	Integer	

Table 1 - 5

Book Code	Title	Author	Year of Publication	Publisher Code	Price	Quantity in Stock
ATL11	Art Through Life	Jane Rick	1994	AW30	$22.95	86
CAL28	Calculus	Henry Slate	1977	TT12	$42.95	152
ECC22	Economically Correct	Lester Dane	1974	CE03	$32.95	81
EMP19	Even More Poems	Sina Grant	1976	BP07	$21.00	47
LOP18	Lots of Poems	Sina Grant	1973	BP07	$18.00	7
LUI81	Look Up In The Sky	Bruce Tipple	1989	TT12	$28.95	63
MOR47	Modern Russian	Igora Bylov	1990	CE03	$28.50	59
MUC17	Music Composition	Eliza Smith	1985	AW30	$32.95	127
MUH16	Music Harmony	Eliza Smith	1986	AW30	$32.95	86
POG17	The Physics of Glass	Kate Rice	1993	BP07	$7.95	80
PWM51	Philosophize With Me	Whyle Jones	1975	TT12	$30.95	115
WOH23	World of History	James Dyce	1988	CE03	$34.95	39
*					$0.00	0

Figure 1 - 19

1. Run *Access*.
2. Maximize the *Access* window if it does not already cover the entire screen.
3. Begin creating a new database to hold the book list (and later the publishers) with **FILE/New Database** or by clicking the **New Database** button on the toolbar.
4. Make certain the drive and directory are correct in the dialog box. If you will be using the A: drive and that is not currently selected, click on the drop-down arrow for the **Drives:** list and click on **A:**.
5. Type the name for the new database, **XERCISE2**, in the File Name box of the New Database dialog box and click the **OK** button.
6. Make sure the **Table** tab is selected and click the **New** button to begin a new table.
7. Click the **New Table** button in the **New Table** dialog box.
8. Fill in the seven fields as shown in Table 1 - 5. Remember to set the Size for each field (except the automatic one) in the lower section of the window.
9. Make **Book Code** the Primary Key by clicking anywhere on its line and clicking the **Primary Key** button on the toolbar. The key icon will appear on the record selector.
10. Save the table by picking **FILE/Save As**, entering the name: **Books**, and clicking the **OK** button.
11. Close the Table Window with **FILE/Close**.
12. With the highlight on **Books**, click the **Open** button to open the table for data entry.
13. Enter the twelve records shown in Figure 1 - 19. Be careful to match the upper or lower case characters for each entry. Some of the entries will scroll and be partially hidden since they are longer than the width that is currently showing for the column. That is perfectly all right. We will correct the situation in the next lesson.
14. When finished, close the table with **FILE/Close**.

    The book store owner comes to you with the realization that she forgot to include the Cost of a book which is an important piece of data. You need to modify the table structure to add the Cost.

15. With the highlight on **Books**, click the **Design** button to open the design of the table.
16. Since Cost should be placed before Price, press the **DOWN ARROW** five times to move onto the line that currently contains the Price field.
17. When on the line with Price, press the **INSERT** key to open a new line, which will push Price down to line 7.
18. Type the field name: **Cost** and press **TAB** to move to the Data Type column.

19. It will be a **Currency** field, so type a **C** and press **TAB**. The size will be automatic. No description is necessary.
20. Save the altered design with **FILE/Save**.
21. Close the table with **FILE/Close**.
22. Click the **Open** button to open Books.
23. Move to the **Cost** column and enter the values shown in the Cost column in Figure 1 - 20.

Book Code	Title	Author	Year of Pub	Publisher Code	Cost	Price	Quantity in Stock
ATL11	Art Through Life	Jane Rick	1994	AW30	$13.50	$22.95	86
CAL28	Calculus	Henry Slate	1977	TT12	$25.40	$42.95	152
ECC22	Economically Correct	Lester Dane	1974	CE03	$19.95	$32.95	81
EMP19	Even More Poems	Sina Grant	1976	BP07	$12.60	$21.00	47
LOP18	Lots of Poems	Sina Grant	1973	BP07	$10.80	$18.00	7
LUI81	Look Up In The Sky	Bruce Tipple	1989	TT12	$17.00	$28.95	63
MOR47	Modern Russian	Igora Bylov	1990	CE03	$17.00	$28.50	59
MUC17	Music Composition	Eliza Smith	1985	AW30	$19.50	$32.95	127
MUH16	Music Harmony	Eliza Smith	1986	AW30	$19.50	$32.95	86
POG17	The Physics of Glass	Kate Rice	1993	BP07	$4.75	$7.95	80
PWM51	Philosophize With Me	Whyle Jones	1975	TT12	$18.50	$30.95	115
WOH23	World of History	James Dyce	1988	CE03	$20.95	$34.95	39

Figure 1 - 20

24. Print the table with **FILE/Print** or the **Print** button on the toolbar. Click on the **OK** button.
25. Close the table with **FILE/Close**.
26. Close the database with **FILE/Close Database**.
27. If you are finished with *Access*, exit from *Access* with **FILE/Exit**.
28. If you are finished with Windows, exit from Windows with **FILE/Exit Windows**.

Independent Project 1.3: The Real Estate Office

During a summer job in a real estate office the manager learns of your work with databases, and asks you to create a database for the listings of commercial properties. He shows you a sample sheet that contains commercial offers and it lists 10 items of data: street address of the building, city, state, zip code, size in square feet, floor of the building, whether it is to purchase or rent, price, date it becomes available, and the code for the agency that holds the listing.

In order to include a Primary Key, a unique code number has been created for each listing. Thus, the 11 fields should be given the names in Table 1 - 6. The data you are given to get started and test the table is shown in Figure 1 - 21

Field Name	Description
Code	2 letters plus 2 digits (Primary Key)
Address	
City	
State	
Zip	
Size	Number of square feet
Floor	Number of the floor in the building
Purchase or Rent	The letter P or R
Price	
Available	Date available for occupancy
Agency Code	2 letters plus 2 digits

Table 1 - 6

	Code	Address	City	State	Zip	Size	Floor	Purchase or Rent	Price	Available	Agency
▶	ES52	5 Elm St.	Greenwich	CT	06830	4800	1	R	$72,000.00	6/1/95	SC18
	FA28	18 Frost Ave.	Greenwich	CT	06830	3700	2	R	$52,000.00	8/1/95	RR11
	GP25	12 Gedney Place	Danbury	CT	06810	8900	3	R	$105,000.00	7/15/95	SC18
	LW17	1 Lewis Way	Danbury	CT	06810	12000	2	R	$140,000.00	7/1/95	PP24
	MC29	Maple Court	New Canaan	CT	06840	450	1	P	$125,000.00	4/1/95	PP15
	MS11	22 Main St.	Stamford	CT	06901	5500	10	R	$75,000.00	5/20/95	RR11
	RP12	2 Research Park	Stamford	CT	06902	18000	1	P	$3,400,000.00	6/1/95	PP15
	RP13	3 Research Park	Stamford	CT	06902	18000	1	P	$3,400,000.00	6/1/95	GW14
	RP15	5 Research Park	Stamford	CT	06902	21000	1	P	$4,100,000.00	8/1/95	RP12
	RR19	952 River Rd.	Stamford	CT	06901	3750	6	R	$49,000.00	9/1/95	PP24
*						0	0		$0.00		

Figure 1 - 21

1. Create a new database named **XERCISE3.MDB** to hold the commercial real estate listings with **FILE/New Database** or by clicking the **New Database** button on the toolbar.
2. In XERCISE3, create a table. Fill in the Primary Key field together with the remaining 10 fields named in Table 1 - 6. Carefully choose a data type for each, and remember to set the size for each text and number field in the lower section of the table design window. Examine the data in Figure 1 - 21 to help decide the sizes. Make certain that the field **Size** (in square feet) is a number field of type **Long Integer**.
3. Save the table with the name: **Commercial Listings** and close the design window.
4. Open **Commercial Listings** for data entry.
5. Enter the ten records shown in Figure 1 - 21.
6. When finished, close the table.

   The manager notices that the agent's name is not included and requests an addition to the table design. A field named Agent should be added to the structure. It will contain the data shown in Figure 1 - 22.

7. Open the design of **Commercial Listings**.
8. Put the new field **Agent** at the end of the table. Examine the names in Figure 1 - 22 to see what size to make the field.
9. Save and close the design.
10. Open the table and enter the values shown in the Agent column in Figure 1 - 22.

	Code	Address	City	State	Zip	Size	Floor	Purc	Price	Available	Agency	Agent
▶	ES52	5 Elm St.	Greenwich	CT	06830	4800	1	R	$72,000.00	6/1/95	SC18	Brown
	FA28	18 Frost Ave.	Greenwich	CT	06830	3700	2	R	$52,000.00	8/1/95	RR11	Funchall
	GP25	12 Gedney Place	Danbury	CT	06810	8900	3	R	$105,000.00	7/15/95	SC18	Equat
	LW17	1 Lewis Way	Danbury	CT	06810	12000	2	R	$140,000.00	7/1/95	PP24	Smith
	MC29	Maple Court	New Canaan	CT	06840	450	1	P	$125,000.00	4/1/95	PP15	Green
	MS11	22 Main St.	Stamford	CT	06901	5500	10	R	$75,000.00	5/20/95	RR11	Wuthen
	RP12	2 Research Park	Stamford	CT	06902	18000	1	P	$3,400,000.00	6/1/95	PP15	Ruth
	RP13	3 Research Park	Stamford	CT	06902	18000	1	P	$3,400,000.00	6/1/95	GW14	Purcell
	RP15	5 Research Park	Stamford	CT	06902	21000	1	P	$4,100,000.00	8/1/95	RP12	Williams
	RR19	952 River Rd.	Stamford	CT	06901	3750	6	R	$49,000.00	9/1/95	PP24	Smith
*						0	0		$0.00			

Figure 1 - 22

11. Print the table.
12. Close the table.
13. Close the database.
14. If you are finished with *Access*, exit from *Access*.
15. If you are finished with Windows, exit from Windows.

Independent Project 1.4: The Veterinarian

The local veterinarian needs you to help with a database of the pets she tends. Since she likes to keep up on the names and ages of each pet she sees, the database will need to include the pet's name, date of birth (as closely as it is known), weight, color, and type of animal, as well as the owner's name, address and phone number. She gives you the list shown in Table 1 - 7 to get started.

In this project you are to do most of the planning as well as the creating of the database and table. While the data is listed in Table 1 - 7, you must determine the table name, field names, and data types. In this project you will build the table for the pets; in Lesson 3 you will include a table for the owners' data.

To include a Primary Key, you must create a unique code number for each pet. Whatever you call that field, you will probably want it to be the first field in the table.

NAME	DATE OF BIRTH	WEIGHT			OWNER CODE
Homer	2/15/94	35	dark brown	dog	AS19
Fifi	9/1/89	14	yellow	cat	AS19
Wild Thing	3/5/94	22	gray	dog	AS19
Runner	10/1/91	840	brown	horse	AS19
Spot	1/1/92	49	brown	dog	DW11
Fluffy	4/1/94	15	white	cat	MU25
George	8/15/91	67	brown	dog	MU25
Kuddles	7/1/92	12	orange	cat	MU25
Sir Strut	5/1/90	915	gray	horse	TR12
Yoshi	6/1/95	0.25	brown	hamster	TR12
Clank	7/1/94	13	gray	armadillo	WE31
Lilly	2/1/93	13	black	cat	PS14
Homer	1/1/92	75	white	dog	PS14
Sneaker	5/15/90	12	orange	cat	PS14

Table 1 - 7

Carry out the following steps using *Access*.

1. Study Table 1 - 7 to plan the structure of the data table.
2. Create a new database to hold the veterinarian's data.
3. In that new database, create the pet table. Be sure to include a Primary Key. IMPORTANT: You must name the field with the codes for the owners **Owner Code** in order to work with the table containing the owners' data that will be added in Lesson 3.
4. Enter the data shown in Table 1 - 7.

   After examining your design, the veterinarian notices that Date of Last Visit needs to be added to the table.

5. Add a field for Date of Last Visit and enter a different date for each pet, but each date must be within the last 12 months.
6. Print the table.
7. Close the database.
8. If you are finished with *Access*, exit from *Access*.
9. If you are finished with Windows, exit from Windows.

Lesson

2 Working with a Table's Data

Objectives

In this lesson you will learn how to:

- Open an existing database
- Move about within an *Access* table
- Size the fields in a table
- Move the fields within a table
- Edit a table's data
- Search for matching listings
- Delete records

PROJECT DESCRIPTION

In this lesson we will change the data within a table and the appearance of the table. Changing the data means editing the table. Since the data is recorded magnetically, editing it is a simple matter of typing the new values over the old data. Usually the appearance of a table will need adjusting by changing the display widths of fields, and sometimes the positions of fields.

While the editing is a straightforward task, locating the record that needs editing is often a bigger challenge. With thousands of listings in a table, you would not want to read every entry searching for the desired record. The computer program must perform that task for you since it can search many times faster than a human. Thus, we will also see how to search for matching records in this lesson.

After sizing the columns, editing some of the data, and deleting one record, the Employee table will look like Figure 2 - 1.

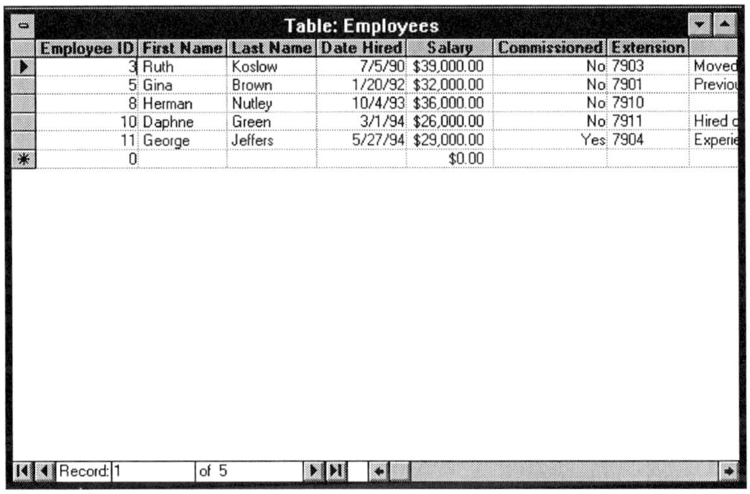
Table: Employees

Employee ID	First Name	Last Name	Date Hired	Salary	Commissioned	Extension	
3	Ruth	Koslow	7/5/90	$39,000.00	No	7903	Moved
5	Gina	Brown	1/20/92	$32,000.00	No	7901	Previo
8	Herman	Nutley	10/4/93	$36,000.00	No	7910	
10	Daphne	Green	3/1/94	$26,000.00	No	7911	Hired c
11	George	Jeffers	5/27/94	$29,000.00	Yes	7904	Experie
0				$0.00			

Record: 1 of 5

Figure 2 - 1

OPENING A DATABASE

To work with the objects in a database you must open that database.

To open an existing database:

- Choose **FILE/Open Database** or click the **Open Database** button on the toolbar.
- Pick the correct drive and directory if they are not already the right choices.
- Click on the desired database name and click **OK**.

Activity 2.1: Opening the SALES Database

1. Pick **FILE/Open Database**.
2. Make certain the correct drive and directory are chosen.
3. Click on **SALES.MDB** and click **OK**.

MOVING ABOUT WITHIN A TABLE

Before you can change any data you must move to the position of that data. There are ways to move about within a table using the mouse or the keyboard. While the arrow keys may be best for navigating short distances, data tables often consist of thousands of records. Moving from the first to the thousandth listing with only the arrow keys would be impractical. Thus, the following methods are important for faster and more efficient navigation.

To move about a table with the mouse:

- Click the mouse on any field that is visible to position the cursor within that field.
- The *Navigation Buttons* are the four buttons with triangles on their faces on the left half of the bottom line of the window frame (see Figure 2 - 2). The first button jumps to record 1 and the fourth button jumps to the last record. The second and third Navigation Buttons jump to the preceding and next records, respectively. The cursor remains in the same field during these moves.

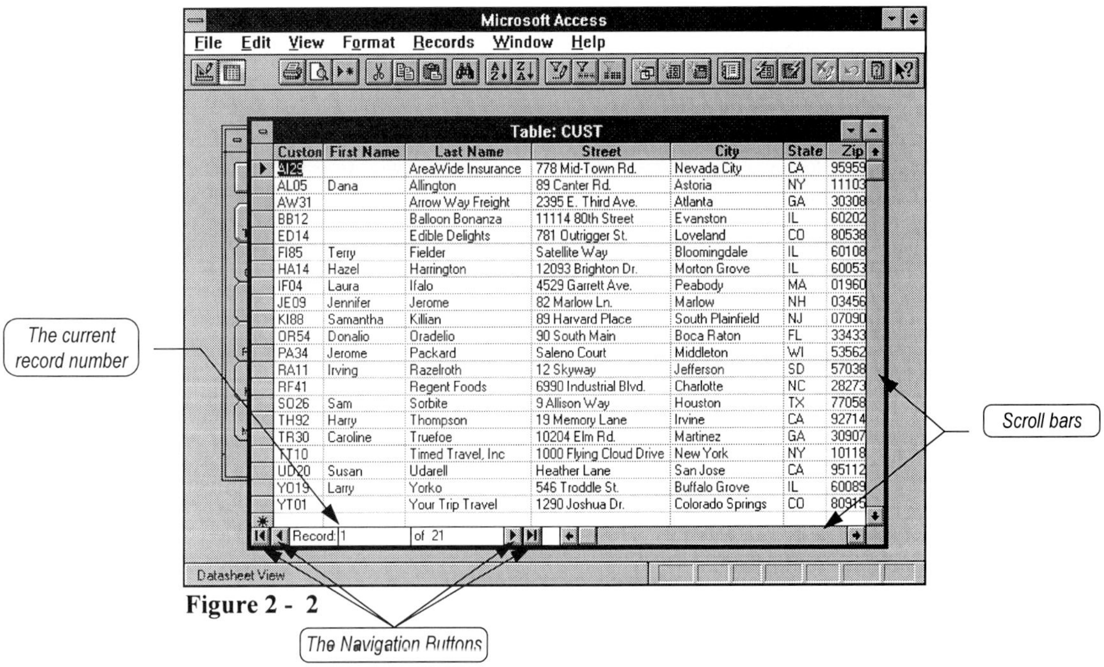

Figure 2 - 2

- Between the two pairs of Navigation Buttons is the current **Record:** number indicator (see Figure 2 - 2). Clicking the mouse on that number places the cursor next to its digits, so that you can delete the current value and type the number of the record to which you want to jump. After pressing **ENTER**, you will be placed on the desired record.
- The *scroll bars* at the right edge of the table window and in the right half of the bottom line of the window frame will scroll to a section of the table not currently showing in the window (see Figure 2 - 2). The scroll bars do not actually move the cursor, and, thus, it is possible to scroll the table so that the cursor cannot be seen. Once you have scrolled far enough to see the desired data, click the mouse on that field to position the cursor there. Each scroll bar only appears when actually needed, that is, when the table actually extends beyond the window boundary.

Activity 2.2: Navigating Within a Table with the Mouse

1. The **SALES** database should be open.
2. Make certain the **Table** tab is selected.
3. Select the **Employees** table and click the **Open** button at the top of the **Database** window to open that table into a window.
4. Notice between the Navigation Buttons that the current record number is **1**.
5. Click the **Last Record** button (fourth Navigation Button) to jump to the last record.

   *The Navigation line should now say **Record 6 of 6** as in* Figure 2 - 3.

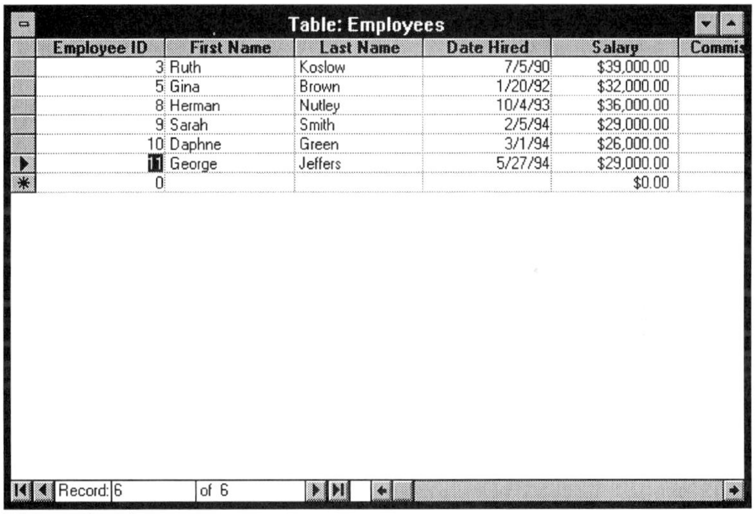

Figure 2 - 3

6. Click the **Previous Record** button (second Navigation Button) to jump to the preceding record.
7. Click the **First Record** button to jump to record 1.
8. Click the mouse on the number **1** of **Record: 1 of 6** between the Navigation Buttons and remove the 1 with either the **BACKSPACE** or the **DELETE** key. Type **4** and press the **ENTER** key to jump to record 4.
9. Click three times the **rightward pointing arrow** at the right end of the scroll bar on the bottom edge of the table's window to scroll to the right so that you can see the last field in the table. Notice that you can no longer see the selection highlight on the Employee ID field (see Figure 2 - 4).

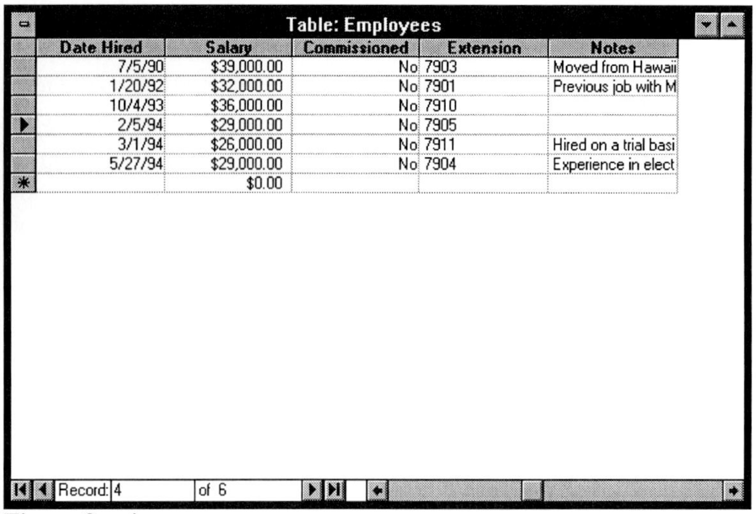

Figure 2 - 4

10. Scroll back to the first field so you can see the cursor and selection highlight in the Employee ID field.

To move about a table with keys:

- The **arrow keys** move one line up or down or one field to the left or right in the direction of the arrow.
- The **TAB** key moves to the next field and **SHIFT+TAB** moves to the previous field. (The **ENTER** key will usually move to the next column, but not in every situation. Thus, **TAB** is preferred.)
- **PGUP** (or **PAGE UP**) and **PGDN** (or **PAGE DOWN**) move up or down the number of records showing in the window; that is, they jump to the next screenful of records.
- **HOME** jumps to the first field and **END** jumps to the last field.
- **CTRL+HOME** jumps to the first field in the first record.
- **CTRL+END** jumps to the last field on the last record.

Activity 2.3: Navigating Within a Table with Keys

1. Press **CTRL+END** to jump to the last field of the last record.
2. Press **CTRL+HOME** to jump to the first field of record 1.
3. Press the **DOWN ARROW** to move to record **2**.
4. Press **END** to jump to the last field within record 2.
5. Press **HOME** to jump to the first field of the current record.
6. Press **TAB** four times to move to the **Salary** field.
7. Close the table with **FILE/Close**.

SIZING FIELDS

When a table is created, all fields, no matter what data type or designed size, are displayed at the default width of 18.8 characters wide. Thus, you usually need to change the display width of the majority of columns. The gray rectangle that contains the field name at the top of each column of data is called the *field selector*. You can use the mouse to either drag the line at the right edge of the field selector until the width looks right, or double click the same line to have *Access* perform a "best fit." *Best fit* means that *Access* will check all entries in the field to determine which is the longest. It will then adjust the field width to either the longest entry in the column or the field name, whichever is longer.

To change the display width of a column:

- Move the mouse pointer on top of the line at the right edge of the desired field selector (see Figure 2 - 5). The mouse pointer will become a double-headed left-and-right pointing arrow. Hold down the mouse button and drag the mouse to the left to narrow the column or to the right to widen it.

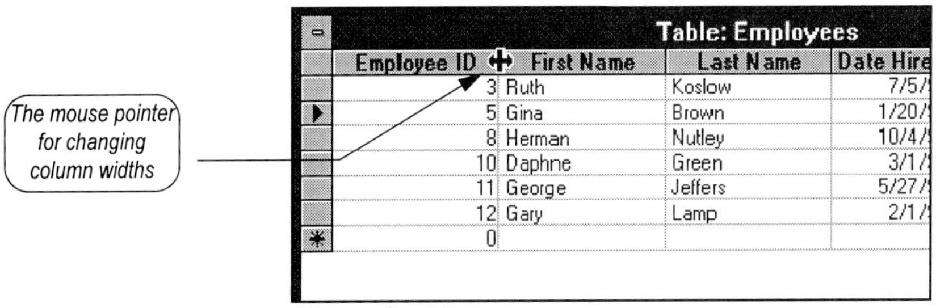

Figure 2 - 5

- To achieve a best fit for the whole column, double-click the line on the right edge of the field selector.

Activity 2.4: Sizing a Table's Fields

1. The **Sales** database should be open.
2. Make certain the **Table** tab is selected.
3. Click on the **Employees** table and click the **Open** button at the top of the database window to open that table into a window.

   SHORTCUT: *To open a table, double-click on the table name.*

4. Move the mouse pointer on top of the right edge of the field selector for the **Employee ID** field. When the mouse cursor shape is a double-headed left-and-right arrow, hold down the mouse button and drag the line to the left until it is between the two letters **pl** of Employee. Release the mouse button.

   Four or five letters will probably now show in the title (see Figure 2 - 6*) since the name had been centered so that there was extra space ahead of the field name. Notice that you may hide part of the field name.*

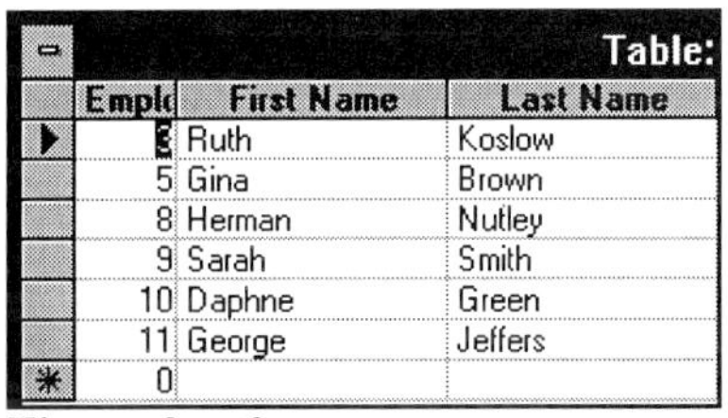

Figure 2 - 6

5. Increase the width of the same field so that the entire field name, **Employee ID**, shows.

6. Narrow the width of the **First Name** field so that the field name just fits (see Figure 2 - 7).

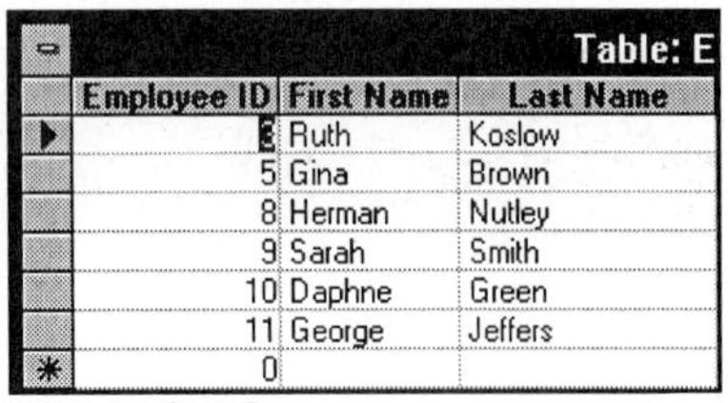

Figure 2 - 7

7. Move the mouse on top of the line at the right edge of the field selector for the **Last Name** column and double-click the mouse button to do a best fit.

   The field width should adjust to the size of the field name since that name is longer than any data item in the column.

8. Perform a best fit on the **Date Hired, Salary, Commissioned,** and **Extension** columns.

   You may need to scroll with the scroll bar to get to the right edge of the ***Extension*** *field's selector box.*

9. Widen the **Notes** field so that it reveals the entire length of every note.

10. Choose **FILE/Save Table** to record the new widths.

MOVING FIELDS

On occasion you may need one or more fields in a different position while viewing the table. Perhaps you need to see the first and last columns simultaneously. You may move fields to new positions either temporarily or permanently. Moving fields does not restructure the table; it only repositions the fields for viewing purposes. To move them, merely select the field and drag the field selector to a new position. When you close the table you will be asked whether or not to save the layout changes and make them permanent.

To move a field:

- Click the mouse on the field selector at the top of the desired column. The entire column will be highlighted.
- Move the mouse cursor back on top of the field selector, hold down the mouse button, and drag the field to a new position. As you drag the field, you will see a thick highlight on top of the line that separates one column from another. When the highlight is in the position that you want the field to occupy, release the mouse button.

Activity 2.5: Moving Fields

We will move the **Notes** field in-between **Last Name** and **Date Hired** so we can see the names and notes simultaneously.

1. The **Employees** table should still be open. If not, open it.
2. Press the **END** key to jump to the **Notes** field.
3. Move the mouse on top of the field selector and click the mouse button to select the entire **Notes** column (see Figure 2 - 8).

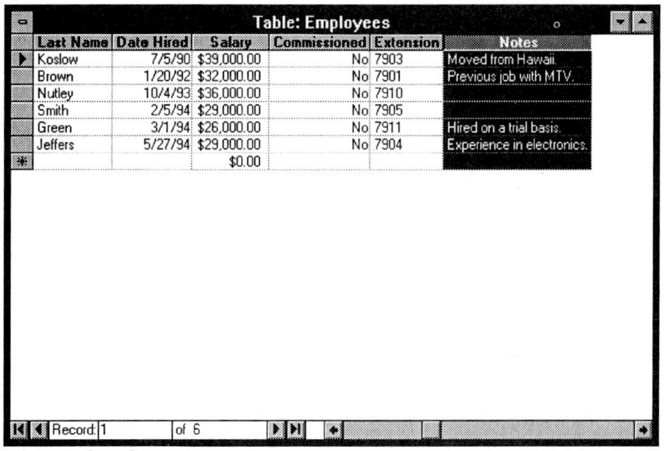

Figure 2 - 8

4. Move the mouse back on top of the field selector and hold down the mouse button. Drag the mouse to the left until the highlight that jumps from separator line to separator between the fields is between **Last Name** and **Date Hired** (see Figure 2 - 9). Release the mouse button.

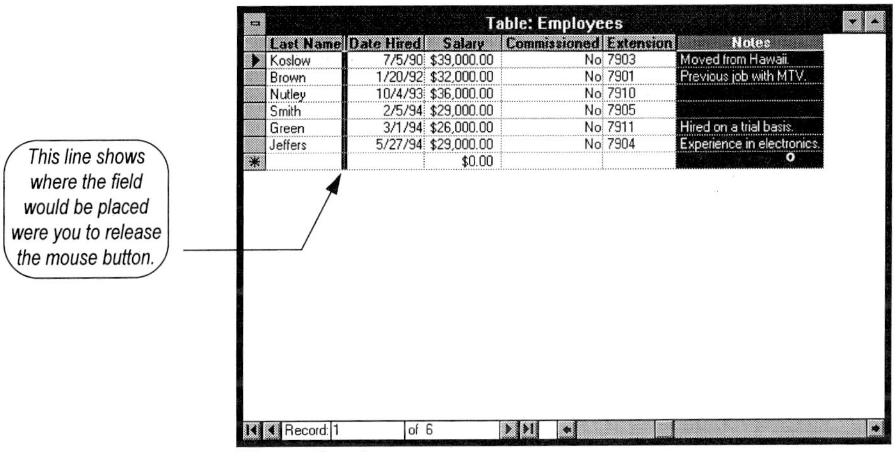

Figure 2 - 9

5. Press the **HOME** key to jump to the first field.

   Notice that you can now see the ID, names, and notes simultaneously.

6. Choose **FILE/Close** to close the table.

7. As the change of position of the **Notes** field was only intended to be temporary, answer **Save layout changes to Table 'Employees'?** by clicking the **No** button (see Figure 2 - 10).

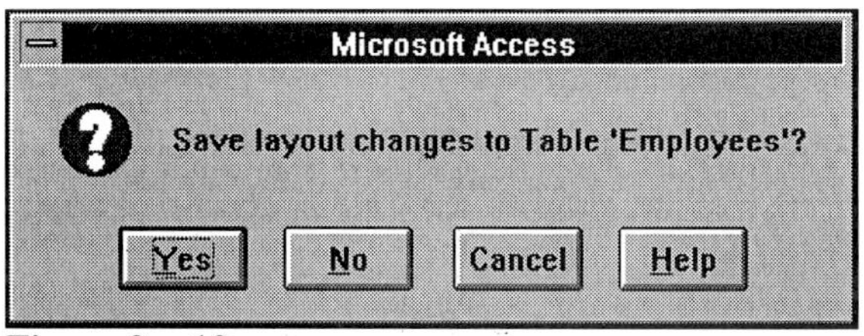

Figure 2 - 10

EDITING A TABLE'S DATA

To edit the data in an *Access* table, move to the data that needs to be changed and type over the old entry with a new entry. The table is always in edit mode unless you uncheck the menu item **RECORDS/Allow Editing**.

To replace an entire field's entry:

- If you use the keys or Navigation Buttons to move to a field, the entire entry in the field will be highlighted (see Figure 2 - 11). While the entry is highlighted, the next character you type would replace the entire entry.

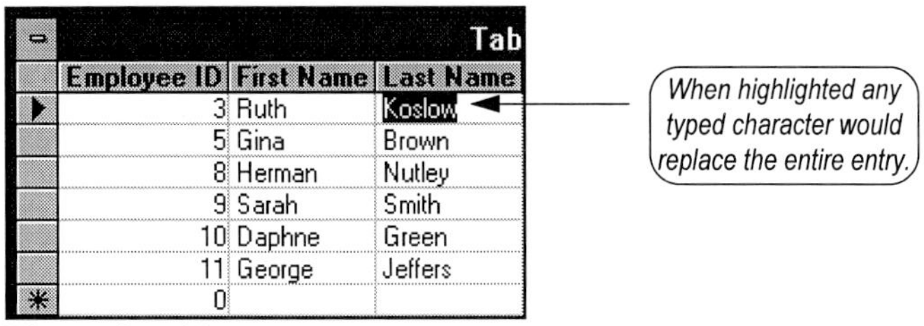

Figure 2 - 11

- Should you accidentally erase an entire entry while it is highlighted, choose **EDIT/Undo Typing** immediately. If you only notice the accident after you have moved to another record, you can still choose **EDIT/Undo Saved Record**, but only if you have not edited any other record yet.

To edit a few characters within a field:

- To switch to a moveable cursor within the field, either press the **F2** Edit Mode key, or click the mouse within the field. Once the cursor is blinking within the field (see Figure 2 - 12), you may use the left and right arrow keys to move from character to character, press **BACKSPACE** or **DELETE** to remove characters, and insert new characters.

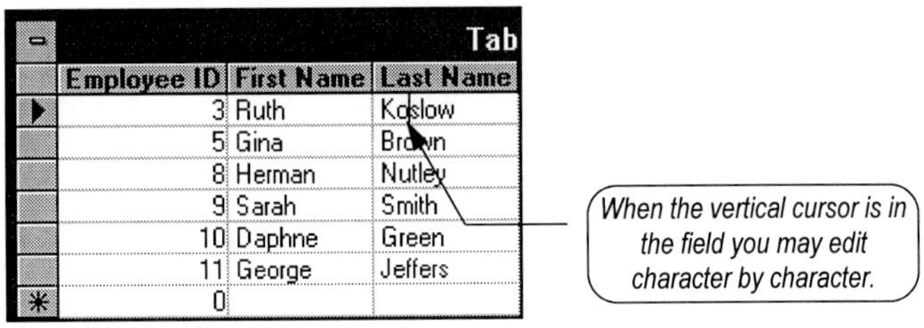

Figure 2 - 12

- To overstrike existing characters and replace them, press the **INSERT** key. **OVR** will appear on the Status Bar. Since you usually need to insert characters, be sure to press **INSERT** again to return to insert mode when you are finished overstriking.
- To return to Navigation Mode so that the entire entry is highlighted and the movement keys function normally, press **F2** again, or move to another field with **TAB**, or the **UP** or **DOWN ARROW** keys.

While editing (or entering) data, you do not need to do anything to save the changes. The moment you move to a different record, any data changes are registered. Thus, at no time is more than one record unsaved.

Activity 2.6: Editing Data

Sarah Smith has received a raise; she now makes $31,000. We need to correct her record. Also, Sarah and George Jeffers are on commission, so we need to update that field. Finally, we will add the note **Looking for a new position** to Sarah's **Notes** field.

1. Select the **Employees** table and click the **Open** button at the top of the **Database** window to open that table into a window.
2. Click the mouse between the **$** and the **2** of Sarah Smith's **Salary** to move to that field and position the cursor (see Figure 2 - 13). If the vertical insertion bar is not blinking between the **$** and **2**, press **ARROW** keys until it is.

Date Hired	Salary	Commissioned
7/5/90	$39,000.00	No
1/20/92	$32,000.00	No
10/4/93	$36,000.00	No
2/5/94	$29,000.00	No
3/1/94	$26,000.00	No
5/27/94	$29,000.00	No
	$0.00	

Click between the $ and the 2.

Figure 2 - 13

3. If the Status Bar shows an **OVR** at the right end, press the **INSERT** key to return to insert mode. The **OVR** should not show.
4. Press the **DELETE** key twice to remove the **29**.
5. Type **31** to insert the new value.
6. Press the **TAB** key to move to the **Commissioned** field.

   *The current value in the field, **No**, should be highlighted.*
7. Type **Yes** to replace the old value in the **Commissioned** field (see Figure 2 - 14).

Salary	Commissioned	Extension
$39,000.00	No	7903
$32,000.00	No	7901
$36,000.00	No	7910
$31,000.00	yes	7905
$26,000.00	No	7911
$29,000.00	No	7904
$0.00		

Figure 2 - 14

8. Press the **TAB** key twice to move to the **Notes** field.
9. Enter: **Looking for a new job.** in the **Notes** field.
10. Click the mouse on the **Commissioned** field of **George Jeffers'** record.

    *If you cannot see the last name Jeffers, press **HOME** to jump to the first field, move onto the record for George Jeffers, and press **TAB** to move to the **Commissioned** field.*
11. Remove the **No** and enter: **Yes**.
12. Press **TAB** to move to the next field.

    *Should the message **The value you entered isn't appropriate for this field** appear, you need to correct the entry so it has exactly the characters **Yes**.*

13. Choose **FILE/Close** to close the table.

    The changes are automatically saved. We will print the new data.

14. With the highlight on the table name, **Employees**, click the **Print** button on the toolbar and click **OK** in the print dialog box.

SEARCHING FOR RECORDS

While the typing of changes to the data in a table is relatively straightforward, finding the record, especially as the table gets large, can be more difficult. With hundreds or thousands of records you cannot take the time (nor would you want to) to read every name or code number looking for a matching value. The program can search much faster and does not tire of reading data.

To search for a value in a table:

- Choose **EDIT/Find** or click the **Find**  button on the toolbar.
- In the Find dialog box (see Figure 2 - 15), type the value to be located in the Find What text box.

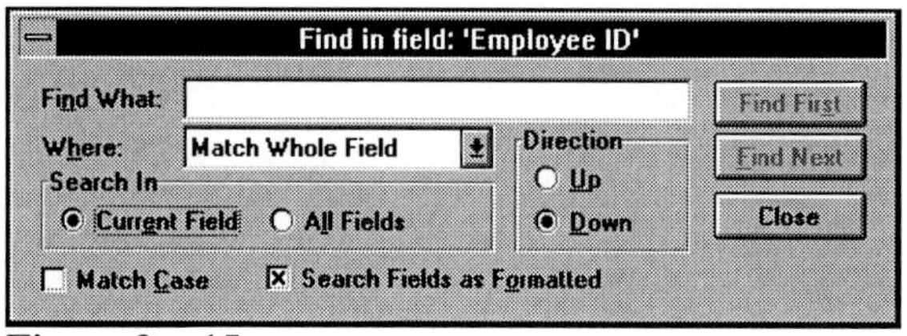

Figure 2 - 15

- In the **Where:** list, pick either **Any Part of Field** to look for the desired characters embedded anywhere within a field's entry, **Match Whole Field** to require an exact match of all characters, or **Start of Field** to match only the starting characters for as many characters as you enter.
- For **Search In** choose either **Current Field** if you positioned the cursor in the appropriate field and want to limit the search to only that field, or **All Fields** to search every column in the table.
- Check **Match Case** only if you have typed correctly capitalized characters and want to restrict matches to that capitalization.
- **Search Fields as Formatted** allows for dollar signs, commas, and other characters that show in the table even though they may not have been typed. If those special characters must be matched, check this option.
- The choice for **Direction** often does not matter as *Access* will ask to continue the search by wrapping from the bottom of the table to the top, and vice versa. Pick whichever direction you think will locate the desired value faster.
- The three command buttons will locate the first match in the table (**Find First**), the next match (**Find Next**), or **Close** the dialog box. Since you might need to continue the search several times to locate a record, the dialog box remains open until you close it.
- Should the dialog box obscure the data that you need to see, drag it higher or lower on the screen by dragging its Title Bar, as you would with any window.

Activity 2.7: Searching for Matching Records

Because of an approaching project, we need to find the two employees with experience in television (with MTV) and electronics.

1. Select the **Employees** table and click the **Open** button at the top of the **Database** window to open that table.
2. Click the **Find** button  on the toolbar.
3. In the **Find** dialog box, type: **mtv** in the **Find What** text box (see Figure 2 - 16).

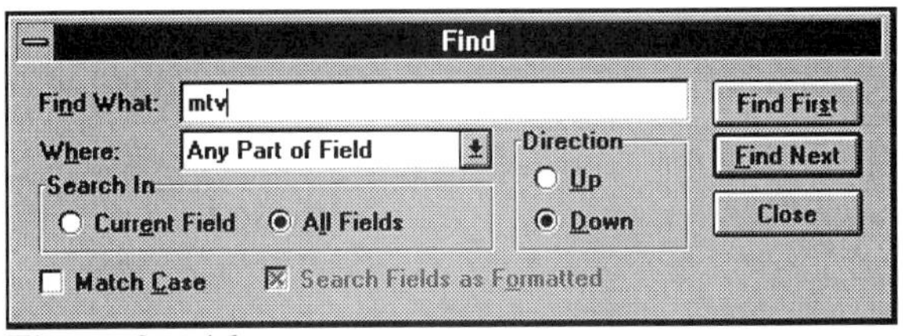

Figure 2 - 16

4. For **Where**, open the drop-down list and choose **Any Part of Field**.
5. Pick **All Fields** for **Search In**.
6. Leave **Match Case** unchecked. **Down** is the best choice for **Direction**. Click the **Find First** button.

   The triangle on the record selectors at the left end of each row will jump to Brown and the record number between the Navigation Buttons will show record 2 (see Figure 2 - 17*) even though the dialog box is obscuring the record.*

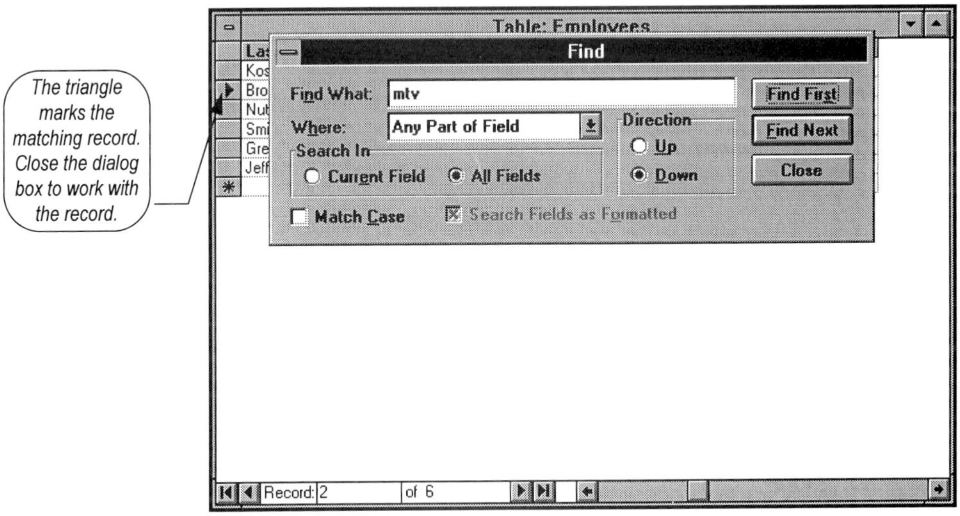

Figure 2 - 17

7. Click the **Close** button.

   ***MTV** should be highlighted.*
8. Click the **Find** button  on the toolbar.

9. Move the mouse cursor on top of the Title Bar at the top of the dialog box, hold down the mouse button, and drag the **Find** dialog box down into the open space in the bottom of the table window so it does not cover the data (see Figure 2 - 18).

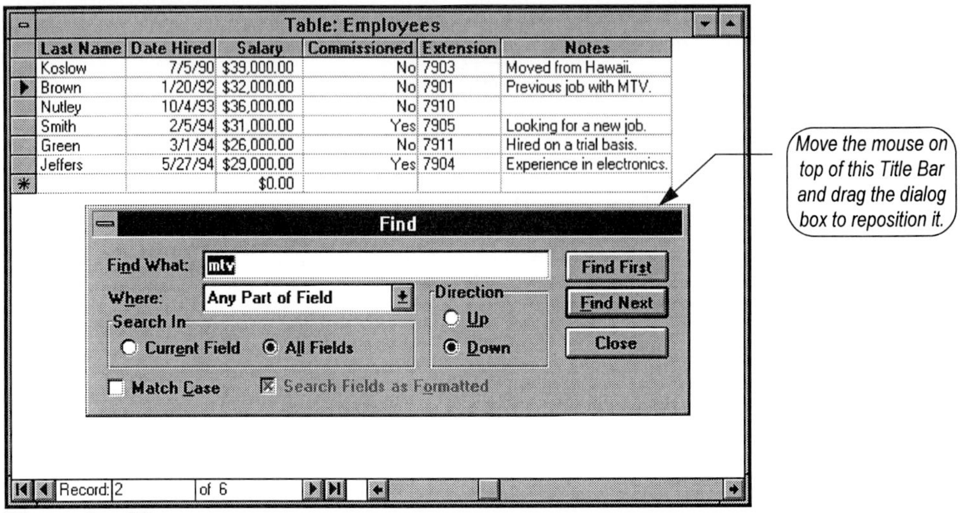

Figure 2 - 18

10. In the **Find** dialog box, type: **electronics** on top of **mtv** in the **Find What** text box to replace the earlier characters.
11. **Where** should remain as **Any Part of Field.**
12. **Search In** should still have **All Fields** selected.
13. Leave **Match Case** unchecked, and **Down** is again the best choice for **Direction**. Click the **Find First** button.

    The triangle on the record selectors at the left end of each listing will jump to Jeffers and the record number between the Navigation Buttons will show 6 (see Figure 2 - 19).

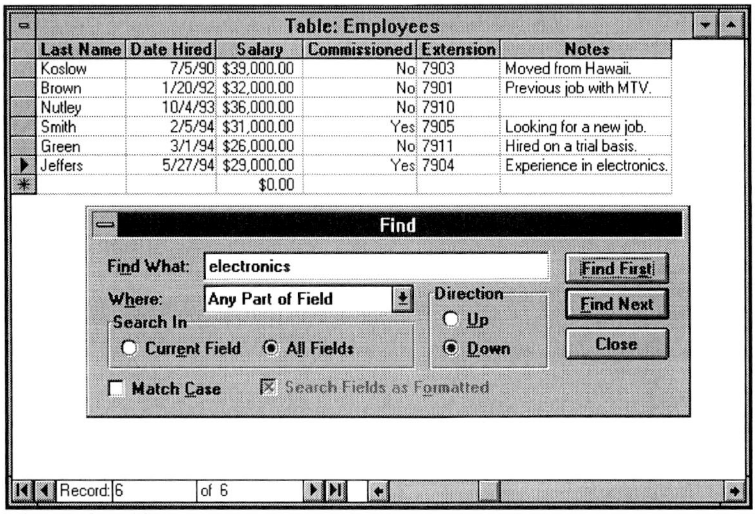

Figure 2 - 19

14. Perhaps there is someone else with electronics experience, so click the **Find Next** button.

    *The message **Microsoft Access reached the end of the records. Do you want to continue searching from the beginning?** appears (see* Figure 2 - 20*). Since we previously found the first match, and there are no additional matches toward the end of the table, there can be no other matches.*

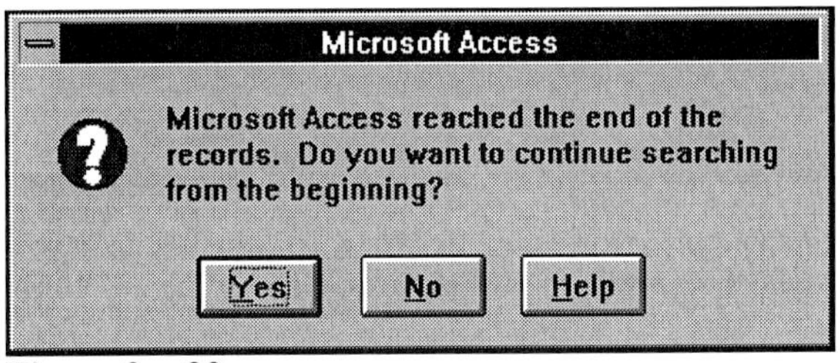

Figure 2 - 20

15. Click **No**.
16. Click the **Close** button to close the **Find** dialog box.
17. Press the **HOME** key to see the full name and Employee ID of the person with electronics experience.

Activity 2.8: Editing a Matching Record

After asking Gina Brown about her MTV experience, it turns out she actually worked for CTW, Children's Television Workshop, not MTV. We need to correct the inaccurate data.

1. If the **Employees** table is not already open, click the **Open** button.
2. Click the **Find** button on the toolbar.
3. In the **Find** dialog box, replace electronics with: **mtv** in the **Find What** text box.

   Access remembers what you searched for the last time in case you need to repeat that search.
4. All other choices are still correct, so click the **Find First** button.

   *Brown will again become the selected record and **MTV** will be highlighted.*
5. Click the **Close** button to close the dialog box.
6. Since **MTV** is highlighted, merely type: **Children's Television Workshop**, and the new name will replace the old (see Figure 2 - 21).

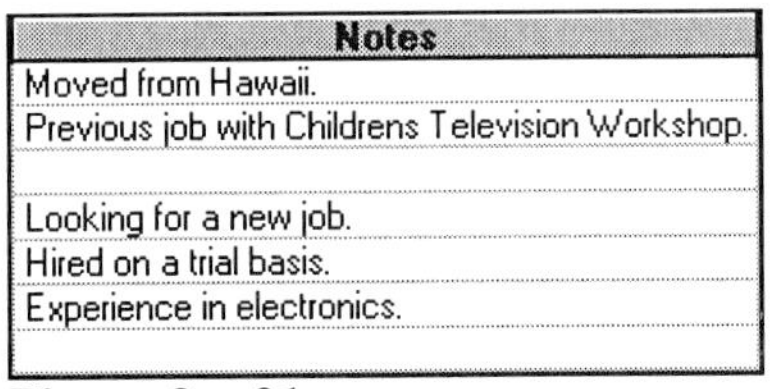

Figure 2 - 21

7. To adjust the column width for this longer note, double-click the line at the right edge of the field selector.

Activity 2.9: Searching for an Exact Match

We need to locate the employee whose ID number is 9. Were we to leave **Any Part of Field** as the choice for **Where,** *Access* would stop at every field that contains a 9. The extensions, salaries, and hired dates have many 9s in them. It would take a while to work through the unwanted 9s before arriving at Employee ID number 9. Therefore, we need to change the choice for **Where** to **Match Whole Field.**

1. If the **Employees** table is not already open, click the **Open** button.
2. Click the **Find** button  on the toolbar.
3. In the **Find** dialog box, replace **mtv** with: **9** in the **Find What** text box.
4. Click on the drop-down arrow for the **Where:** list and pick **Match Whole Field** (see Figure 2 - 22).

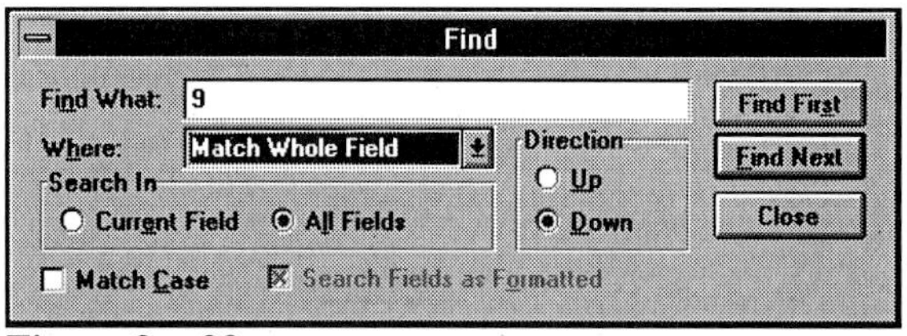

Figure 2 - 22

5. Click **Find First.**

   The Employee ID for Sarah Smith should be highlighted on record 4.
6. Close the **Find** dialog box by clicking the **Close** button.
7. Close the table with **FILE/Close.**

   Because you have made changes to the column width of the ***Notes*** *field, the message for saving the layout changes appears.*
8. Click **Yes** to save the layout changes.

DELETING RECORDS

Records can be deleted by merely selecting the record or records, and either pressing the **DELETE** key or choosing **EDIT/Delete** in the menu. When you delete, *Access* will ask you to confirm or cancel the deletion. If you confirm the deletion with the **OK** button, the record(s) are permanently erased, and the operation cannot be undone. If you select the **Cancel** button, the records are restored and no deletion takes place.

Selecting one or more records is accomplished by moving the mouse on top of the *record selector* (the gray block at the left edge of each record) and clicking the mouse button for a single record, or dragging the mouse across several rows' selectors to select a group of neighboring records. The **EDIT** menu also has two selection choices. **Select Record** will select the current record and **Select All Records** will select every record.

To delete a record:

- Select the record or records to be deleted.
- Press the **DELETE** key or choose **EDIT/Delete** in the menu.
- Confirm the deletion by clicking the **OK** button.

Activity 2.10: Deleting a Record

Sarah Smith has left the company. We need to delete her record.

1. Select the **Employees** table and click the **Open** button at the top of the **Database** window to open that table.
2. Click the mouse on the record selector at the left edge of the line for Sarah Smith (see Figure 2 - 23).

Click on the record selector to select the entire record.

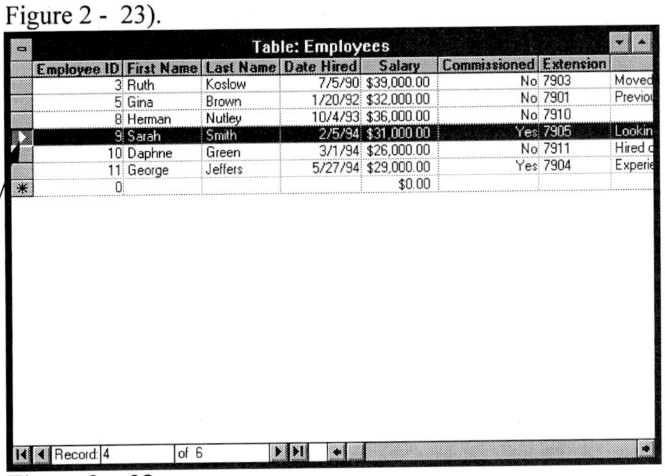

Figure 2 - 23

The mouse pointer will become a rightward pointing arrow on top of the record selector. The entire row will be highlighted when you click the mouse button.

3. Press the **DELETE** key.
4. Confirm the deletion by clicking the **OK** button in the **You've just deleted 1 record(s)...** alert box (see Figure 2 - 24).

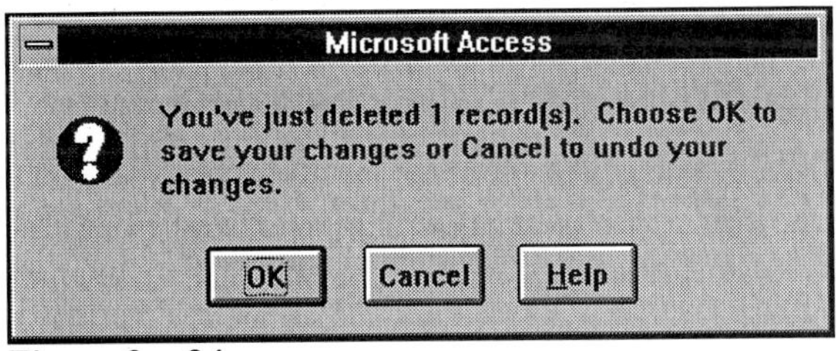

Figure 2 - 24

5. Print the table by clicking the **Print** button on the toolbar and clicking **OK**.
6. Close the table with **FILE/Close**.

SUMMARY

In this project you have made several different types of changes to a table. You have sized the fields and moved them into different positions. You have edited the data and searched for the listings that needed editing. You have deleted a record. In Lesson 3 you will add additional tables to the database, and in Lesson 4 you will find complete sets of matching records and work with multiple tables at one time.

KEY TERMS

Best-fit
Field Selector
Navigation Buttons
Record Selector
Undo

INDEPENDENT PROJECTS

Independent Project 2.1: The School Newspaper

This Independent Project continues the Newspaper Ad database you began in Independent Project 1.1. In this project you will edit the table to make some changes to the data, size the fields, move a field, delete a record, and search for listings.

The following changes need to be made. When finished, the table should look like Figure 2 - 25.

- Pizza Plus has changed their ad number 2389 to a Full Page. They paid the larger fee on 5/11/95.
- The Student Grill paid for ad number 2396 on 5/12/95.
- College Movies has cancelled its ad number 2392.

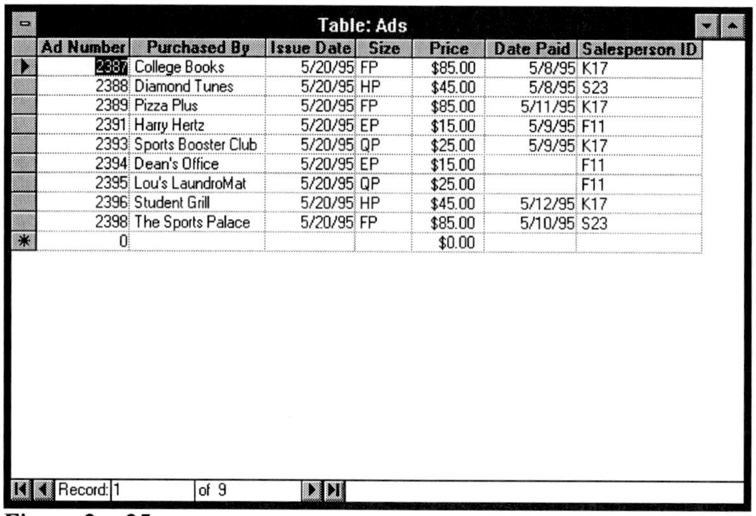
Table: Ads

Ad Number	Purchased By	Issue Date	Size	Price	Date Paid	Salesperson ID
2387	College Books	5/20/95	FP	$85.00	5/8/95	K17
2388	Diamond Tunes	5/20/95	HP	$45.00	5/8/95	S23
2389	Pizza Plus	5/20/95	FP	$85.00	5/11/95	K17
2391	Harry Hertz	5/20/95	EP	$15.00	5/9/95	F11
2393	Sports Booster Club	5/20/95	QP	$25.00	5/9/95	K17
2394	Dean's Office	5/20/95	EP	$15.00		F11
2395	Lou's LaundroMat	5/20/95	QP	$25.00		F11
2396	Student Grill	5/20/95	HP	$45.00	5/12/95	K17
2398	The Sports Palace	5/20/95	FP	$85.00	5/10/95	S23
0				$0.00		

Record: 1 of 9

Figure 2 - 25

1. Run *Access*.
2. Maximize the *Access* window if it does not already cover the entire screen.
3. Begin opening the **xercise1.mdb** database with **FILE/Open Database** or by clicking the **Open Database** tool on the toolbar.
4. Click on the name **xercise1.mdb** and click the **OK** button.
5. Open the **Ads** table by clicking on the name in the list of tables and clicking the **Open** button.
6. To change Pizza Plus' ad number 2389 to a Full Page, begin by searching for that ad number. Click the **Find** button on the toolbar, type **2389** into the Find What text box, and click the **Find First** button.
7. The triangle record marker should already have moved to record 3, but to see the record click the **Close** button.

8. Press **TAB** twice to move to the **Size** field.
9. The **HP** should be highlighted, so merely type: **FP** to replace the old value.
10. Press **TAB** again to jump to the Price column and enter: **85**
11. Press **TAB** once more and change the Date Paid to **5/11/95**. You can either retype the entire date, or press **F2** to switch into edit mode and change the 9 to an 11.
12. To fill in the Date Paid for the Student Grill ad number 2396, begin by searching for that ad number. Click the **Find** button on the toolbar, type **2396** into the Find What text box, click the **All Fields** option button, and click the **Find First** button.
13. The triangle record marker should already have moved to record 9, but to see the record click the **Close** button.
14. Press **TAB** four times to move to the **Date Paid** field.
15. Enter: **5/12/95**
16. To remove the College Movies ad number 2392, begin by searching for that ad number. Click the **Find** button on the toolbar, type **2392** into the Find What text box, check that the **All Fields** option button is still selected, and click the **Find First** button.
17. The triangle record marker should already have moved to record 5, but to see the record click the **Close** button.
18. Click the mouse on the gray **selector box** at the left end of that record to select the entire listing.
19. Press the **DELETE** key and click the **OK** button in the alert box that appears.
20. Press the **END** key to jump to the Issue Date field.
21. Click the mouse on the gray **selector** at the top of the column (where the field name is) to select the entire column.
22. Move the mouse back on top of the selector, hold down the left mouse button and drag that field to the left until the dark highlight is between Purchased By and Size. Release the mouse button to drop the field and reposition it there.
23. Press the **HOME** key to jump to the first field.
24. Resize the **Ad Number** field by moving the mouse on top of the right edge of its selector (at the top of that column) and either dragging the line until it's the proper size or double-clicking to do a best fit.
25. Similarly, resize the remaining fields (see Figure 2 - 25).
26. Print the table by clicking the **Print** button on the toolbar. Print **1** copy of **All** pages at the appropriate Print Quality. Click **OK**.
27. Close the table with **FILE/Close**. Answer **Save layout changes to Table 'Ads'?** by clicking **Yes**.
28. Close the database with **FILE/Close Database**.
29. If you need to exit from *Access* and/or Windows, do so properly.

Independent Project 2.2: The Book Store

This Independent Project continues the Book Store database you began in Independent Project 1.2. In this project you will edit the table to make some changes to the data, size the fields, delete a record, and search for listings.

The following changes need to be made:

- The book with code ALT11 ("Art Through Life") has the wrong publisher code. Instead of AW30, it should be TT12.
- The music students have purchased their texts so that the Quantity in Stock of MUC17 ("Music Composition") has dropped from 127 to 85, and the Quantity in Stock of MUH16 ("Music Harmony") has dropped from 86 to 48.
- The Author of LUI81 ("Look Up In The Sky") is incorrect. Instead of Bruce Tipple, it should be Bruce Tiggle.
- LOP18 ("Lots of Poems") is being discontinued, so it should be deleted.

When finished, the table should look like Figure 2 - 26.

	Book Code	Title	Author	Year of Pub	Publisher Code	Cost	Price	Quantity in Stock
	ATL11	Art Through Life	Jane Rick	1994	TT12	$13.50	$22.95	86
	CAL28	Calculus	Henry Slate	1977	TT12	$25.40	$42.95	152
	ECC22	Economically Correct	Lester Dane	1974	CE03	$19.95	$32.95	81
	EMP19	Even More Poems	Sina Grant	1976	BP07	$12.60	$21.00	47
▶	LUI81	Look Up In The Sky	Bruce Tiggle	1989	TT12	$17.00	$28.95	63
	MOR47	Modern Russian	Igora Bylov	1990	CE03	$17.00	$28.50	59
	MUC17	Music Composition	Eliza Smith	1985	AW30	$19.50	$32.95	85
	MUH16	Music Harmony	Eliza Smith	1986	AW30	$19.50	$32.95	48
	POG17	The Physics of Glass	Kate Rice	1993	BP07	$4.75	$7.95	80
	PWM51	Philosophize With Me	Whyle Jones	1975	TT12	$18.50	$30.95	115
	WOH23	World of History	James Dyce	1988	CE03	$20.95	$34.95	39
*						$0.00	$0.00	0

Figure 2 - 26

1. Run *Access.*
2. Maximize the *Access* window if it does not already cover the entire screen.
3. Begin opening the **xercise2.mdb** database with **FILE/Open Database** or by clicking the **Open Database** tool on the toolbar.
4. Click on the name **xercise2.mdb** and click the **OK** button.
5. Open the **Books** table by clicking on the name in the list of tables and clicking the **Open** button.
6. Maximize the table window by clicking it's **Maximize Button**.
7. To change the publisher code for ALT11 ("Art Through Life") from AW30 to TT12, you need to locate the record. It is the first record, so you don't need to search.
8. Press **TAB** four times to move to the **Publisher Code** field.
9. The **AW30** should be highlighted, so merely type: **TT12** to replace the old value.
10. To update the Quantity in Stock for the two music texts, begin by searching for the first book's code number. Click the **Find** button on the toolbar, type **MUC17** into the Find What text box, and click the **All Fields** option button. Where: should say **Match Whole Field**, Match Case should not be checked, and Direction can be **Down**. Click the **Find First** button.
11. The triangle record marker should already have moved to record 8, but to see the record click the **Close** button.
12. Press the **END** key to jump to the **Quantity in Stock** field.
13. The **127** should be highlighted, so merely type: **85** to replace the old value.

14. To update the Quantity in Stock for the second music text, search for the Book Code by clicking the **Find** button on the toolbar, typing **MUH16** into the Find What text box, and clicking the **Find First** button. All the other options remain the same as in the first search.
15. The triangle record marker should moved to record 9. To see the record click the **Close** button.
16. Press the **END** key to jump to the **Quantity in Stock** field.
17. The **86** should be highlighted, so merely type: **48** to replace the old value.
18. To correct the Author's name for LUI81 ("Look Up In The Sky"), click the **Find** button on the toolbar, type **LUI81** into the Find What text box, and click the **Find First** button.
19. The triangle record marker will jump to record 6. Click the **Close** button.
20. Press **TAB** twice to move to the **Author** field.
21. You only need to correct two letters, so press the **F2** key to get an insertion bar rather than the full field highlight.
22. Move over to the **pp** and delete those two characters. Then type: **gg** in their place so the name becomes Bruce Tiggle.
23. LOP18 ("Lots of Poems") is being discontinued and should be deleted. Since it is the preceding record (record 5), merely click the mouse on the gray **selector box** at the left end of LOP18 (record 5) to select the entire listing.
24. Press the **DELETE** key and click the **OK** button in the alert box that appears.
25. Resize the **Year of Publication** field so that only **Year of Pub** shows. To do this, move the mouse on top of the right edge of its selector (at the top of the Year of Publication column) and drag that line to the left until it is between the **b** and **l** of the word Publication (see Figure 2 - 26).
26. Resize the remaining fields to a Best Fit by double-clicking on the right edge of the field selector box of each field (see Figure 2 - 26).
27. Print the table by clicking the **Print** button on the toolbar. Print **1** copy of **All** pages at the appropriate Print Quality. Click **OK**.
28. Close the table with **FILE/Close**. Answer **Save layout changes to Table 'Books'?** by clicking **Yes**.
29. Close the database with **FILE/Close Database**.
30. If you need to exit from *Access* and/or Windows, do so properly.

Independent Project 2.3: The Real Estate Office

This Independent Project continues the Real Estate Office database you began in Independent Project 1.3. In this project you will edit the table to make some changes to the data, size the fields, move a field, delete a record, and search for listings.

The following changes need to be made.

- Property MC29 will take longer to prepare than was originally estimated, so the date when it will be available should be 5/15/95 instead of 4/1/95.
- The rental price on 1 Lewis Way, Danbury has been lowered to $125,000.
- MS11 has been leased and should be deleted.

When finished, the table should look like Figure 2 - 27.

Code	Address	City	State	Zip	Size	Floor	Purc	Price	Available	Agency Code	Agent
ES52	5 Elm St.	Greenwich	CT	06830	4800	1	R	$72,000.00	6/1/95	SC18	Brown
FA28	18 Frost Ave.	Greenwich	CT	06830	3700	2	R	$52,000.00	8/1/95	RR11	Funcha
GP25	12 Gedney Place	Danbury	CT	06810	8900	3	R	$105,000.00	7/15/95	SC18	Equat
LW17	1 Lewis Way	Danbury	CT	06810	12000	2	R	$125,000.00	7/1/95	PP24	Smith
MC29	Maple Court	New Canaan	CT	06840	450	1	P	$125,000.00	5/15/95	PP15	Green
RP12	2 Research Park	Stamford	CT	06902	18000	1	P	$3,400,000.00	6/1/95	PP15	Ruth
RP13	3 Research Park	Stamford	CT	06902	18000	1	P	$3,400,000.00	6/1/95	GW14	Purcell
RP15	5 Research Park	Stamford	CT	06902	21000	1	P	$4,100,000.00	8/1/95	RP12	Williams
RR19	952 River Road	Stamford	CT	06901	3750	6	R	$49,000.00	9/1/95	PP24	Smith
					0	0		$0.00			

Figure 2 - 27

1. Run *Access* and maximize the window.
2. Open **xercise3.mdb**.
3. Open the **Commercial Listings** table.
4. Change the **Available** date for MC29 (Maple Court, New Canaan) from 4/1/95 to **5/15/95**.
5. Locate **1 Lewis Way** in Danbury and change its **Price** to **$125,000**.
6. To remove the listing for **MS11** (22 Main St., Stamford), click on its **selector**, then press the **DELETE** key and click the **OK** button in the alert box that appears.
7. Resize all fields to a Best Fit by double-clicking on the right edge of the field selector box of each field (see Figure 2 - 27).
8. Resize **Purchase or Rent** so that only **Purc** shows in the title (see Figure 2 - 27).
9. Move the **Available** field between **Zip** and **Size**.
10. Print the table.
11. Close the table. Save layout changes.
12. Close the database.
13. If you need to exit from *Access* and/or Windows, do so properly.

INDEPENDENT PROJECT 2.4: The Veterinarian

This Independent Project continues the veterinarian database you began in Independent Project 1.4. In this project you will edit the table to make some changes to the data, size the fields, move a field, delete a record, and search for listings.

Make the following changes.

- Wild Thing's weight has increased to 30 pounds.
- Spot is much older than his family thought; change his date of birth to 1/1/88.
- The owner of Sir Strut has sold the horse to a breeder several hundred miles away. Delete that record from the table.
- Set the width of each field in the table to fit the data as closely as possible.
- Move the field that contains the type of animal (dog, cat, etc.) immediately to the right of the name field.

Lesson

3 Multiple Tables

Objectives

In this lesson you will learn how to:

- Import tables from other *Access* databases
- Attach tables from other *Access* databases
- Rename a table
- Design a multiple table system
- Create a form
- Use a form

PROJECT DESCRIPTION

In this lesson we will begin to explore the need for multiple tables to hold the data that a typical business generates. Usually it is neither efficient nor desirable to combine all of the data into a single table. To obtain the extra data needed to work with multiple tables, we will build upon the **Sales** database by *importing* and *attaching* existing tables of data from other *Access* databases that are supplied on the student diskette. Once we have several tables of data, we will see how the tables fit together in a system of tables, a Relational Database System. We will also create and use forms, an alternative way to view and work with the data in a single table or a pair of related tables.

When this lesson concludes, the **Sales** database will contain five tables, as shown in Figure 3 - 1.

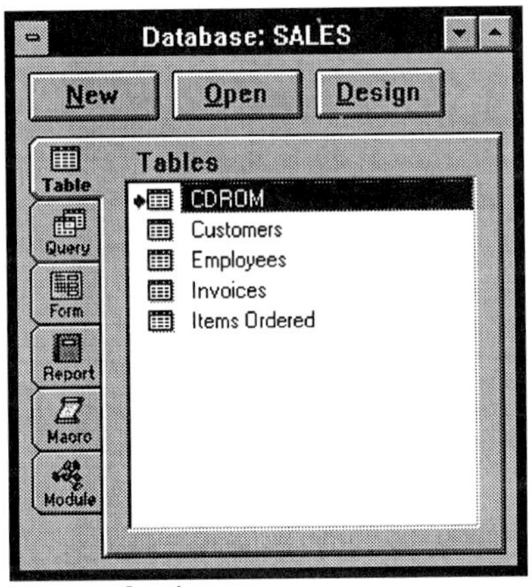

Figure 3 - 1

IMPORTING A TABLE FROM ANOTHER *ACCESS* DATABASE

Our need to acquire additional tables is not the only reason to copy a table from one database to another. In *Access* only one database may be open at a time. Because of this, if there is a table of data that will be needed in two different databases, you must either make a second copy of the table by importing the table into the second database, or link by attaching from the second database to the original copy of the table in the first database.

Importing a table will make a new copy of the table. Of course, if you create a second copy of a table, you must keep both copies up to date by editing them. Since that is usually an undesirable task, attaching is commonly employed. We will discuss attaching in the next section of this lesson.

Sometimes you need a second copy of a table of data, either to work with separately, or as a model from which to continue. Importing the table structure or the structure together with the data will produce that second copy of a table. Possibly someone else in the office has created the very table you need, but it resides in another *Access* database. Whatever the reason, you may often need to import a copy of a table from a different *Access* database.

To import a table from another *Access* database:

- Select **FILE/Import** in the menu, or click the **Import** button  on the toolbar.
- In the **Import** dialog box, pick **Microsoft Access** as the desired source of the data and click the **OK** button.
- In the **Select Microsoft Access Database** dialog box, pick the desired drive, directory, and database name, and click the **OK** button.
- In the **Import Objects** dialog box, select the **Object Type**, click on the name of the object itself and pick **Structure Only** or **Structure and Data.**
- Click the **Import** button.
- When the import is finished, click **OK** in the **Successfully imported...** alert box.
- Unless there is another table to import, click the **Close** button in the **Import Objects** dialog box. The table should be included in the list of tables in the database window.

Activity 3.1: Importing a Table

1. The **Sales** database should be open.
2. Choose **FILE/Import** or click the **Import** toolbar button.
3. In the **Import** dialog box, pick **Microsoft Access** as the desired source of the data (see Figure 3 - 2) and click the **OK** button.

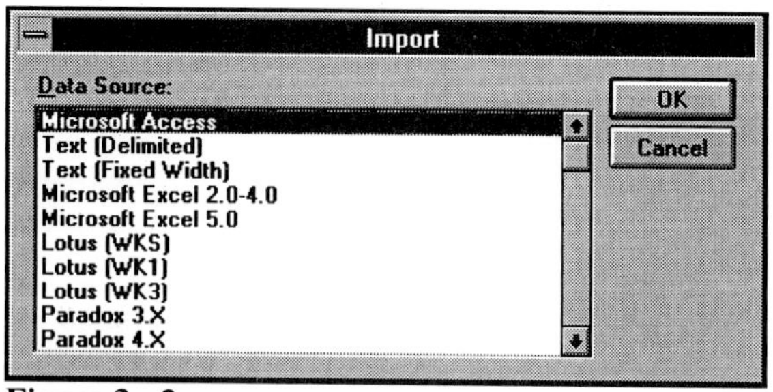

Figure 3 - 2

4. Click on **marketng.mdb** and click **OK**.
5. The **Object Type** should be **Tables** and **Structure and Data** should be selected. Pick **Invoices** in the **Objects** list and click the **Import** button (see Figure 3 - 3).

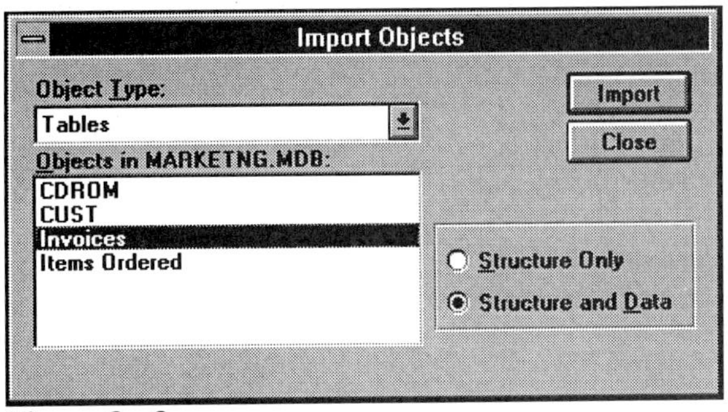

Figure 3 - 3

6. When the import is finished, click **OK** in the **Successfully imported...** alert box (see Figure 3 - 4).

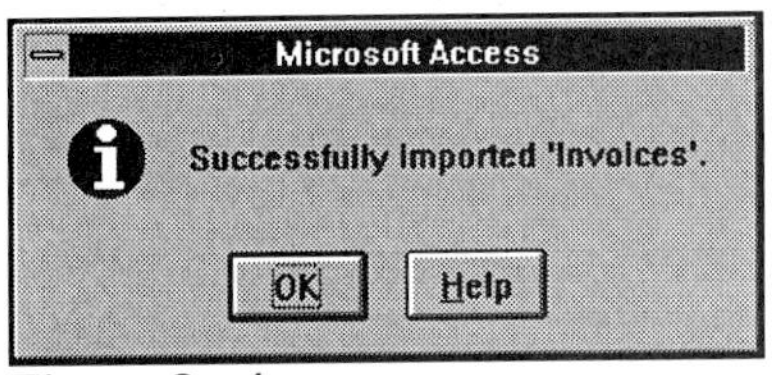

Figure 3 - 4

7. Click the **Close** button in the **Import Objects** dialog box.
8. Click on the new name **Invoices** to select it, and click the **Open** button to examine the imported data.

   The new data table should look like Figure 3 - 5.

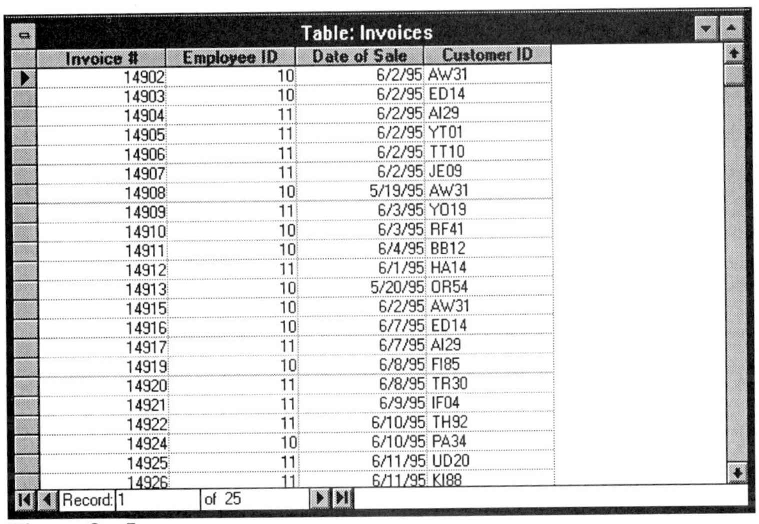

Invoice #	Employee ID	Date of Sale	Customer ID
14902	10	6/2/95	AW31
14903	10	6/2/95	ED14
14904	11	6/2/95	AI29
14905	11	6/2/95	YT01
14906	11	6/2/95	TT10
14907	11	6/2/95	JE09
14908	10	5/19/95	AW31
14909	11	6/3/95	YO19
14910	10	6/3/95	RF41
14911	10	6/4/95	BB12
14912	11	6/1/95	HA14
14913	10	5/20/95	OR54
14915	10	6/2/95	AW31
14916	10	6/7/95	ED14
14917	11	6/7/95	AI29
14919	10	6/8/95	FI85
14920	11	6/8/95	TR30
14921	11	6/9/95	IF04
14922	11	6/10/95	TH92
14924	10	6/10/95	PA34
14925	11	6/11/95	UD20
14926	11	6/11/95	KI88

Figure 3 - 5

9. After looking at the new table, close it with **FILE/Close**.

Importing Additional Tables

We will import two more tables from the **marketng.mdb** database.

Activity 3.2: Importing Additional Tables

1. Select **FILE/Import** or click the **Import** toolbar button.
2. In the **Import** dialog box, pick **Microsoft Access** as the desired source of the data and click the **OK** button.
3. Click on **marketng.mdb** and click **OK**.
4. The **Object Type** should be **Tables** and **Structure and Data** should be selected. Pick **Items Ordered** in the **Objects** list and click the **Import** button.
5. When the import is finished, click **OK** in the **Successfully imported...** alert box.
6. Do not close the **Import Objects** dialog box, but choose **CUST** as a second table to import and click the **Import** button.
7. When the import is finished, click **OK** in the **Successfully imported...** alert box.
8. Click the **Close** button in the **Import Objects** dialog box.
9. Click on the new name **Items Ordered** to select it, and click the **Open** button to examine the imported data (see Figure 3 - 6).

Table: Items Ordered

Invoice #	Line #	Quantity Sold	CD ID	Back Ordered	Expected Delivery
14902	1	20	F01	N	
14902	2	100	E04	N	
14902	3	25	C01	N	
14903	1	20	C01	N	
14903	2	5	F01	N	
14903	3	10	E04	N	
14903	4	5	P02	N	
14904	1	55	E04	N	
14904	2	3	P02	N	
14904	3	100	C01	N	
14905	1	10	C02	N	
14905	2	5	C01	N	
14906	1	2	E04	N	
14907	1	1	T02	Y	6/11/95
14907	2	1	E06	N	
14908	1	125	E04	N	
14909	1	1	E07	N	
14909	2	1	E06	N	
14909	3	1	F02	N	
14909	4	1	E05	N	
14910	1	30	P02	N	
14911	1	5	E04	N	

Record: 1 of 45

Figure 3 - 6

10. After looking at the new data, close the table with **FILE/Close**.
11. Click on the new name **CUST** to select it, and click the **Open** button to examine its data (see Figure 3 - 7).
12. Click the **Print** button on the toolbar to begin printing the table and click the **OK** button in the Print dialog box.
13. Close the table with **FILE/Close**.

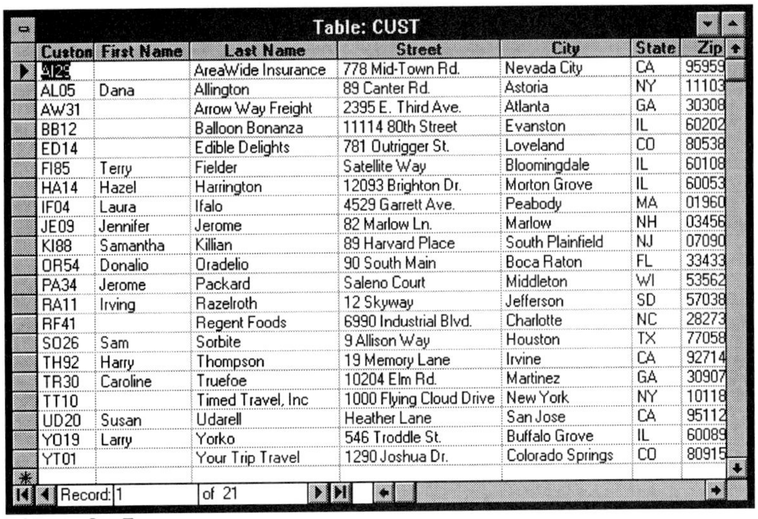

Table: CUST

Custon	First Name	Last Name	Street	City	State	Zip
AI26		AreaWide Insurance	778 Mid-Town Rd.	Nevada City	CA	95959
AL05	Dana	Allington	89 Canter Rd.	Astoria	NY	11103
AW31		Arrow Way Freight	2395 E. Third Ave.	Atlanta	GA	30308
BB12		Balloon Bonanza	11114 80th Street	Evanston	IL	60202
ED14		Edible Delights	781 Outrigger St.	Loveland	CO	80538
FI85	Terry	Fielder	Satellite Way	Bloomingdale	IL	60108
HA14	Hazel	Harrington	12093 Brighton Dr.	Morton Grove	IL	60053
IF04	Laura	Ifalo	4529 Garrett Ave.	Peabody	MA	01960
JE09	Jennifer	Jerome	82 Marlow Ln.	Marlow	NH	03456
KI88	Samantha	Killian	89 Harvard Place	South Plainfield	NJ	07090
OR54	Donalio	Oradelio	90 South Main	Boca Raton	FL	33433
PA34	Jerome	Packard	Saleno Court	Middleton	WI	53562
RA11	Irving	Razelroth	12 Skyway	Jefferson	SD	57038
RF41		Regent Foods	6990 Industrial Blvd.	Charlotte	NC	28273
SO26	Sam	Sorbite	9 Allison Way	Houston	TX	77058
TH92	Harry	Thompson	19 Memory Lane	Irvine	CA	92714
TR30	Caroline	Truefoe	10204 Elm Rd.	Martinez	GA	30907
TT10		Timed Travel, Inc	1000 Flying Cloud Drive	New York	NY	10118
UD20	Susan	Udarell	Heather Lane	San Jose	CA	95112
YO19	Larry	Yorko	546 Troddle St.	Buffalo Grove	IL	60089
YT01		Your Trip Travel	1290 Joshua Dr.	Colorado Springs	CO	80915

Record: 1 of 21

Figure 3 - 7

ATTACHING A TABLE FROM ANOTHER *ACCESS* DATABASE

To avoid having to keep both an imported copy of a table and the original table up-to-date, attaching can be used. Attaching a table establishes a link to the original table without producing another copy of it. Once linked, you can use the data in all of the normal ways like editing, printing reports, and adding new listings from either database.

The only restriction on an attached table is that you may not restructure the table within the database in which it is linked; you would need to open the database that actually contains the table to change the table's design.

To attach a table from another *Access* database:

- Select **FILE/Attach Table** in the menu, or click the **Attach Table** button on the toolbar.
- In the **Attach** dialog box, pick **Microsoft Access** as the desired source of the data and click the **OK** button.
- In the **Select Microsoft Access Database** dialog box pick the desired drive, directory, and database name, and click the **OK** button.
- In the **Attach Tables** dialog box, select the **Table** from the list.
- Click the **Attach** button.
- When the attaching is finished, click **OK** in the **Successfully Attached...** alert box.
- Unless there is another table to attach, click the **Close** button in the **Attach Tables** dialog box. The table should be included in the list of tables in the **Database** window. It will show an arrow at the left of the name and icon indicating that this is only a link to the table.

Activity 3.3: Attaching a Table

1. Select **FILE/Attach Table** or click the **Attach Table** toolbar button.
2. In the **Attach** dialog box, pick **Microsoft Access** as the desired source of the data and click the **OK** button (see Figure 3 - 8).

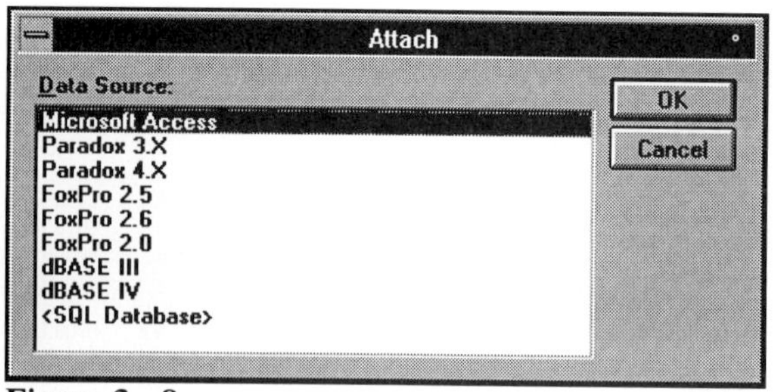

Figure 3 - 8

3. Click on **marketng.mdb** and click **OK**.
4. Pick **CDROM** in the **Tables** list and click the **Attach** button (see Figure 3 - 9).

Figure 3 - 9

5. When the attaching is finished, click **OK** in the **Successfully Attached...** alert box (see Figure 3 - 10).

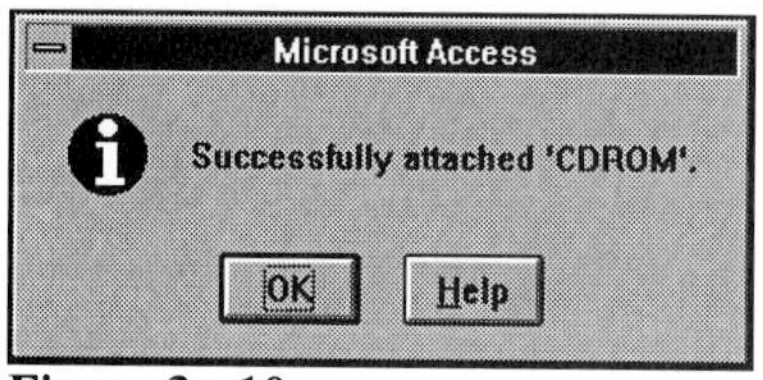

Figure 3 - 10

6. Click the **Close** button in the **Attach Tables** dialog box.
7. Click on the name **CDROM** to select the table.
8. Choose **Open** to view the table (see Figure 3 - 11).

   The table appears normal in every way, and is, except that you cannot restructure it. You may, of course, add new data, edit the existing records, print reports, and query its data in the regular ways.
9. Click the **Print** button on the toolbar to begin printing the table and click the **OK** button in the Print dialog box.
10. Close the table with **FILE/Close**.

    Notice that the icon in front of the table name has an arrow signifying that a link points to the original table.

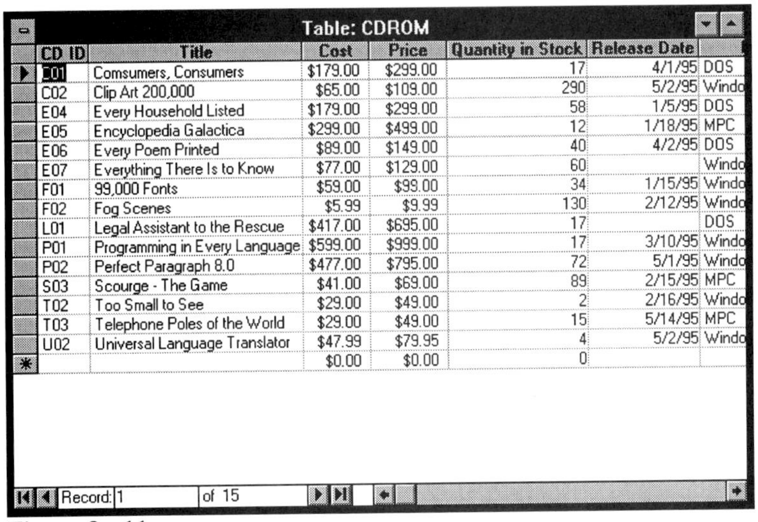

Table: CDROM

CD ID	Title	Cost	Price	Quantity in Stock	Release Date	
C01	Comsumers, Consumers	$179.00	$299.00	17	4/1/95	DOS
C02	Clip Art 200,000	$65.00	$109.00	290	5/2/95	Windo
E04	Every Household Listed	$179.00	$299.00	58	1/5/95	DOS
E05	Encyclopedia Galactica	$299.00	$499.00	12	1/18/95	MPC
E06	Every Poem Printed	$89.00	$149.00	40	4/2/95	DOS
E07	Everything There Is to Know	$77.00	$129.00	60		Windo
F01	99,000 Fonts	$59.00	$99.00	34	1/15/95	Windo
F02	Fog Scenes	$5.99	$9.99	130	2/12/95	Windo
L01	Legal Assistant to the Rescue	$417.00	$695.00	17		DOS
P01	Programming in Every Language	$599.00	$999.00	17	3/10/95	Windo
P02	Perfect Paragraph 8.0	$477.00	$795.00	72	5/1/95	Windo
S03	Scourge - The Game	$41.00	$69.00	89	2/15/95	MPC
T02	Too Small to See	$29.00	$49.00	2	2/16/95	Windo
T03	Telephone Poles of the World	$29.00	$49.00	15	5/14/95	MPC
U02	Universal Language Translator	$47.99	$79.95	4	5/2/95	Windo
*		$0.00	$0.00	0		

Record: 1 of 15

Figure 3 - 11

RENAMING A TABLE

An imported copy of a table may have a different purpose from the original and, thus, needs a new name. Or the original name may have been created by someone else who was not descriptive enough. Perhaps the table you need to import has the same name as one of your existing tables. Whatever the reason, you may need to rename a table.

As a quick reminder, *Access*' rules allow up to 64 characters in a name, with any characters except the five between the parenthesis (` . [ ] !) being legal.

To rename a table:

- Make certain the table is not open. A table cannot be renamed while it is open.
- The highlight must be on top of the name in the **Database** window.
- Select **FILE/Rename**.
- In the **Rename...** dialog box, type the new name and click the **OK** button.

Activity 3.4: Renaming a Table

Whoever created the **CUST** table did not name it very well. CUST could be an abbreviation for several things. A fully spelled out name would be much more descriptive and useful.

1. If the **CUST** table is open on the workspace, close it with **FILE/Close**.
2. Click once on the name **CUST** so that it is highlighted in the table list of the **Sales** database.
3. Select **FILE/Rename**.
4. In the **Rename...** dialog box, type the new name **Customers** (see Figure 3 - 12) and click the **OK** button.

Figure 3 - 12

The table names are kept in alphabetical order in the ***Database*** *window list. Thus, when you rename a table, the order of the tables may change.*

A RELATIONAL SYSTEM OF TABLES

As you gain experience developing tables of data, you will encounter situations that cause various design problems. For example, suppose the CDROM company asks you to design a table to record customer purchases. You might try a single table like Figure 3 - 13, but when you begin filling in the data an immediate problem occurs. Data begins to get duplicated. Redundant data usually signals a poor design and taxes the system in the following five ways.

- A data entry person is wasting time and effort retyping every character that is duplicate data.
- Disk space is wasted recording the redundant data.
- Inconsistencies will occur among the duplicated data when changes are made, as some of it will get updated and some may not.
- *Access* will slow down as it works its way through more data than is necessary.
- Typing errors will proliferate since more data entry is being done than is required.

A poor table design because of all the duplication

Customer	Employee	Last Nam	Invoice #	Quantity Sold	Title	Price
Arrow Way Freight	Daphne	Green	14902	20	99,000 Fonts	$99.00
Arrow Way Freight	Daphne	Green	14902	100	Every Household Listed	$299.00
Arrow Way Freight	Daphne	Green	14902	25	Comsumers, Consumers	$299.00
Edible Delights	Daphne	Green	14903	20	Comsumers, Consumers	$299.00
Edible Delights	Daphne	Green	14903	5	99,000 Fonts	$99.00
Edible Delights	Daphne	Green	14903	10	Every Household Listed	$299.00
Edible Delights	Daphne	Green	14903	5	Perfect Paragraph 8.0	$795.00
AreaWide Insurance	George	Jeffers	14904	55	Every Household Listed	$299.00
AreaWide Insurance	George	Jeffers	14904	3	Perfect Paragraph 8.0	$795.00
AreaWide Insurance	George	Jeffers	14904	100	Comsumers, Consumers	$299.00
Your Trip Travel	George	Jeffers	14905	10	Clip Art 200,000	$109.00
Your Trip Travel	George	Jeffers	14905	5	Comsumers, Consumers	$299.00
Timed Travel, Inc	George	Jeffers	14906	2	Every Household Listed	$299.00
Jerome	George	Jeffers	14907	1	Too Small to See	$49.00
Jerome	George	Jeffers	14907	1	Every Poem Printed	$149.00
Arrow Way Freight	Daphne	Green	14908	125	Every Household Listed	$299.00
Yorko	George	Jeffers	14909	1	Everything There Is to Know	$129.00
Yorko	George	Jeffers	14909	1	Every Poem Printed	$149.00
Yorko	George	Jeffers	14909	1	Fog Scenes	$9.99
Yorko	George	Jeffers	14909	1	Encyclopedia Galactica	$499.00
Regent Foods	Daphne	Green	14910	30	Perfect Paragraph 8.0	$795.00
Balloon Bonanza	Daphne	Green	14911	5	Every Household Listed	$299.00
Balloon Bonanza	Daphne	Green	14911	2	Perfect Paragraph 8.0	$795.00
Harrington	George	Jeffers	14912	1	Every Poem Printed	$149.00
Oradelio	Daphne	Green	14913	1	Too Small to See	$49.00
Arrow Way Freight	Daphne	Green	14915	50	Comsumers, Consumers	$299.00

Figure 3 - 13

To eliminate data duplication, divide some of the data into separate tables. While entire books are devoted to this topic, there are two fundamental situations which with experience you can begin to recognize.

- When an indeterminate number of fields needs to be included.
- When data items will occur over and over again.

As an example of the first situation, suppose you need to record customer purchases of CDROMs. You will need to record the customer's name and address, of course, but how many CDROMs will the customer purchase at a time? There is no way of telling. Therefore, you cannot design a table based on the customer, with a separate column for each CDROM ordered (see Figure 3 - 14). You don't know how many columns to create. If you create too few columns, the remainder of the order will not fit, and if you create too many fields, every order for a single CDROM will waste the space reserved in each additional column. Such a design fails either way.

Customer	Street	State	Title1	Qty1	Title2	Qty2	Title3	Qty3
Arrow Way Freight	2395 E. Third Ave.	GA	Comsumers, Consu	25	Every Household L	100	99,000 Fonts	20
Edible Delights	781 Outrigger St.	CO	Perfect Paragraph :	5	Every Household L	10	99,000 Fonts	5
AreaWide Insurance	778 Mid-Town Rd.	CA	Comsumers, Consu	100	Perfect Paragraph :	3	Every Household L	55
Your Trip Travel	1290 Joshua Dr.	CO	Comsumers, Consu	5	Clip Art 200,000	10		
Timed Travel, Inc	1000 Flying Cloud D	NY	Every Household L	2	Every Poem Printec	1		
Jerome	82 Marlow Ln.	NH	Too Small to See	125				
Arrow Way Freight	2395 E. Third Ave.	GA	Every Household L	125				
Yorko	546 Troddle St.	IL	Encyclopedia Gala	1	Everything There Is	1	Every Poem Printec	1
Regent Foods	6990 Industrial Blvd.	NC	Perfect Paragraph :	30				
Balloon Bonanza	11114 80th Street	IL	Every Household L	5	Perfect Paragraph :	2		
Harrington	12093 Brighton Dr.	IL	Every Poem Printec	1				
Oradelio	90 South Main	FL	Too Small to See	1				
Edible Delights	781 Outrigger St.	CO	Clip Art 200,000	25				
AreaWide Insurance	778 Mid-Town Rd.	CA	Clip Art 200,000	50				
Fielder	Satellite Way	IL	Programming in Any	1				
Truefoe	10204 Elm Rd.	GA	Everything There Is	1	Encyclopedia Gala	1		
Ifalo	4529 Garrett Ave.	MA	Fog Scenes	1				
Thompson	19 Memory Lane	CA	Too Small to See	1	Encyclopedia Gala	1	Scourge - The Gam	1
Packard	Saleno Court	WI	Every Household L	110				
Udarell	Heather Lane	CA	Fog Scenes	1				
Killian	89 Harvard Place	NJ	Encyclopedia Gala	1				
Allington	89 Canter Rd.	NY	Legal Assistant to tl	1				
Sorbite	9 Allison Way	TX	Programming in Any	1				
						0		0

A poor table design because there is no way to anticipate how many Titles a customer will order.

Figure 3 - 14

On the other hand, and as an example of the second situation where data will repeat over and over, you might try to record each CDROM ordered in a separate record (see Figure 3 - 13). But then, if you keep track of the customer's name and address, a customer who orders ten CDROMs will have ten records with his or her name and address repeated on every line! That design fails because of redundancy.

The solution to both design problems is to split the data into separate tables (see Figure 3 - 15). Record each customer only once in a separate customer table. Do not enter the CDROM order there, but give each customer a code number and enter that code on each order. Since the code number will be very short, we will not mind typing it on each order, even if the same customer orders over and over so that his or her code is repeated many times.

Customer ID	First Name	Last Name	Street	State
AI29		AreaWide Insurance	778 Mid-Town Rd.	CA
AL05	Dana	Allington	89 Canter Rd.	NY
AW31		Arrow Way Freight	2395 E. Third Ave.	GA
BB12		Balloon Bonanza	11114 80th Street	IL
ED14		Edible Delights	781 Outrigger St.	CO
FI85	Terry	Fielder	Satellite Way	IL
HA14	Hazel	Harrington	12093 Brighton Dr.	IL
IF04	Laura	Ifalo	4529 Garrett Ave.	MA
JE09	Jennifer	Jerome	82 Marlow Ln.	NH
KI88	Samantha	Killian	89 Harvard Place	NJ
OR54	Donalio	Oradelio	90 South Main	FL
PA34	Jerome	Packard	Saleno Court	WI
RF41		Regent Foods	6990 Industrial Blvd.	NC
SO26	Sam	Sorbite	9 Allison Way	TX
TH92	Harry	Thompson	19 Memory Lane	CA
TR30	Caroline	Truefoe	10204 Elm Rd.	GA
TT10		Timed Travel, Inc	1000 Flying Cloud Drive	NY
UD20	Susan	Udarell	Heather Lane	CA
YO19	Larry	Yorko	546 Troddle St.	IL
YT01		Your Trip Travel	1290 Joshua Dr.	CO

Invoice #	Date of Sale	Customer ID
14902	6/2/95	AW31
14903	6/2/95	ED14
14904	6/2/95	AI29
14905	6/2/95	YT01
14906	6/2/95	TT10
14907	6/2/95	JE09
14908	5/19/95	AW31
14909	6/3/95	YO19
14910	6/3/95	RF41
14911	6/4/95	BB12
14912	6/1/95	HA14
14913	5/20/95	OR54
14915	6/2/95	AW31
14916	6/7/95	ED14
14917	6/7/95	AI29
14919	6/8/95	FI85
14920	6/8/95	TR30
14921	6/9/95	IF04
14922	6/10/95	TH92
14924	6/10/95	PA34
14925	6/11/95	UD20
14926	6/11/95	KI88
14927	6/12/95	AL05
14928	6/12/95	SO26

Enter each customer once in a separate Customer table.

Repeat only the Customer ID in a separate Orders table, not the entire customer name, address, and phone number.

Figure 3 - 15

Since we cannot anticipate how many items will be on an order, make one table for the customer's order as a whole (an invoice with order number, date, sales person, etc.—each item that has a predetermined number of entries), and a separate table that lists the items on the order with one item in each record (see Figure 3 - 16). To know which order an item belongs to, record the order number along with each item. Since the order number will be short, we won't mind if it is repeated on each of the ten lines of an order for ten items.

Enter each invoice once in a separate table.

Invoice #	Employee ID	Date of Sale	Customer ID
14902	10	6/2/95	AW31
14903	10	6/2/95	ED14
14904	11	6/2/95	AI29
14905	11	6/2/95	YT01
14906	11	6/2/95	TT10
14907	11	6/2/95	JE09
14908	10	5/19/95	AW31
14909	11	6/3/95	YO19
14910	10	6/3/95	RF41
14911	10	6/4/95	BB12
14912	11	6/1/95	HA14
14913	10	5/20/95	OR54
14915	10	6/2/95	AW31
14916	10	6/7/95	ED14
14917	11	6/7/95	AI29
14919	10	6/8/95	FI85
14920	11	6/8/95	TR30
14921	11	6/9/95	IF04
14922	11	6/10/95	TH92
14924	10	6/10/95	PA34
14925	11	6/11/95	UD20
14926	11	6/11/95	KI88
14927	10	6/12/95	AL05
14928	11	6/12/95	SO26
	0		

Invoice #	Line #	Quantity	CD ID	Back Ordered
14902	1	20	F01	N
14902	2	100	E04	N
14902	3	25	C01	N
14903	1	20	C01	N
14903	2	5	F01	N
14903	3	10	E04	N
14903	4	5	P02	N
14904	1	55	E04	N
14904	2	3	P02	N
14904	3	100	C01	N
14905	1	10	C02	N
14905	2	5	C01	N
14906	1	2	E04	N
14907	1	1	T02	Y
14907	2	1	E06	N
14908	1	125	E04	N
14909	1	1	E07	N
14909	2	1	E06	N
14909	3	1	F02	N
14909	4	1	E05	N
14910	1	30	P02	N
14911	1	5	E04	N
14911	2	2	P02	N
14912	1	1	E06	N
14913	1	1	T02	Y
14915	1	50	C01	N

Because there could be any number of items ordered on an invoice, enter the items in a separate table.

Figure 3 - 16

To test your understanding of these two database design problems, try determining which of the two problems each of the following examples resembles.

- A design to keep track of the computer equipment each employee is using. How many pieces of equipment (computer, printer, screen, mouse, etc.) would each employee have?
- One or more tables to keep track of the publisher's name and address for each CDROM title, where many CDROMs may come from the same publisher.
- A list of the people who are contacts at each publisher. Could there be more than one contact?
- A design for the family members (dependents) of each employee. Could a family have 10 members? 12? 14?

Now that you understand the necessity for multiple tables, we will actually use multiple tables in the next sections with forms, as well as in most of the remaining lessons.

CREATING A FORM

A form is an alternative arrangement of the fields in a table (see Figure 3 - 17). Rather than the straight columns and rows of a table, a form may have any field placed anywhere you please. Normally a form displays only one record at a time so the user can focus on a single listing. Because a form allows great freedom in design, you may not only arrange some or all of the fields in any order on the screen, but you may add titles, instructions, boxes and lines, colors, calculations, and graphics to enhance the design. Forms can also display two related tables at a time.

Designing a form from scratch would be a lengthy and tedious process as you would need to place every field and every label individually, adjust the appearance and alignment of those items, and add any other details you wanted. Fortunately there is a *Wizard* that can perform all of the tedious work for you. The *FormWizard* is a built-in set of instructions that is programmed to help you design a form. The *Wizard* offers a number of options, then creates the form for you based on your choices. We will make use of the *FormWizard* and save a great deal of time and effort.

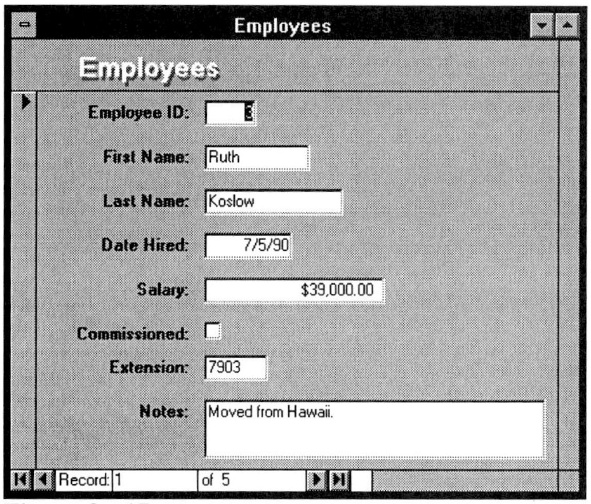

Figure 3 - 17

To create a form:

- Click on the **Form** tab at the left edge of the **Database** window.
- Click the **New** button at the top of the **Database** window.
- Select a table from the **Select A Table/Query** drop-down list.
- Click the **FormWizards** button.
- Choose the type of form and click **OK**.
- Select the desired options in each step of the *FormWizard.*
- Click the **Finish** button.

Activity 3.5: Creating a Form

We will create a standard form (see Figure 3 - 17) for the Employees table that includes all eight fields. The choice **AutoForm** uses all fields in the most common design, thus creating the form without asking for any selection of options.

1. Click on the **Form** tab at the left edge of the **Database** window (see Figure 3 - 18).

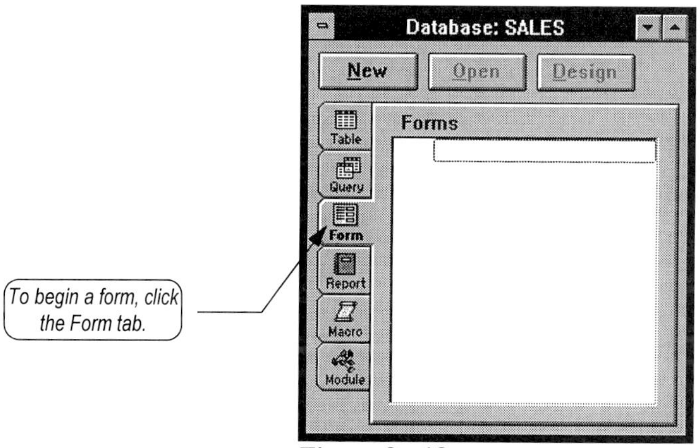

Figure 3 - 18

2. Click the **New** button at the top of the **Database** window.
3. Select **Employees** from the **Select A Table/Query** drop-down list (see Figure 3 - 19).

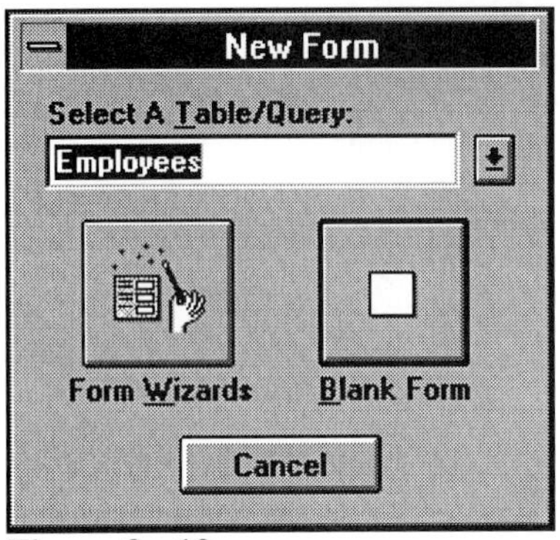

Figure 3 - 19

Be careful not to double-click the table name since the next set of buttons is directly behind the list. The first click would pick the table name and the second would click one of the buttons behind the list.

4. Click the **FormWizards** button (see Figure 3 - 19).
5. Choose **AutoForm** (see Figure 3 - 20) and click **OK**.

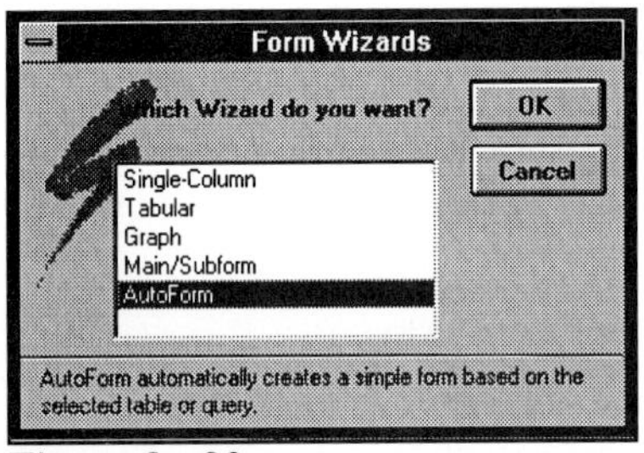

Figure 3 - 20

After a brief delay while the FormWizard does all of the design work, the form will appear on the workspace ready to use (see Figure 3 - 17).

6. To save the design choose **FILE/Save Form**, then type the name **Employees** and click **OK** (see Figure 3 - 21).

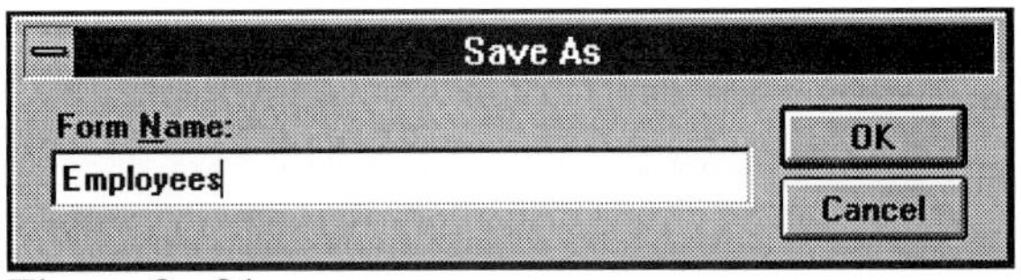

Figure 3 - 21

7. Do not close the form.

USING A FORM

You work with this form the same way you do in a table, except that the movement is mostly vertical instead of horizontal. The data is the same; editing is the same; searching is the same. It is the same table of data, just reorganized visually.

To use a form:

- Open the form.
- View the data, edit the existing data, or type new data.
- The form may be printed.
- Close the form.

Activity 3.6: Using a Form

A form is used to view or edit the data, or to enter new data. A form may also be printed. We will view the existing listings in **Employees**, then enter a new record on the form.

1. If the **Employees** form is not already open on the screen, click on the **Form** tab at the left edge of the **Database** window, click on the name **Employees** to highlight it, and click the **Open** button at the top of the **Database** window.

   The current record number between the Navigation Buttons should say Record: 1 of 5 (see Figure 3 - 22).

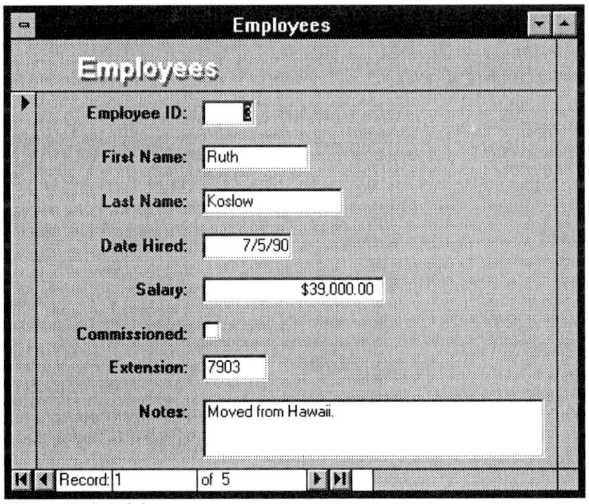

Figure 3 - 22

2. View record 2 by pressing the **PGDN** (or **PAGE DOWN**) key.
3. View record 3 by clicking the **Next Record** Navigation Button ▶.
4. Jump to the last record by clicking the **Last Record** Navigation Button ▶|.
5. To begin a new record, press the **PGDN** key or click the **Next Record** button ▶.

   *The record number should be **Record: 6 of 6** (see Figure 3 - 23).*

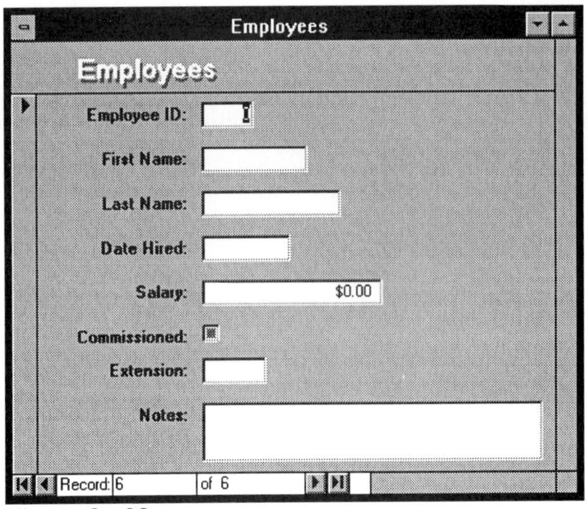

Figure 3 - 23

6. For the **Employee ID**, enter: **12** and press **TAB** to move to the next field.
7. Fill in the **First Name** by typing: **Gary** and press **TAB.**
8. For **Last Name** type: **Lamp** and press **TAB.**
9. His **Date Hired** is: **2/1/95.**
10. Enter: **28,000** for **Salary.**
11. The **Commissioned** field is a check box just like those in a dialog box. Check the box for this new employee since he is on commission. Press **TAB** to continue.
12. The **Extension** is: **7905**
13. There are no Notes for this employee yet, so we are finished (see Figure 3 - 24). Close the form with **FILE/Close.**

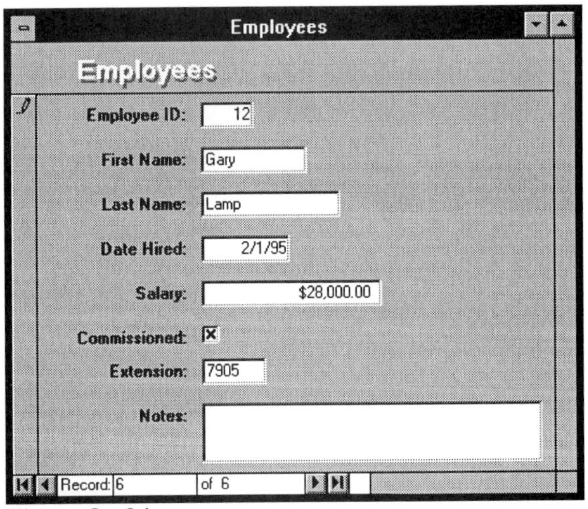

Figure 3 - 24

*The new form **Employees** will be listed in the Form section of the **Database** window. If you were to view the Employees table, you would, of course, see the new record there, too.*

A MULTI-TABLE FORM

Two tables can be displayed on the same form with a Main/Subform FormWizard design. One of the tables would be the main table; the other would be the secondary table (see Figure 3 - 25). The two tables would be related by a field that was common to both tables. That common field is the basis of the link or relationship between the pair of tables. Once there is such a link, *Access* will display only the records from the secondary table that go with the current record in the main table. *Access* figures out which records go together (are related) and displays them on the form simultaneously.

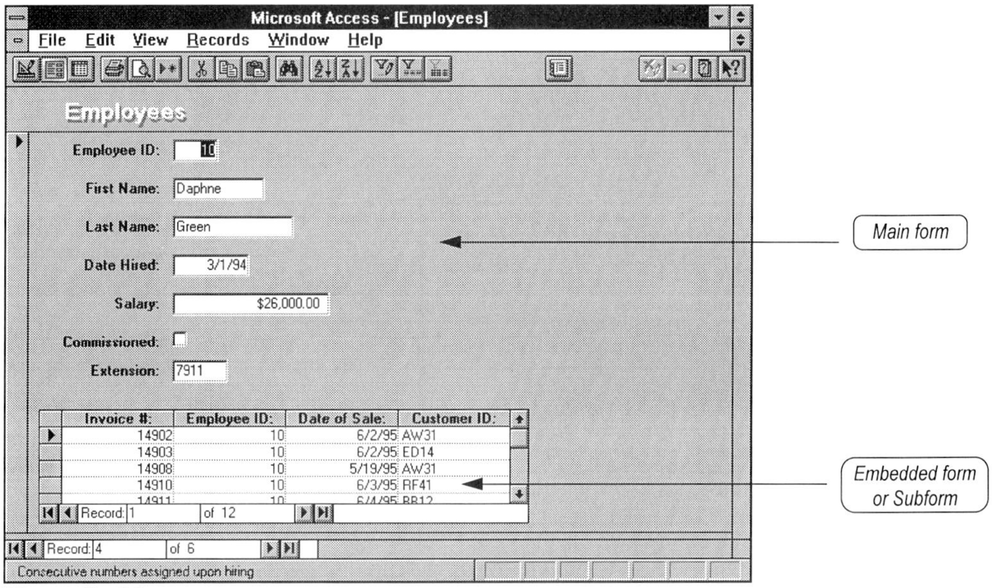

Figure 3 - 25

Remembering the discussion of relational tables two sections ago, we will create a form with data from both the **Employees** and the **Invoices** tables. Both tables contain the linking field **Employee ID**. **Employees** will be the main table, and a subform listing **Invoices** will be embedded on it (see Figure 3 - 25).

To create a Main/Subform form:

- Click on the **Form** tab at the left edge of the **Database** window.
- Click the **New** button at the top of the **Database** window.
- Select a table from the **Select A Table/Query** drop-down list.
- Click the **FormWizards** button.
- Choose **Main/Subform** for the type of form and click **OK**.
- Select the desired fields from the main table.
- Select the desired fields from the secondary table.
- Choose the desired style for the form.
- Click the **Finish** button.
- Type a name for the subform.
- Save the main form with whatever name you desire.

Activity 3.7: Creating a Main/Subform Form

We need to work with the employees and the invoices they have sold, so we will create a Main/Subform where **Employees** is the main table and **Invoices** is the subform. This form will display the employees one at a time, with the invoices they sold in the subform embedded on the main form.

1. Click on the **Form** tab at the left edge of the **Database** window followed by the **New** button at the top of the **Database** window.
2. Pick **Employees** as the table from the drop-down list.
3. Click the **FormWizard** button.
4. Choose **Main/Subform** from the list of Wizards and click the **OK** button (see Figure 3 - 26).

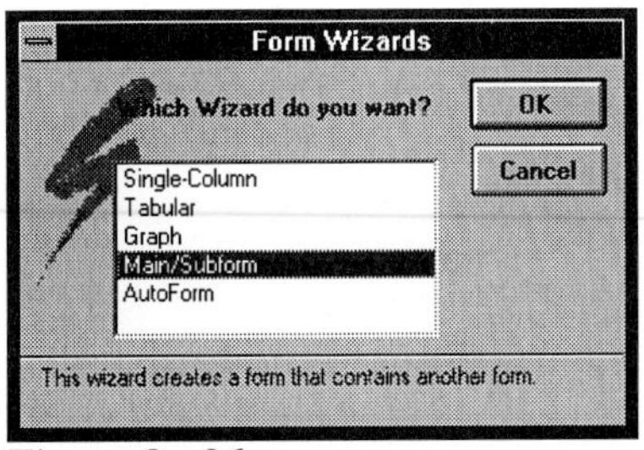

Figure 3 - 26

5. Select **Invoices** as the choice for **Which table or query contains the data for the subform?** in the first **Main/Subform Wizard** dialog box (see Figure 3 - 27), and click the **Next>** button.

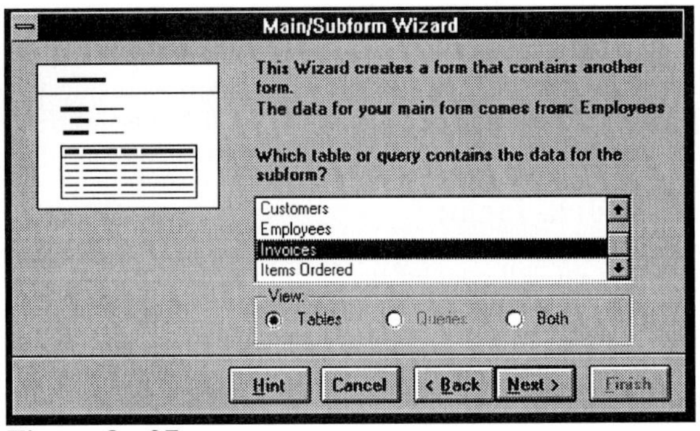

Figure 3 - 27

6. Click the >> button in answer to **Which fields do you want on your main form?** in the second **Main/Subform Wizard** dialog box (see Figure 3 - 28). Do **not** click the **Next>** button yet.

   Notice that the arrow in the diagram in the top left corner of the dialog box points to the main section of the sample form.

   We do not want the ***Notes*** *field, so we must remove it.*

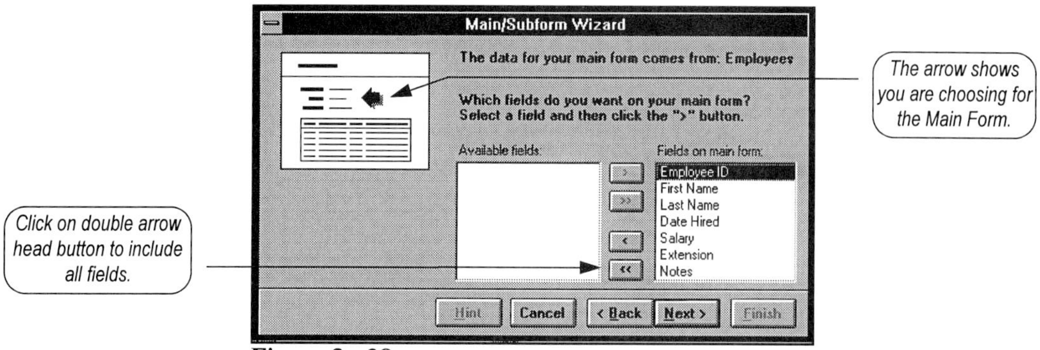

Figure 3 - 28

7. In the **Fields on Main Form** list, scroll down until you see **Notes**. Click on **Notes** to highlight it and click the < button to remove it from the list.

   __Notes__ will appear back in the __Available fields__ list (see Figure 3 - 29).

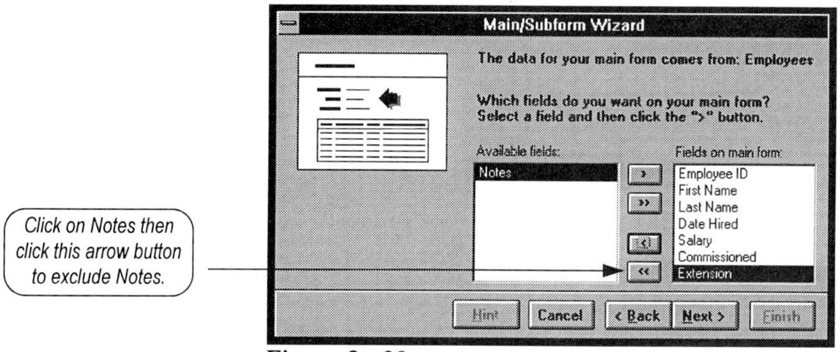

Figure 3 - 29

8. Click **Next>**.
9. Click the >> button in answer to **Which fields do you want on your subform?** and click the **Next>** button (see Figure 3 - 30).

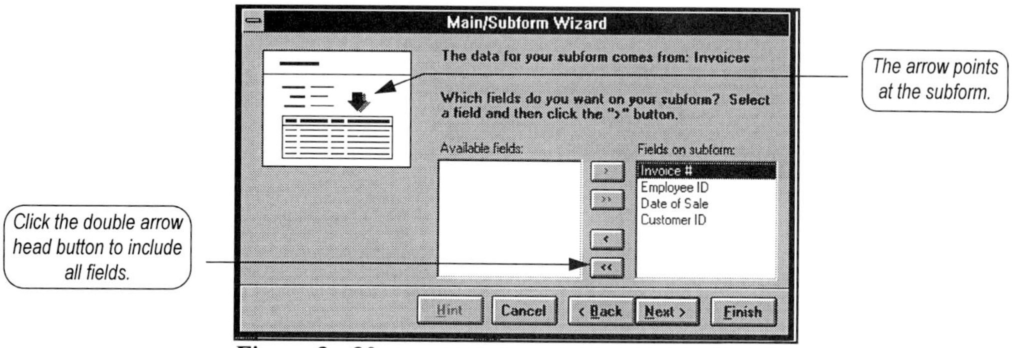

Figure 3 - 30

Notice that the arrow in the diagram in the top left corner of the dialog box points to the subform section of the sample form.

10. Click on **Embossed** as the style when the Wizard asks **What style do you want for your form?** and click the **Next>** button (see Figure 3 - 31).

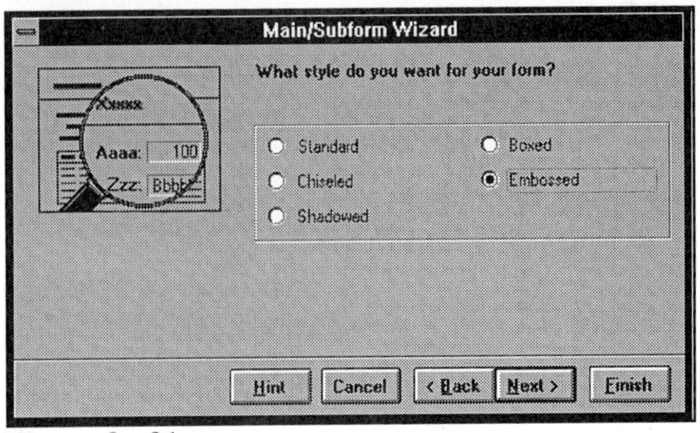

Figure 3 - 31

To view each of the available styles, click on each choice in turn and examine the sample in the top left corner of the dialog box.

11. We need make no changes in the final dialog box (note the checkered finish flag!), so click the **Finish** button (see Figure 3 - 32).

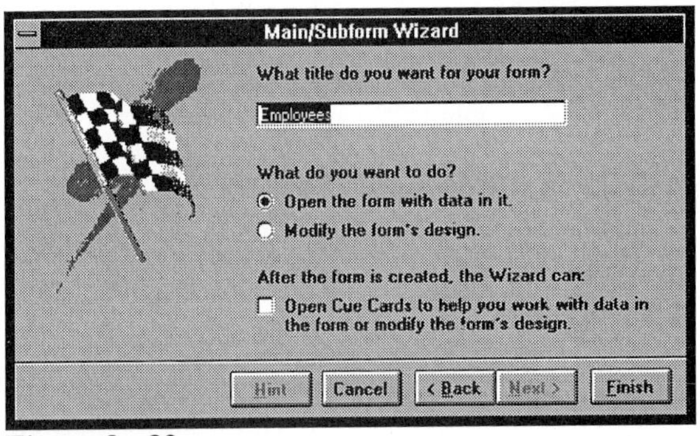

Figure 3 - 32

12. Click **OK** to answer **You must save the subform before the Main/Subform FormWizard can proceed** (see Figure 3 - 33).

Figure 3 - 33

Access considers the subform to be a separate design, even though it will embed it on the main table's form.

13. Enter **Invoices Subform** as the name in the **Save As** dialog box (see Figure 3 - 34). Click the **OK** button.

Figure 3 - 34

There may be a delay while Access assembles the forms and ascertains that the ***Employee ID*** *field in* ***Employees*** *matches the* ***Employee ID*** *field in* ***Invoices****.*

14. Maximize the form window.

    The first employee, Ruth Koslow, doesn't have any invoice sales, so the secondary form below the ***Extension*** *field is empty. The next two employees are not salespeople, either.*

15. Press **PGDN** (or **PAGE DOWN**) three times to get to **Daphne Green** (see Figure 3 - 25).

    As Daphne is a salesperson, she has invoices associated with her Employee ID number. Notice that her number, 10, is listed on every one of the invoices that shows in the embedded subform.

16. Press **PGDN** (or **PAGE DOWN**) once to get to **George Jeffers**. He is in sales and has many invoices listed.

17. Press **PGDN** (or **PAGE DOWN**) once more to get to **Gary Lamp**. He is in sales, but is so new he does not have any sales yet.

18. Save the design with **FILE/Save Form**. Type the name: **Employees and Their Invoices** in the **Save As** dialog box (see Figure 3 - 35) and click the **OK** button.

Figure 3 - 35

19. Close the form with **FILE/Close**.

    Both new forms plus the Invoices Subform will be listed in the ***Database*** window.

20. Restore the size of the **Database** window.

Operations with multiple tables like this multi-table form are much simpler if you name the matching fields in each table the exact same thing. In this past example, *Access* figured out that Employee ID was the common field because the field name was the same in both tables. You are not required to make the names identical, but it makes many operations for multiple tables much simpler.

SUMMARY

In this lesson we have assembled a group of tables to compliment the **Employees** table that we created in Lesson 1, by importing and attaching from other *Access* databases. Once we had the tables, we began to work with multiple tables, examining the need for common fields between pairs of tables and creating a form that displayed data from two tables simultaneously.

In the next two lessons we will carry the multiple table idea one step further by seeing how to join separate but related tables. We will also learn how to select subsets of the data in a table based on matching specified values.

KEY TERMS

Attach
Form
Form Wizard
Import
Relational Database System
Subform
Wizard

INDEPENDENT PROJECTS

Independent Project 3.1: The School Newspaper

This Independent Project continues the Newspaper Ad database from Independent Project 2.1. In this project you will import the table containing the salespersons' names, rename the table, and create a form that includes both the sales persons' names and the sales data on one screen. Finally, you will use that form to enter a new ad.

The table of names was typed by someone else who works for the newspaper and saved as SF (short for Sales Force) in the IND-PROJ database that is on the Student Data Diskette. You might ask why are the salespersons' names in a separate table? Why not include them right in the Ads table? Because the same sales people sell many ads, and their names would be repeated over and over in Ads. In SF, each salesperson is entered just once and given a code number. Only the short code number is included on each ad. Of course, to combine both SF and Ads on the same form, the matching code numbers must be in the Ads table, too. You can check Ads to make certain they are.

The table of names looks like Figure 3 - 36. When finished with the form, it should resemble Figure 3 - 37.

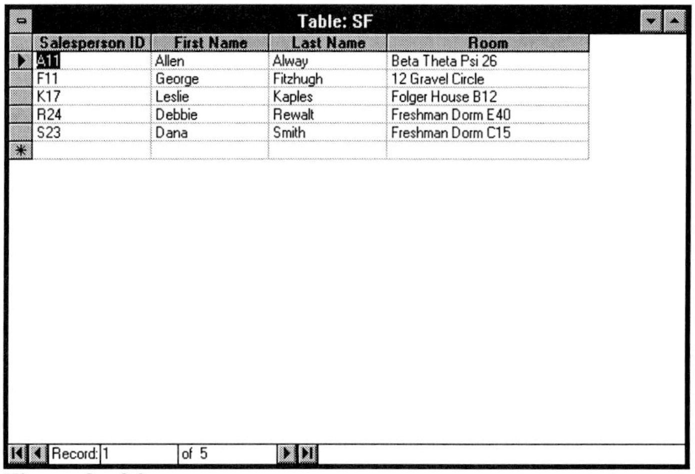
Table: SF

Salesperson ID	First Name	Last Name	Room
A11	Allen	Alway	Beta Theta Psi 26
F11	George	Fitzhugh	12 Gravel Circle
K17	Leslie	Kaples	Folger House B12
R24	Debbie	Rewalt	Freshman Dorm E40
S23	Dana	Smith	Freshman Dorm C15

Record: 1 of 5

Figure 3 - 36

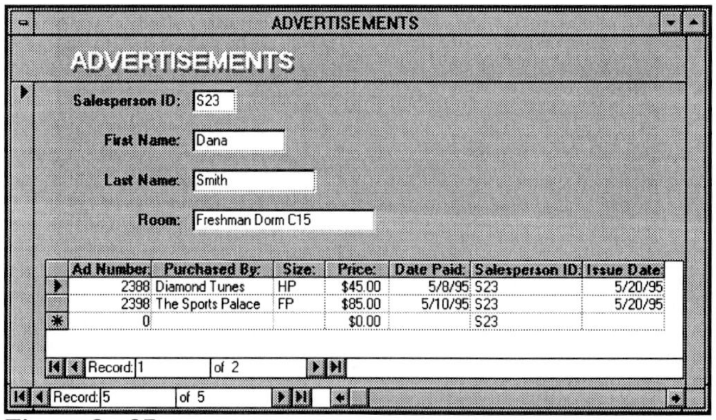

Figure 3 - 37

1. Run *Access*.
2. Maximize the *Access* window if it does not already cover the entire screen.
3. Begin opening the **xercise1.mdb** database with **FILE/Open Database** or by clicking the **Open Database** tool on the toolbar.
4. Click on the name **xercise1.mdb** and click the **OK** button.
5. Begin importing the **SF** (Sales Force) table from the **Ind-Proj** database on the Student Data Diskette by picking **FILE/Import** or clicking the **Import** button on the toolbar.
6. In the Import dialog box, click on **Microsoft Access** and click the **OK** button.
7. From the list of available databases, click on **ind-proj.mdb** and click the **OK** button.
8. The Object Type should say **Tables** and the option **Structure and Data** should be selected. From the list of Objects in IND-PROJ.MDB, click on **SF** and click the **Import** button.
9. Click **OK** in the "Successfully imported 'SF'". alert box.
10. Click **Close** in the Import Objects dialog box.
11. Click once on the name **SF** to highlight it.
12. To rename the table pick **FILE/Rename** and enter the new name **Sales Force** in the text box. Click **OK**.
13. Open **Sales Force** by clicking the **Open** button. It should look like Figure 3 - 36.
14. Close **Sales Force** by picking **FILE/Close**.
15. Begin creating the form by clicking on the **Form** tab at the left edge of the database window.
16. Click the **New** button.
17. Open the list of tables by clicking the drop-down arrow and, remembering to carefully click just once, choose **Sales Force**. Click on the **Form Wizards** button.
18. In the list of form types, click on **Main/Subform** and click the **OK** button.
19. In the first Main/Subform dialog box, click on **Ads** as the subform and click the **Next** button.
20. In the second Main/Subform dialog box you pick the fields for the main form. Click on the **double arrow head button pointing to the right** to select all fields and click **Next**.
21. In the third Main/Subform dialog box you pick the fields for the subform. Click on the **double arrow head button pointing to the right** to select all fields and click **Next**.
22. In the fourth Main/Subform dialog box you pick the style for the form. Click on **Embossed** and click **Next**.
23. In the final Main/Subform dialog box you enter the title and choose whether to go to the design window or the form window. Enter the title **ADVERTISEMENTS**, make certain "Open the form with data in it." is the selected option, and click the **Finish** button.
24. Click the **OK** button in the "You must save the subform before the Main/Subform Form Wizard can proceed." alert box.
25. Enter the Form Name **Ads Subform** for the name and click the **OK** button.
26. When the form appears on the desktop, it is designed, but has not been saved yet. Save the design with **FILE/Save Form As**, and enter the name **Ad Sales by Salesperson**. Click **OK**.
27. Press the **PGDN** key four times, pausing between each press to examine the data. Notice that two salespersons have no sales (records 1 and 4). The other three should have sales.
28. Press **PGUP** to jump to record 4, the record for **Debbie Rewalt**.

29. She has made her first sale, so click the mouse on the typing box below **Ad Number** in the subform.
30. Enter Ad Number **2399**. It was purchased by **College Movies** as a **QP** (Quarter Page Size) at **$25** and was paid on **5/12/95**. Enter each data item in the appropriate field.
31. Since these are only sales for Debbie whose ID number is R24, the Salesperson ID is already typed and must not be changed. Press **TAB** twice to jump to Issue Date.
32. Enter **5/20/95** as the Issue Date.
33. Close the form with **FILE/Close**.
34. Close the database with **FILE/Close Database**.
35. If you need to exit from *Access* and/or Windows, do so properly.

Independent Project 3.2: The Book Store

This Independent Project continues the Book Store database from Independent Project 2.2. In this project you will import the table containing the publishers' names, rename the table, and create a form that includes both the book data and the publishers' names on one screen. Finally you will use that form to enter a new book and a new publisher.

The table of publishers was typed by a clerk at the book store and saved as PUB (short for Publishers) in the IND-PROJ database that is on the Student Data Diskette. You might ask why are the publishers' names in a separate table? Why not include them right in the Books table? Because the same publishers supply many books, and their names would be repeated over and over in the Books table. In PUB, each publisher is entered just once and given a code number. Only the short code number is included on each book listing. Of course, to combine both PUB and Books on the same form, the matching code numbers must be in the Books table, too. You can check Books to make certain they are.

The table of publishers' names looks like Figure 3 - 38. When finished with the form, it should resemble Figure 3 - 39.

1. Run *Access*.
2. Maximize the *Access* window if it does not already cover the entire screen.
3. Begin opening the **xercise2.mdb** database with **FILE/Open Database** or by clicking the **Open Database** tool on the toolbar.
4. Click on the name **xercise2.mdb** and click the **OK** button.
5. Begin importing the **PUB** (Publishers) table from the **Ind-Proj** database on the Student Data Diskette by picking **FILE/Import** or clicking the **Import** button on the toolbar.
6. In the Import dialog box, click on **Microsoft Access** and click the **OK** button.
7. From the list of available databases, click on **ind-proj.mdb** and click the **OK** button.
8. The Object Type should say **Tables** and the option **Structure and Data** should be selected. From the list of Objects in IND-PROJ.MDB, click on **PUB** and click the **Import** button.
9. Click **OK** in the "Successfully imported 'PUB'". alert box.
10. Click **Close** in the Import Objects dialog box.
11. Click once on the name **PUB** to highlight it.
12. To rename the table pick **FILE/Rename** and enter the new name **Publishers** in the text box. Click **OK**.
13. Open **Publishers** by clicking the **Open** button. It should look like Figure 3 - 38. Press the **END** key to jump to the last field.

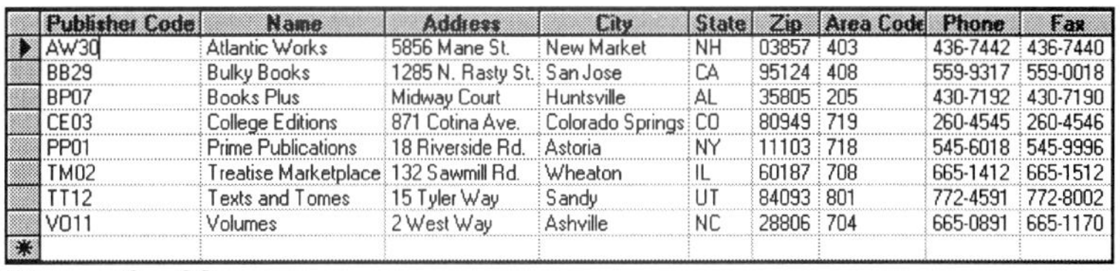

Publisher Code	Name	Address	City	State	Zip	Area Code	Phone	Fax
AW30	Atlantic Works	5856 Mane St.	New Market	NH	03857	403	436-7442	436-7440
BB29	Bulky Books	1285 N. Rasty St.	San Jose	CA	95124	408	559-9317	559-0018
BP07	Books Plus	Midway Court	Huntsville	AL	35805	205	430-7192	430-7190
CE03	College Editions	871 Cotina Ave.	Colorado Springs	CO	80949	719	260-4545	260-4546
PP01	Prime Publications	18 Riverside Rd.	Astoria	NY	11103	718	545-6018	545-9996
TM02	Treatise Marketplace	132 Sawmill Rd.	Wheaton	IL	60187	708	665-1412	665-1512
TT12	Texts and Tomes	15 Tyler Way	Sandy	UT	84093	801	772-4591	772-8002
VO11	Volumes	2 West Way	Ashville	NC	28806	704	665-0891	665-1170

Figure 3 - 38

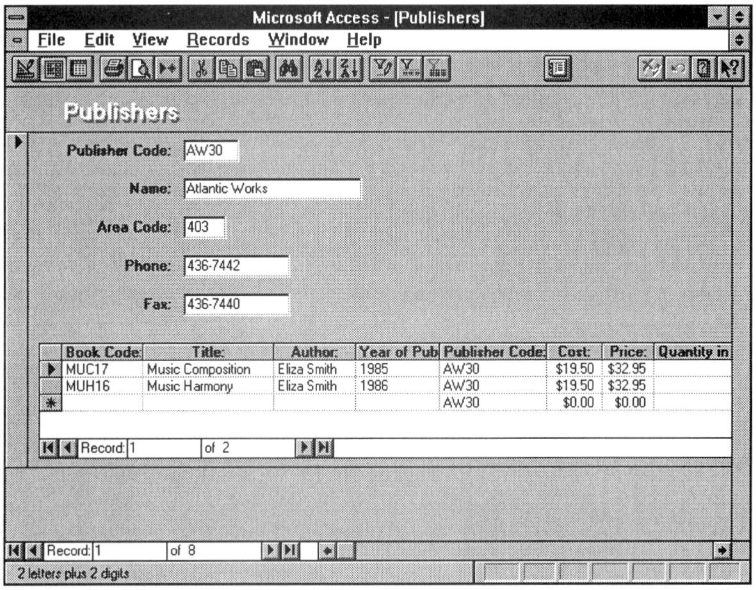

Figure 3 - 39

14. Close **Publishers** by picking **FILE/Close**.
15. Begin creating the form by clicking on the **Form** tab at the left edge of the database window.
16. Click the **New** button.
17. Open the list of tables by clicking the drop-down arrow and, remembering to carefully click just once, choose **Publishers**. Then, click on the **Form Wizards** button.
18. In the list of form types, click on **Main/Subform** and click the **OK** button.
19. In the first Main/Subform dialog box, click on **Books** as the subform and click the **Next** button.
20. In the second Main/Subform dialog box you pick the fields for the main form. Since we will include only the Publisher Code, Name, Area Code, Phone, and Fax fields on this form, make certain the highlight is on **Publisher Code** and click on the **single arrow head button pointing to the right** to start with that one field.
21. Click on the **single arrow head** once more to send the **Name** field to the Fields on main form: list.
22. Click on the field name **Area Code** and click on the **single arrow head** to include it.
23. Similarly, click the **single arrow head** two more times to send the next two fields, **Phone** and **Fax** over to the Fields on main form: list.
24. Click **Next**.
25. In the third Main/Subform dialog box you pick the fields for the subform. Click on the **double arrow head button pointing to the right** to select all fields and click **Next**.

26. In the fourth Main/Subform dialog box you pick the style for the form. Click on **Embossed** and click **Next**.
27. In the final Main/Subform dialog box you enter the title and choose whether to go to the design window or the form window. The title **Publishers** is already in the text box so leave it alone. Make certain "Open the form with data in it." is the selected option, and click the **Finish** button.
28. Click the **OK** button in the "You must save the subform before the Main/Subform Form Wizard can proceed." alert box.
29. Enter: **Books Subform** for the Form Name and click the **OK** button.
30. When the form appears on the desktop (see Figure 3 - 39), it is designed, but has not been saved yet. Save the design with **FILE/Save Form As**, and enter the name **Books by Publisher**. Click **OK**.
31. Maximize the form window.
32. Press the **PGDN** key seven times, pausing between each press to examine the data. Notice that four publishers have no books in the Books table yet. The other four have from two to four each.
33. To make sure the form works, you will enter one new book and one new publisher. To start the new book, you must search for the correct publisher. Click the **Find** button on the toolbar, enter: **BB29** (the code for Bulky Books) in the Find What text box, click on the **All Fields** option, and click the **Find First** button.
34. **Close** the Find dialog box.
35. Click the mouse on the typing box below **Book Code** in the subform.
36. Enter Book Code **CHC18**. The Title is **Chemical Compendium**. There is no Author. Type in the Year of Publication as **1995** and skip over the Publisher Code as that is already filled in. The Cost is **34.50** and the Price is **49.95**. Leave the Quantity in Stock as **0**.
37. To enter the new publisher, click the mouse on the current Publisher Code, click the **Last Record** navigation button at the very bottom of the screen (not in the subform) to jump to the final record, and press **PAGE DOWN** for a new record.
38. Type: **AA15** for the Publisher Code, **Authors Away** as the Name, **415** for the Area Code, **326-8899** in the Phone field, and **326-9988** for the Fax number.
39. Close the form with **FILE/Close**.
40. Close the database with **FILE/Close Database**.
41. If you need to exit from *Access* and/or Windows, do so properly.

Independent Project 3.3: The Real Estate Office

This Independent Project continues the Real Estate Office database from Independent Project 2.3. In this project you will import the table containing the agencies' names and create a form that includes both the properties and the agencies' names on one screen. Finally you will use that form to enter a new commercial real estate listing and a new agency.

The table of agencies was typed by a colleague at the real estate office and saved as Agencies in the IND-PROJ database that is on the Student Data Diskette. You might ask why are the agencies' names in a separate table? Why not include them right in the Commercial Listings table? Because the same agency supplies many commercial listings, and their names would be repeated over and over in the Commercial Listings table. In Agencies, each office and its associated data are entered just once and given a code number. Only the short code number is included on each commercial property listing. Of course, to combine both Agencies and

Commercial Listings on the same form, the matching code numbers must be in the Commercial Listings table, too. You can check Commercial Listings to make certain they are.

The table of agencies' names looks like Figure 3 - 40. When finished with the form, it should resemble Figure 3 - 41.

Agency Code	Agency Name	Address	City	State	Zip	Area Code	Phone 1	Phone 2	Fax
GW14	George Winkle	80 N. Main St.	New Canaan	CT	06840	203	972-9538		972-9625
PP15	Priceless Properties	817 Glable Lane	Stamford	CT	06903	203	359-1111		359-1212
PP24	Profitable Properties	452 Elm Ave.	Danbury	CT	06810	203	748-3471	748-3472	748-0102
RP12	Right Properties	125 Ridgeway	Danbury	CT	06810	203	748-9410	748-9010	748-9411
RR11	Regal Real Estate	17 North Way W.	Stamford	CT	06905	203	359-0050	359-0060	359-0055
SC18	Smith and Cross	7612 Main St.	Greenwich	CT	06830	203	661-2831		661-2001

Figure 3 - 40

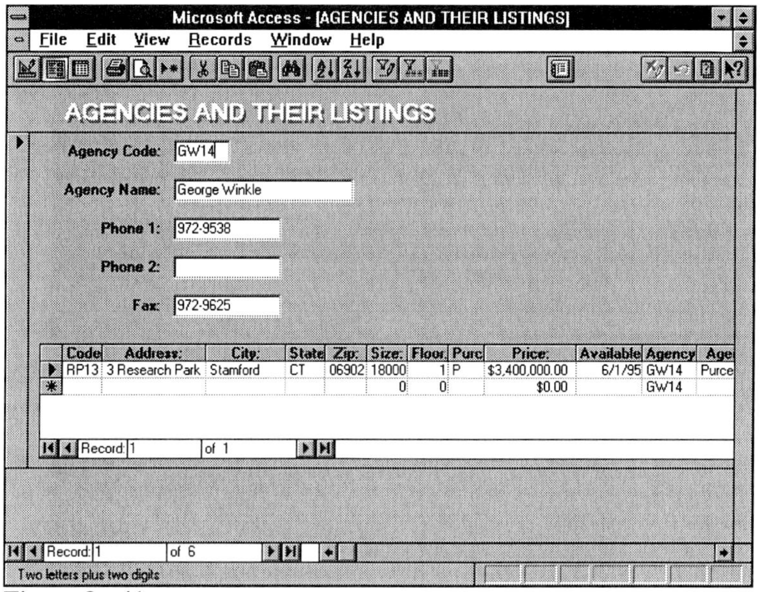

Figure 3 - 41

1. Run *Access* and maximize the window.
2. Open the **xercise3.mdb** database.
3. Import the **Agencies** table (with data) from the **Microsoft Access** database named **Ind-Proj** on the Student Data Diskette.
4. Open **Agencies**. It should look like Figure 3 - 40.
5. Close **Agencies**.
6. Begin creating the form by clicking on the **Form** tab at the left edge of the database window.
7. Use the **Form Wizard** to create a **Main/Subform** form for the **Agencies** table.
8. **Commercial Listings** will be the table in the subform.
9. From **Agencies** include the **Agency Code**, **Agency Name**, **Phone 1, Phone 2**, and **Fax** fields.
10. For the subform include all fields in the Commercial Listings table.
11. Pick **Embossed** as the style.
12. Make the title **AGENCIES AND THEIR LISTINGS** and open the form window with data in it.

13. Click the **OK** button in the "You must save the subform before the Main/Subform Form Wizard can proceed." alert box.
14. Enter the Form Name **Commercial Listings Subform**.
15. When the form appears on the desktop (see Figure 3 - 41), save it as **Agencies and Their Listings**.
16. Maximize the form window.
17. Press the **PGDN** key five times, pausing between each press to examine the data.
18. A new listing at 6 Research Park, Stamford has been announced. The listing agent will be RP12, Right Properties. Locate that real estate agency in the top portion of the form, then enter the new listing from the data shown in Table 3 - 1 into the embedded portion of the form. You may need to scroll across the embedded form to see all the fields.

Field Name	Data
Code	RP16
Address	6 Research Park
City	Stamford
State	CT
Zip	06902
Size	19,000
Floor	1
Purchase or Rent	P
Price	$3,900,000
Available	10/1/95
Agency Code	RP12
Agent	Williams

Table 3 - 1

19. To enter the new real estate agency, move to the final record (SC18), click on the **Agency Code**, and press **PAGE DOWN** for a new record.
20. Type **CP19** for the Agency Code, **Colonial Properties** as the Agency Name, **359-8372** for Phone 1, and **359-0573** in the Fax field.
21. Close the form with **FILE/Close**.
22. Close the database with **FILE/Close Database**.
23. If you need to exit from *Access* and/or Windows, do so properly.

Independent Project 3.4: The Veterinarian

This Independent Project continues the veterinarian database from Independent Project 2.4. In this project you will import the table containing the owners' names and create a form that includes both the pets and the owners' names on one screen. Finally, you will use that form to enter a new owner and her pet.

The table of owners is already typed and has been saved as **Pet Owners** in the IND-PROJ database that is on the Student Data Diskette. Be sure you can answer the question of why the owners' names and addresses are in a separate table rather than included right in the pets table.

Complete the following tasks:

1. Import the **Pet Owners** table from the Student Data Diskette.

2. Open **Pet Owners** and examine the data in it.
3. Use the **Form Wizard** to create a **Main/Subform** form for the **Pet Owners** table that will include **Pets** as the subform. It should match the form illustrated in Figure 3 - 42, except that the embedded subform will have the field names you made up and the Code and Date of Last Visit fields will have the dates you entered.

IMPORTANT: This will only work if you named the field with the codes for the owners in the pets table ***Owner Code****. If you named the owner's code field anything else you will get a "The Main/Subform Form Wizard couldn't establish a link between the main form and the subform." message, meaning the link between the tables has been unsuccessful. To fix this problem, close this form design without saving, delete the subform that the Wizard just saved, restructure the Pets table and make the name of the owner's code* ***Owner Code****, and redo the form design.*

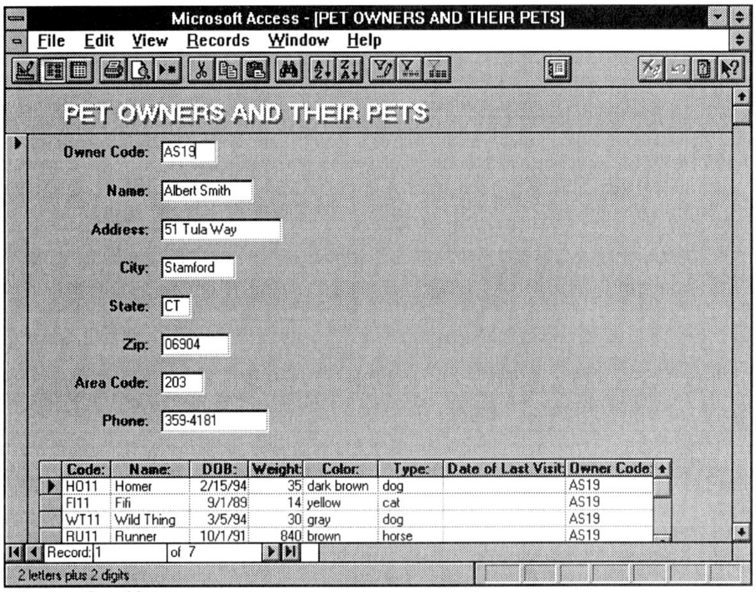

Figure 3 - 42

4. Use the form to enter a new pet for Dan Wilson. The pet is a black horse named Wilhelm that weighs 940 pounds. It was born about 6/15/90.
5. Use the form to enter a new owner. He is Monty Wright and he lives at 56 Wildwood Terrace, Stamford, CT, 06905. His phone is (203) 359-4415.

Lesson 4 Queries

Objectives

In this lesson you will learn how to:

- Set up a select query
- Select the fields to be included
- Sort the query result
- Specify single criteria for selecting records

PROJECT DESCRIPTION

A *query* is a search for all of the records within a table that contain a specific value. For example, you might need a list of all of your customers who ordered a particular CDROM title.

In this lesson, we will run several queries based on the CDROM table in order to extract various groups of listings, check inventory levels, and gather other pertinent information. We will match a single value at a time in this lesson. In the next lesson, we will use queries with multiple matching values, as well as multiple tables to access data from more than one source.

When you complete this lesson, you will have two queries listed in the database window (see Figure 4 - 1).

Figure 4 - 1

QUERYING A TABLE

During editing we searched for matching listings one at a time; with queries you get the complete set of matches all at once. A query also allows sorting the resulting listings, as well as selecting which fields will be included and in what order. Once designed, a query may be saved, or merely used temporarily and discarded. If saved, reports and forms can be designed for queries, the same as for tables. Since we are selecting the fields and records, this type of query is called a *Select Query*.

Access uses what is called *Query by Example*. This means that, rather than type out a lengthy instruction in words, in Access you merely fill in a diagram by giving an example of the value you want matched. For example, to work with only records of customers who live in New York, you would type the example "NY" in the State field. The example of what you want matched is also called the *criterion*. Query by Example is abbreviated QBE, and, thus, the grid in the bottom half of the Select Query window is called the *QBE grid* (see Figure 4 - 2).

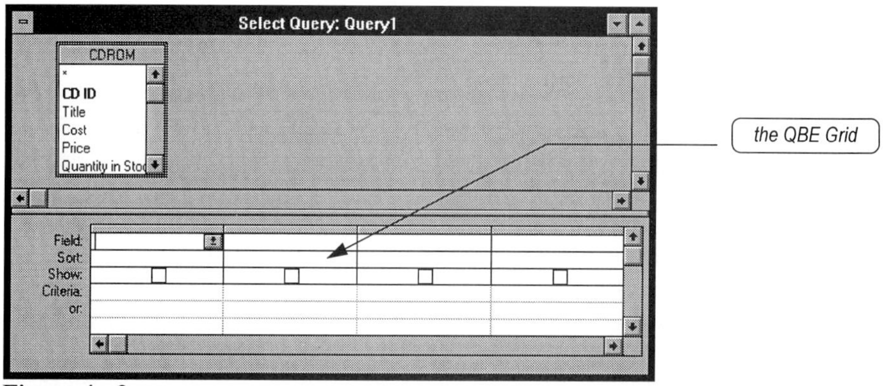

Figure 4 - 2

The resulting answer from a select query is called a *dynaset*. Dynaset stands for dynamically linked datasheet, which is a fancy way of saying that the listings resulting from a query can be directly edited and any changes to the data will automatically be made in the original table as well.

A SINGLE TABLE QUERY

For our first query we will produce a list of each CDROM Title and its Quantity in Stock. We begin by opening the Select Query window.

To set up a Select Query:

- Click the **Query** tab on the left edge of the database window.
- Click the **New** button at the top of the database window.
- Choose the **New Query** button to set up your own query, or the **Query Wizards** button to pick a pre-designed query.

- If you chose **New Query**, add the desired table or tables from the **Add Table** dialog box.

Activity 4.1: Setting up a Select Query

The first step is to initiate the query and choose the table whose data will be the basis of the search.

1. Open the **SALES** database with **FILE/Open**, then click on **SALES.MDB** and click on **OK**.

   Before clicking on sales you may need to pick the correct drive and directory.

2. Click on the **Query** tab (see Figure 4 - 3).

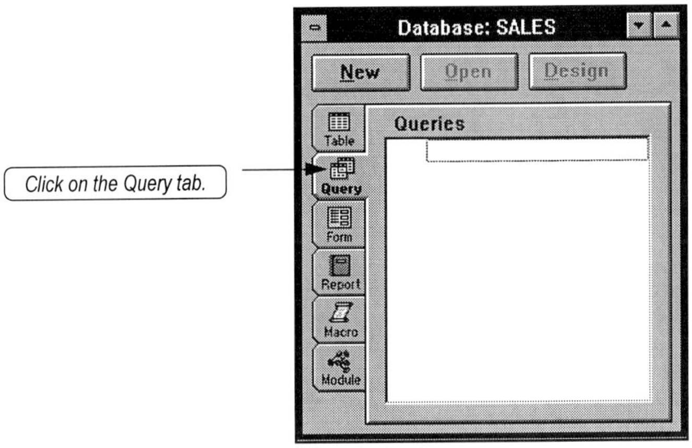

Figure 4 - 3

3. Click the **New** button at the top of the database window.
4. In the **New Query** dialog box, click on the **New Query** button (see Figure 4 - 4).

   *While many of the Wizards are of enormous help, the **Query Wizards** button offers several very complicated queries that would be handy for the advanced user, but are far more complex than we need.*

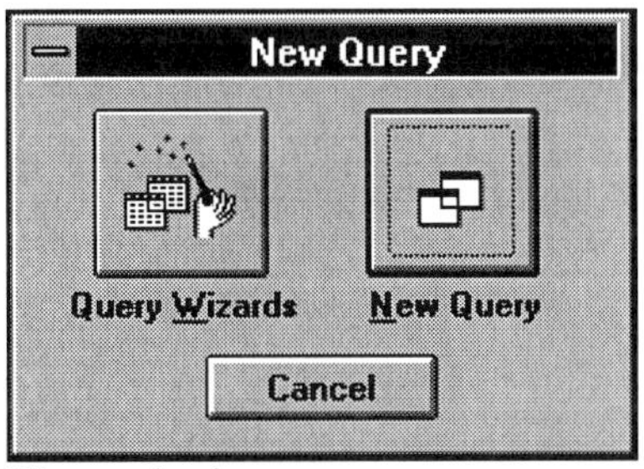

Figure 4 - 4

*The **Select Query** window opens with the **Add Table** dialog box on top of it (see* Figure 4 - 5*).*

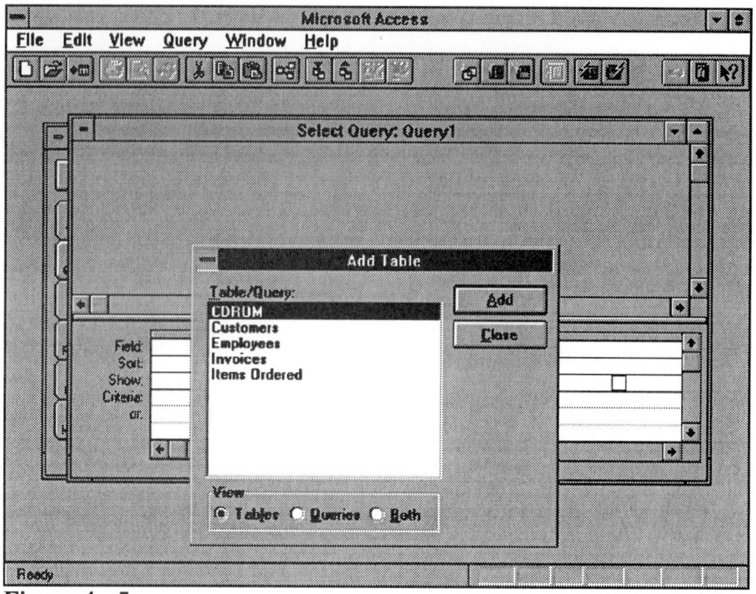

Figure 4 - 5

5. Since we are interested in selected data from the CDROM table, pick **CDROM** and click the **Add** button to place a list of its fields in the top half of the Select Query window (see Figure 4 - 6).

6. Since CDROM is the only table in which we are interested, click the **Close** button to close the **Add Table** dialog box.

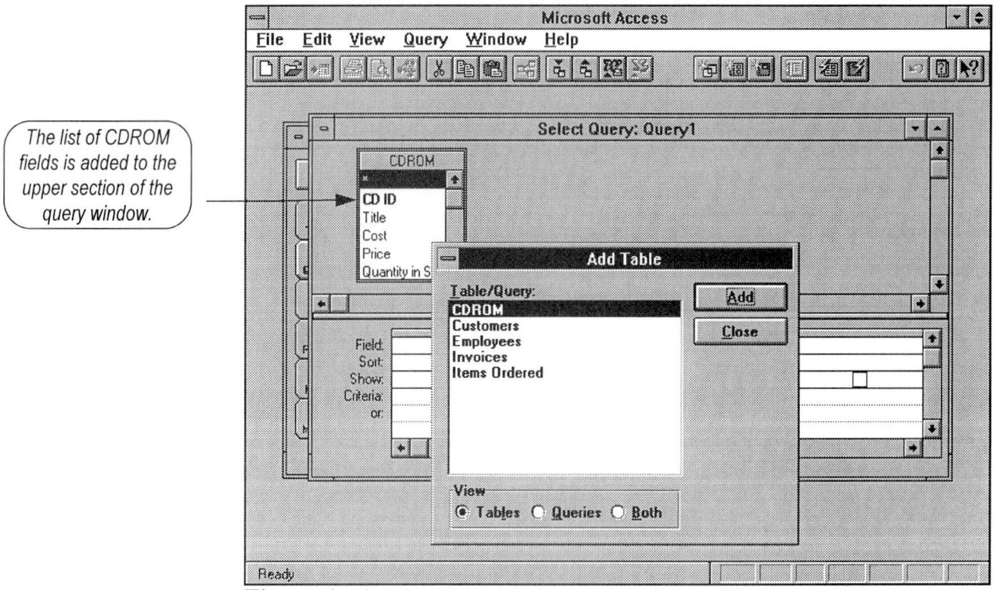

Figure 4 - 6

SELECTING THE FIELDS

There are four methods for choosing the fields that you want to see in the result.

To select the fields to be included in the result:

- Double click the name in the field list in the top half of the query window. That field name will occupy the next available column in the QBE grid. This is probably quickest.
- Click on and drag the name from the field list down to the QBE grid. Either drag the name to an empty column, or, if the column is already occupied, the new name will be inserted and the existing name will be pushed to the right. This method is best for controlling the placement of a field.
- In the desired column in the QBE grid, click on the **Field:** line. Then, click the drop-down arrow to open the list of available fields and select the field name from the list. This is a good method for changing a field selection.
- Type the desired field name directly on the **Field:** line in the desired column. This is the slowest method, but does not require the mouse.

To view the resulting dynaset:

- Click the **Datasheet View** button  on the toolbar or pick **VIEW/Datasheet** in the menus.

To return to the query design:

- Click the **Design View** button  on the toolbar or pick **VIEW/Query Design** in the menus.

Activity 4.2: Selecting the Desired Fields and Viewing the Result

Since we need only the Title and Quantity in Stock, we will select only those two fields to be included in the field list. For the first field we will drag the field name down into the QBE Grid. For the second field we will speed things up by double-clicking to include the field name.

1. In the list of fields in the top half of the **Select Query** window, click on the name **Title** to highlight it.
2. Move the mouse cursor back on top of the highlighted name, hold down the mouse button, and drag its icon (it will become a small rectangle) down onto the **Field:** line in the first column of the QBE Grid. Release the mouse button.

   While dragging the mouse, wherever a circle with a slash appears, that is an inappropriate area for the field name. Do not release the mouse button in such an area.

   *The name **Title** will appear on the Field line in the first column and an X will check the box on the Show: line indicating that the field will be shown in the result (see Figure 4 - 7).*

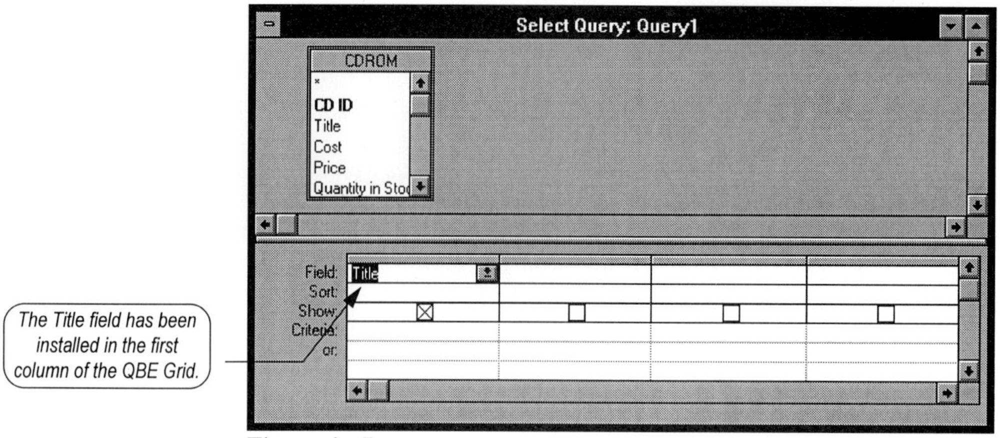

Figure 4 - 7

3. In the list of fields in the top half of the **Select Query** window, double-click on the name **Quantity in Stock** to include it in the second column of the QBE Grid (see Figure 4 - 8).

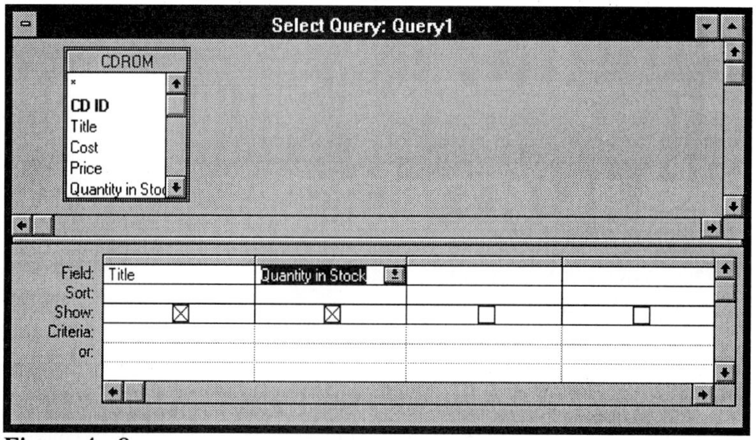

Figure 4 - 8

4. Click the **Datasheet View** button  on the toolbar to view the result.

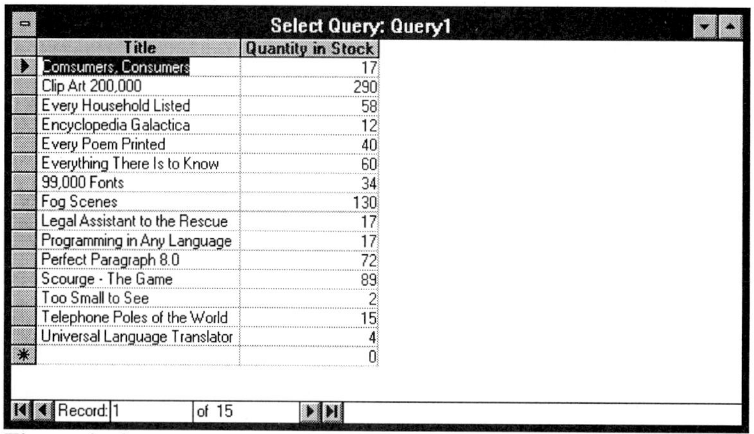

Figure 4 - 9

*All 15 records are listed, but only the two selected fields are included (*Figure 4 - 9*). This result is a dynaset.*

5. Click the **Design View** button on the toolbar to return to the Select Query window and the query design.

SORTING THE DYNASET

A query can sort the resulting dynaset based on any field or combination of fields in the table. You fill in the Sort: line in the QBE Grid in one or more columns. With a multiple field sort, the column furthest on the left will be sorted first, followed by each additional column that contains a sort specification from left to right. The column(s) used to sort may be shown in the dynaset by leaving the Show box checked, or hidden by unchecking the Show box.

To sort a dynaset:

- Include the field you wish to sort by in the QBE Grid.
- Move onto the **Sort:** line of the column you wish to sort by. A drop-down list arrow will appear.
- Open the drop-down list by clicking its arrow and choose either **Ascending** or **Descending**.

Activity 4.3: Sorting by Quantity In Stock

1. We want to sort the dynaset by the Quantity in Stock field. Since the **Quantity In Stock** field is already in the QBE Grid, click the mouse on the **Sort:** line in that column.
2. Click on the drop-down arrow to open the list of sort options (see Figure 4 - 10).

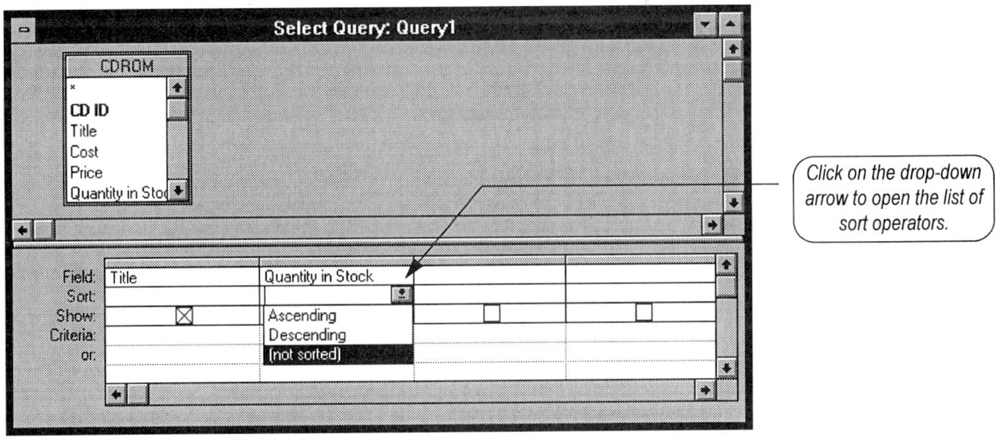

Figure 4 - 10

3. Choose **Descending** to sort the quantities from largest to smallest.
4. Click the **Datasheet View** button on the toolbar to view the result (see Figure 4 - 11).

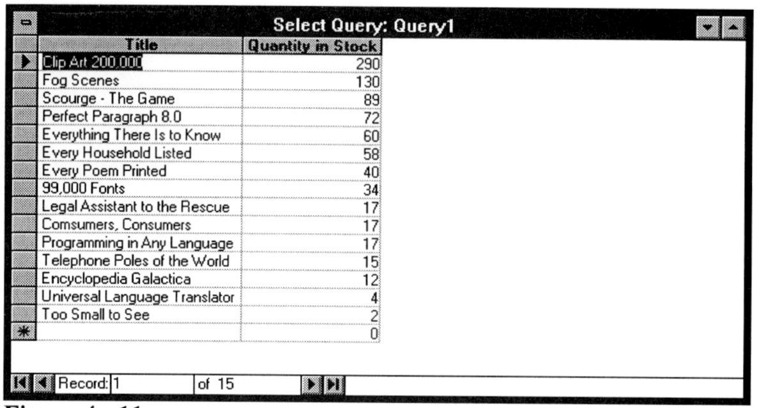

Figure 4 - 11

All 15 records are still listed, but they are now sorted into order by descending quantity.

5. Print this result by clicking the **Print** button and clicking **OK** in the Print dialog box.
6. Click the **Design View** button on the toolbar to return to the Select Query window and the query design.

Activity 4.4: Inserting a Field and Sorting by Two Fields

The Price field is not in the QBE Grid yet, so we must add it. We could easily put it in the third column, but we want it in the second column. To insert a field, drag its name down to the QBE Grid on top of an existing name on the Field line and release the mouse button. The field that was in that column will move to the right to make room for the new field.

1. Click the mouse once on the field name **Price** in the list in the top section of the window to highlight that name.
2. Drag **Price** down to the QBE Grid and drop it on top of **Quantity In Stock**.

   Quantity In Stock will move over to the third column (see Figure 4 - 12*).*

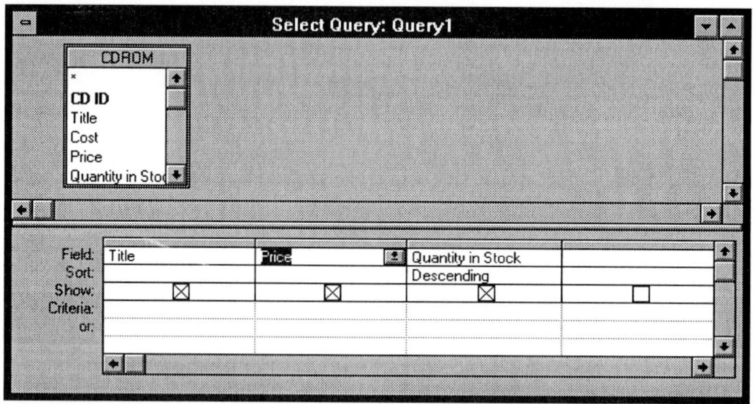

Figure 4 - 12

3. Click the mouse on the **Sort:** line in the **Price** column.

4. Open the list of sort options by clicking the drop-down list arrow and choose **Ascending**.

   Because we have two columns being sorted, Access will sort first by the column on the left. Thus, the prices will be in ascending order. Then, whenever two products have the same price, those two will be in descending quantity order.

5. Click the **Datasheet View** button on the toolbar to view the result (Figure 4 - 13).

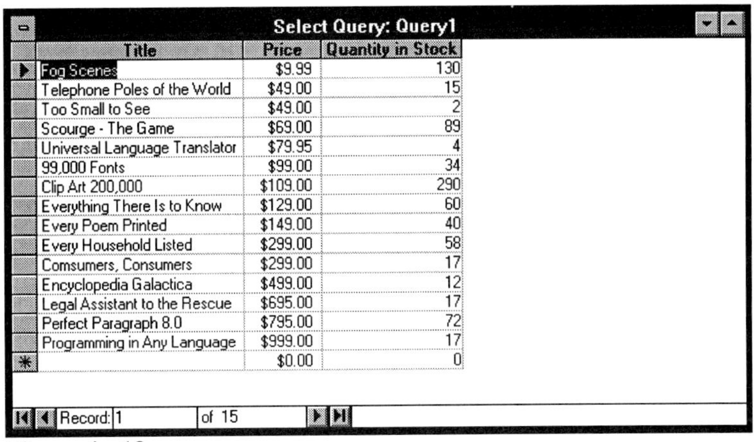

Select Query: Query1

Title	Price	Quantity in Stock
Fog Scenes	$9.99	130
Telephone Poles of the World	$49.00	15
Too Small to See	$49.00	2
Scourge - The Game	$69.00	89
Universal Language Translator	$79.95	4
99,000 Fonts	$99.00	34
Clip Art 200,000	$109.00	290
Everything There Is to Know	$129.00	60
Every Poem Printed	$149.00	40
Every Household Listed	$299.00	58
Comsumers, Consumers	$299.00	17
Encyclopedia Galactica	$499.00	12
Legal Assistant to the Rescue	$695.00	17
Perfect Paragraph 8.0	$795.00	72
Programming in Any Language	$999.00	17
	$0.00	0

Record: 1 of 15

Figure 4 - 13

Note the pair of products with a price of $49.00 and check that their two quantities are in descending order. Also examine the pair priced at $299.00.

6. Print this result by clicking the **Print** button and clicking **OK** in the Print dialog box.
7. Click the **Design View** button on the toolbar to return to the Select Query window and the query design.

REMOVING A FIELD FROM THE QBE GRID

The thin gray bar immediately above the name of each field in the QBE Grid is the *selector*. It is used to delete fields. It can also be used to move fields in exactly the same way we moved fields in a table.

To delete a field from the QBE Grid:

- Click the selector above the field name in the QBE Grid. The entire column will be highlighted.
- Press the **DELETE** key or choose **EDIT/Delete** in the menu.
- To delete all fields from the QBE Grid, pick **EDIT/Clear Grid**.

Activity 4.5: Deleting the Price field

1. Click the **selector** above the **Price** field.

   The entire Price field will be highlighted (see Figure 4 - 14*).*

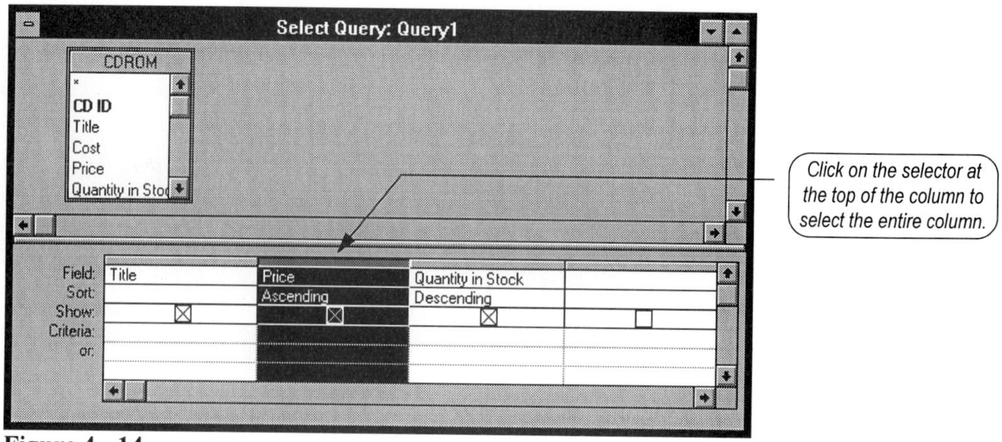

Figure 4 - 14

2. Press the **DELETE** key to remove the Price field.

   The Quantity In Stock field slides back over to the second column.

SORTING BY TWO FIELDS THAT ARE NOT IN LEFT TO RIGHT ORDER

Since Access sorts the fields that have sort specifications in the QBE Grid from left to right, what if that is not the desired order? To see how to accomplish this we will sort by Quantity In Stock in descending order and Title in ascending order even though Title will be the first field displayed in the dynaset.

To sort by fields that are not in left to right order:

- Place the fields you want to see in the dynaset in the desired order.
- Insert a second copy of the field that is the most important field for sorting, placing it to the left of the second most important field for sorting.
- Set the sort order specification (ascending or descending) in this new copy of the most important field, but uncheck the Show box so that the field will not show in the result. Thus it will sort, but not show.
- In the original copy of the most important field for sorting, leave the Show box checked so it will display, but do not set a sort option.

Activity 4.6: Sorting by Quantity, then Title

1. The query design with Title in the first column and Quantity In Stock in the second column should still be open.
2. Click on the **Quantity In Stock** field name in the list in the upper section of the window.
3. Drag that field name down into the QBE Grid and drop it on top of **Title** in the first column.

   Title will move over to the second column (see Figure 4 - 15*).*
4. Click on the **Sort:** line in the first column (the first Quantity In Stock), and open the drop-down list, and choose **Descending**.
5. Remove the check on the **Show:** line for this first column (the first Quantity In Stock) so it will sort but not display.

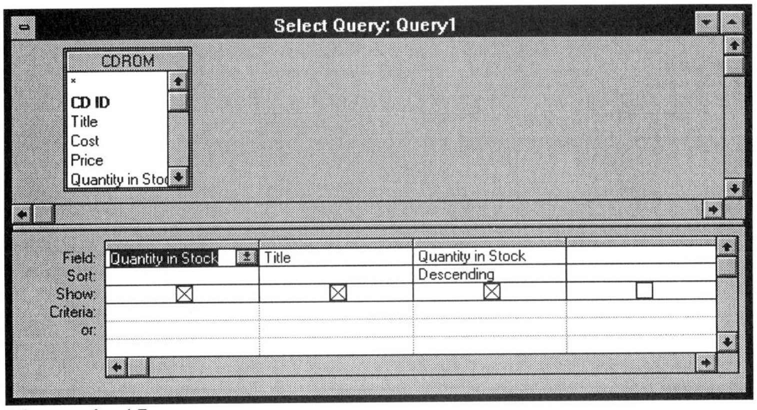

Figure 4 - 15

6. Click on the **Sort:** line under the third column (the second Quantity In Stock) and delete the word **Descending** (see Figure 4 - 16).

   Leave the check in the Show box of this second Quantity In Stock field as this one, which is to the right of Title, should display.

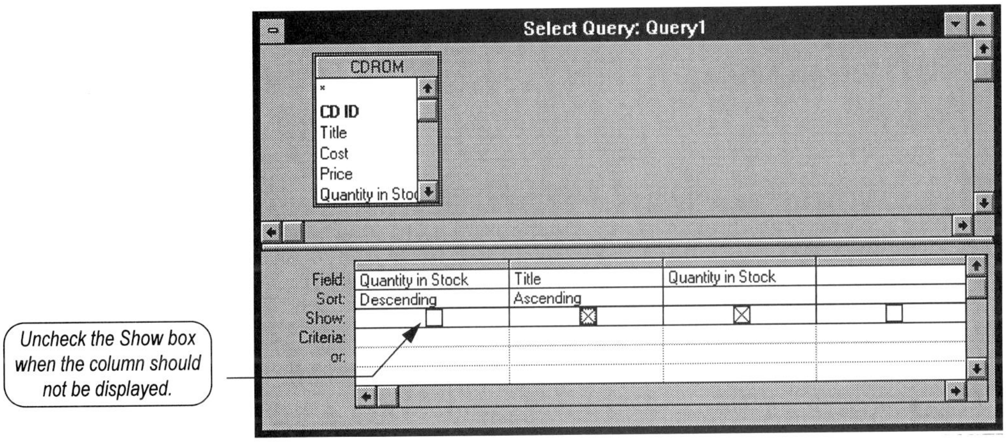

Figure 4 - 16

7. Click on the **Sort:** line under **Title** and pick **Ascending** (see Figure 4 - 16).
8. Click the **Datasheet View** button on the toolbar to view the result (Figure 4 - 17).

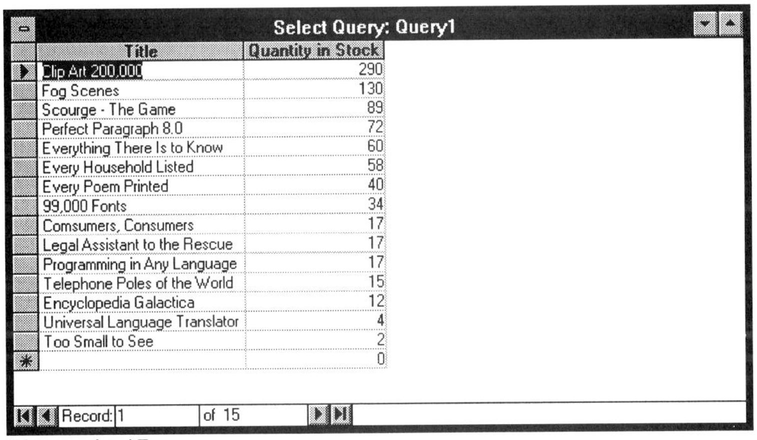

Figure 4 - 17

Examine the three listings with a quantity of 17. They should be in alphabetical order by Title.

9. Print this result by clicking the **Print** button and clicking **OK** in the Print dialog box.
10. Click the **Design View** button on the toolbar to return to the Select Query window and the query design.

SAVING A QUERY DESIGN

While a query is often used to temporarily view a result, sometimes the answer is important or useful enough to save the query so it can be rerun whenever needed.

To save a query:

- Choose **FILE/Save As.**
- Type the desired name (up to 64 characters) in the **Query Name** text box of the **Save As** dialog box.
- Click **OK.**

Activity 4.7: Saving the Query

1. Choose **FILE/Save As.**
2. Type the name: **Quantity and Title Sort** and click **OK** (see Figure 4 - 18).

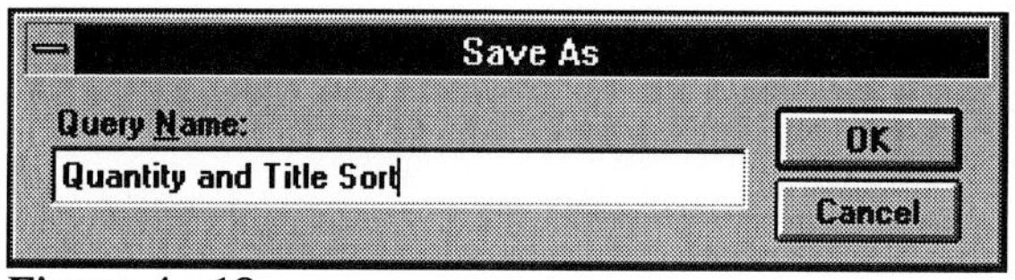

Figure 4 - 18

3. Choose **FILE/Close.**

   The name will appear in the Query list of the database window, and could be reopened any time that query was needed again.

SELECTING MATCHING RECORDS WITH A QUERY

Perhaps the most valuable ability of a query is to select only those records that match some criterion that you specify. You specify the value to be matched by typing an example of it (thus Query By Example). You type the example on the **Criteria:** line in the QBE Grid under the column that would contain the matching values.

In this lesson, we will search for matching values in a single field. In the next lesson, we will use multiple criteria.

To select records with matching values through a query:

- Open the query window and choose a table as discussed previously.
- Pick the desired fields.
- Enter the example of the value to be matched on the **Criteria:** line in the column that would contain that value.
- Click the Datasheet View button to see the resulting dynaset.

Activity 4.8: Using Numerical Criteria in a Query

We need a listing of the CDROMs that cost $179.

1. The **SALES** database should be open.
2. Click on the **Query** tab.
3. Click the **New** button at the top of the database window.
4. In the **New Query** dialog box, click on the **New Query** button.
5. Pick **CDROM** and click the **Add** button to place a list of its fields in the top half of the Select Query window.
6. Since CDROM is the only table in which we are interested, click the **Close** button to close the **Add Table** dialog box.
7. Double-click on **Title** in the list in the upper section of the window to place it in the first column of the QBE Grid.

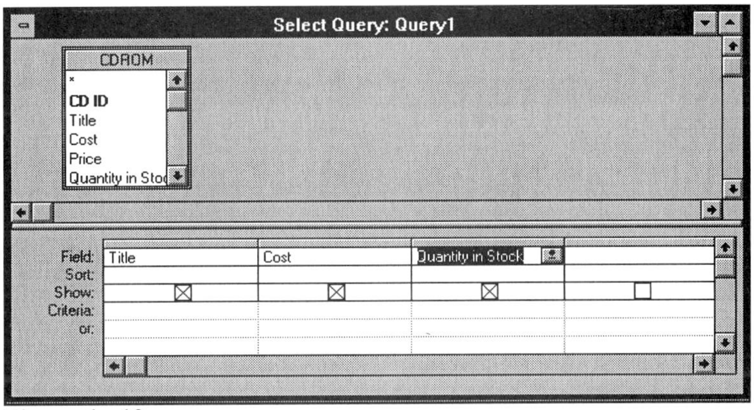

Figure 4 - 19

8. Double-click on **Cost** to put it in the second column of the QBE Grid.
9. Double-click on **Quantity In Stock** to position it in the third column of the QBE Grid (see Figure 4 - 19).
10. Click on the **Criteria:** line in the **Cost** column of the QBE Grid.
11. Type: **179** (see Figure 4 - 20).

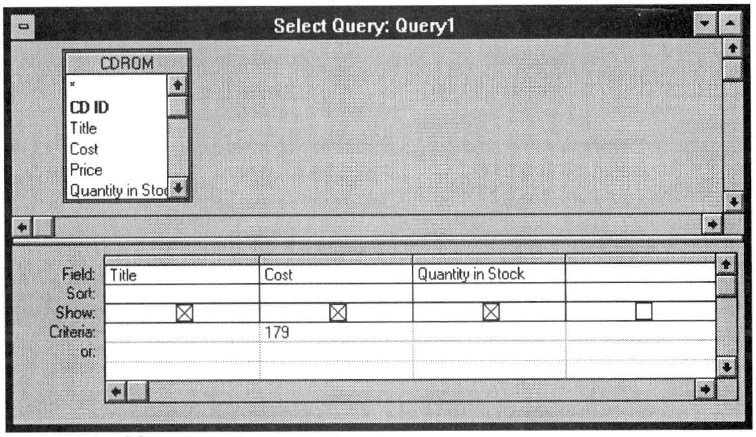

Figure 4 - 20

Do not type the dollar sign or any commas in numbers in a criterion. If you should get a "Type Mismatch" error, check your typing very carefully and correct the entry.

12. Click the **Datasheet View** button on the toolbar to view the result (see Figure 4 - 21).

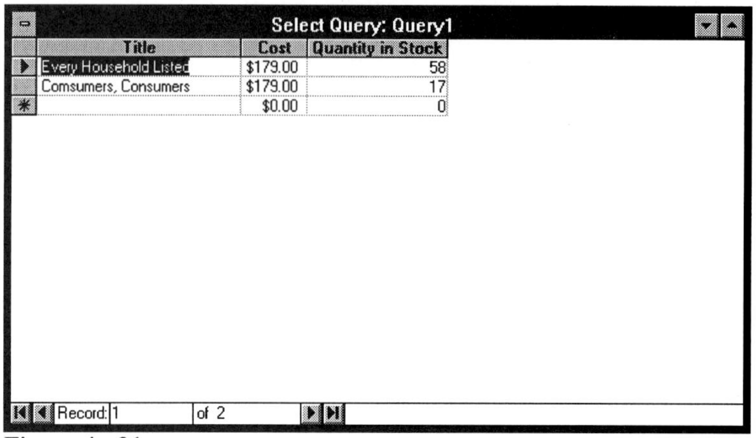

Figure 4 - 21

Examine the values for Cost. They should both be equal to $179.

13. Click the **Design View** button on the toolbar to return to the query design. Do not close the query.

THE INEQUALITY SYMBOLS IN QUERIES

Access interprets a single value on the Criteria: line as requiring an exact match, that is the value in the table must **equal** the example. While you could type the equal sign, it is always optional. Other *operators* are allowed besides an equal sign. These inequality symbols are listed in Table 4 - 1.

Symbol	Meaning with Numbers	Meaning with Dates	Meaning with Text
>	greater than	after	alphabetically after
<	less than	before	alphabetically before
>=	greater than or equal to	on or after	alphabetically after or equal to
<=	less than or equal to	on or before	alphabetically before or equal to
not	not equal to	not on	not equal to
or	or	or	or

Table 4 - 1

To search for a range of values:

- Set up the query as we have done previously.
- Enter the inequality symbol and value on the **Criteria:** line in the column that would contain those values.
- Click the Datasheet View button to see the resulting dynaset.

Activity 4.9: Using a Numerical Range in a Query

We need a listing of any CDROMs that have dropped below the reorder point of 20 pieces in stock.

1. The previous query should still be open.

   If the previous query is not still open, follow steps 1-9 from Activity 4-8 and proceed to step 3 in this activity.

2. Erase the **179** on the Criteria line under Cost.
3. Click on the **Criteria:** line in the **Quantity In Stock** column of the QBE Grid.
4. Type: **<20** (see Figure 4 - 22).

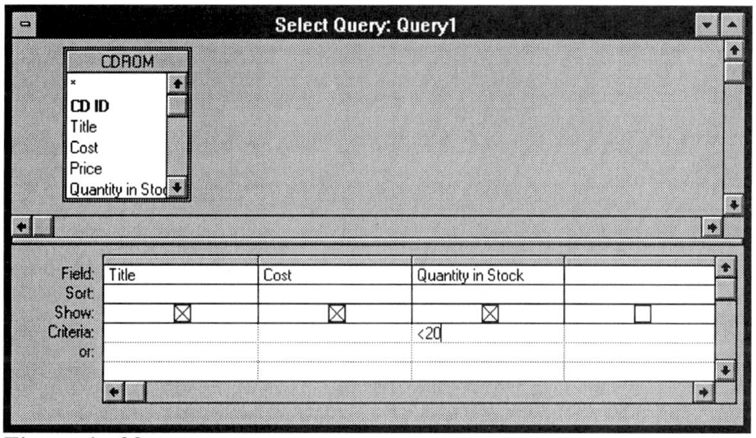

Figure 4 - 22

5. Click the **Datasheet View** button on the toolbar to view the result (see Figure 4 - 23).

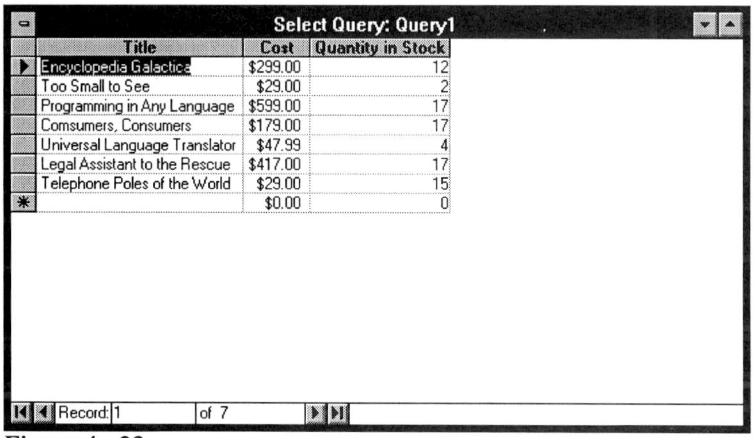

Figure 4 - 23

Examine the quantities. All seven should be less than 20.

6. Click the **Design View** button on the toolbar to return to the query design.

PRINT PREVIEWING A QUERY RESULT

Since a reorder list could be extremely valuable, you would probably want to print the dynaset. Before you commit it to paper, however, you might want to see on the screen how a printout would look. The toolbar contains a Print Preview button (as well as a Print button).

To print preview a dynaset:

- Click the Print Preview button on the toolbar while viewing a dynaset.

Activity 4.10: Printing a Dynaset

So we would not have to remember the reorder list, we could print that result. To view it first we will use Print Preview.

1. Click the **Print Preview** button on the toolbar (see Figure 4 - 24).

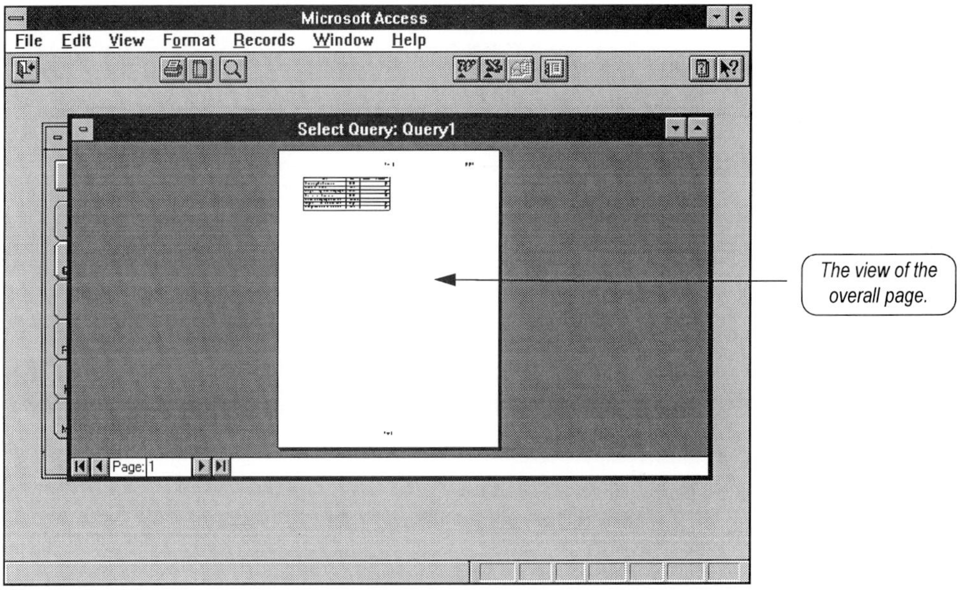

Figure 4 - 24

Notice there is a Print button on this screen should you decide to print during Print Preview.

2. The mouse cursor will become a magnifying glass shape while on top of the preview page. Move that cursor on top of the text and click the mouse button to enlarge the preview to 100% size (see Figure 4 - 25).

   *You can move about the page with the **ARROW** keys or the Scroll Bars.*

3. To return to the full page, click the mouse on the white space of the page, or click the **Zoom** button. on the toolbar.
4. After examining the preview, click the **Close Window** button on the toolbar to return to the dynaset.
5. Click the **Design View** button to return to the query design.

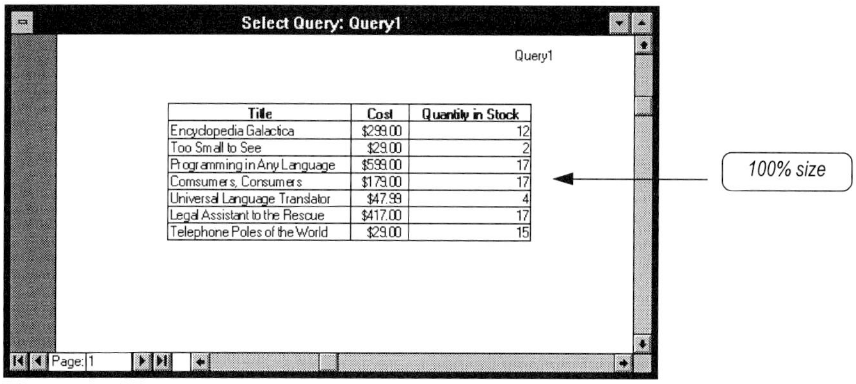

Figure 4 - 25

TEXT CRITERIA IN A QUERY

The only difference between searching for matching text values and numeric values is that text criteria must be typed between quotation marks. For example, you would type "NY" for the abbreviation for the state of New York. Often the quotes are optional as Access will fill them in for you. But Access does not always correctly guess where the quotes belong. For example, if the word **and** or the word **or** is within the text as with "Research and Development" or "Wet or Dry Vacuum," Access will not place the quotes correctly. Get in the habit of typing the quotes yourself and you will not fall into the misplaced quotes trap.

To search for matching text:

- Set up the query as we have done previously.
- Enter the example of the text value to be matched on the **Criteria:** line in the column that would contain that value, being careful to type quotes at the beginning and end of the set of characters.
- Click the Datasheet View button to see the resulting dynaset.

Activity 4.11: Searching for matching text

We need to look up the price of the "Too Small To See" CDROM. Since we will not need the Cost or Quantity In Stock fields, we could remove those two, or it might be easier to simply clear the entire QBE Grid and start fresh.

To clear the QBE Grid:

- Choose **EDIT/Clear Grid**.

Now we are ready to find the price of that CDROM.

1. Double-click the field named **CD ID** in the list of fields to place it in the first column.
2. Similarly, double-click **Title** and **Price**.
3. Click on the **Criteria:** line in the **Title** column and enter: **"Too Small To See"** including the quotes (see Figure 4 - 26).

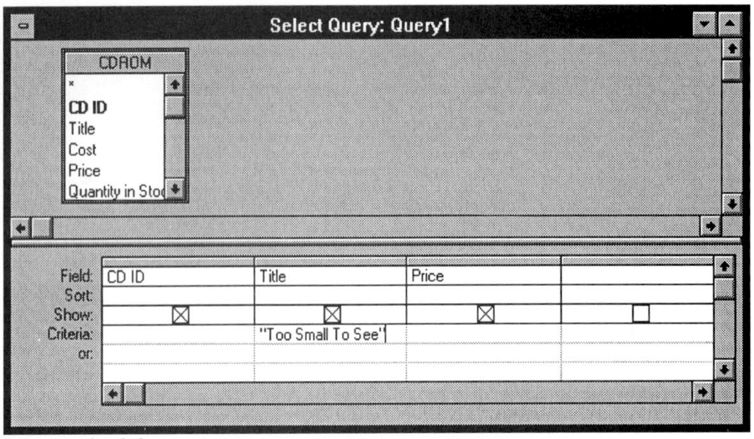

Figure 4 - 26

The text is not sensitive to the case that you type, thus, "too small to see" or "TOO SMALL TO SEE" or the mixed case example above will all succeed.

4. Click the **Datasheet View** button on the toolbar to view the result.

   We do not need to print the $49 price.

5. Click the **Design View** button on the toolbar to return to the query design.

DATE CRITERIA IN A QUERY

Enter dates in the QBE Grid in slash format. Access will surround the date with pound signs. For example, July 4, 1995 would be represented as #7/4/95#. Since the inclusion of the pound signs is totally automatic you do not need to be concerned about them, except to recognize that they will appear whenever you type a date criterion.

To search for a matching date:

- Set up the query as we have done previously.
- Enter the example of the date value to be matched on the **Criteria:** line in the column that would contain that value as M/D/YY.
- Click the Datasheet View button to see the resulting dynaset.

Activity 4.12: Searching for matching dates

We need to look up the titles of the CDROMs that were released before 5/2/95. Since we have not yet placed the Release Date field in the QBE Grid, we must add it.

1. Erase the "Too Small To See" criterion from the Title column.
2. Double-click the field named **Release Date** in the list of fields to place it in the next available column.

   You may need to scroll downward in the field list to find Release Date.

3. On the **Criteria:** line in the **Release Date** column, enter: **<5/2/95** (see Figure 4 - 27).
4. Click the **Datasheet View** button on the toolbar to view the result (see Figure 4 - 28).

   Ten titles were released before 5/2/95.

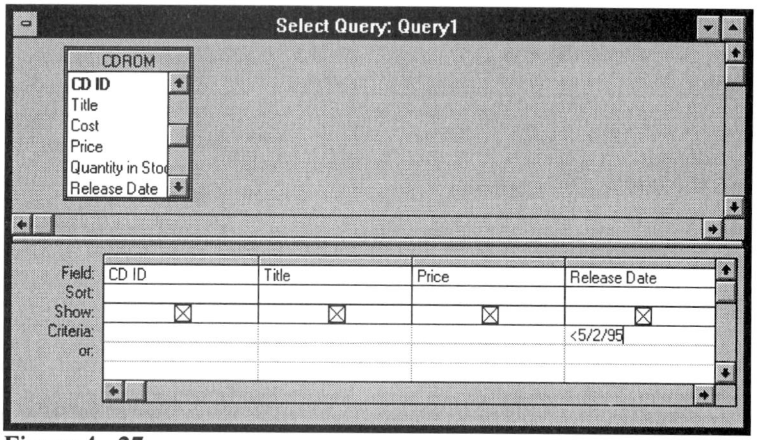

Figure 4 - 27

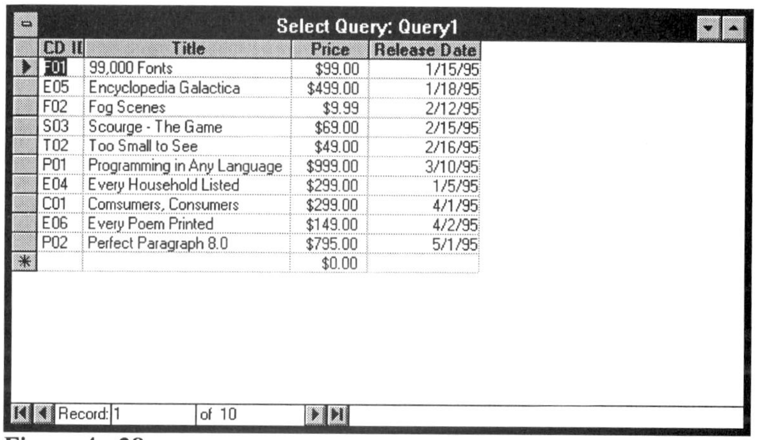

Figure 4 - 28

5. Click the **Design View** button  on the toolbar to return to the query design.

   Notice the pound signs that Access has added around the date.

6. Change the criterion to: **<=#5/2/95#**

7. Click the **Datasheet View** button  on the toolbar to view the result (see Figure 4 - 29).

   Twelve titles were released on or before 5/2/95.

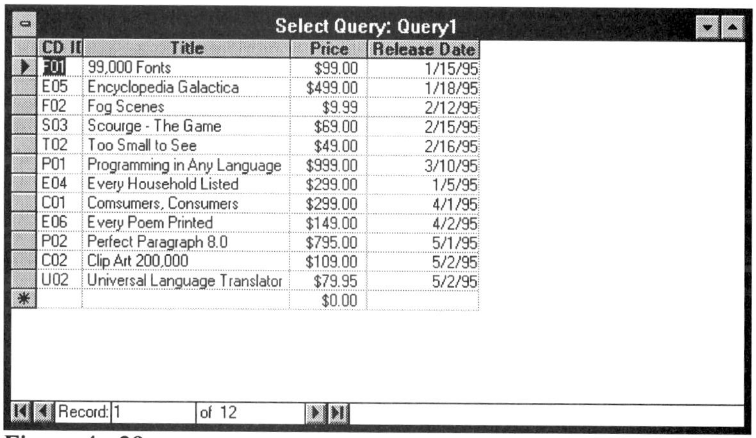

Figure 4 - 29

8. Print this result by clicking the **Print** button and clicking **OK** in the Print dialog box.
9. Click the **Design View** button on the toolbar to return to the query design.
10. Choose **FILE/Save As**.
11. Type: **Before or on 5/2/95** (see Figure 4 - 30).

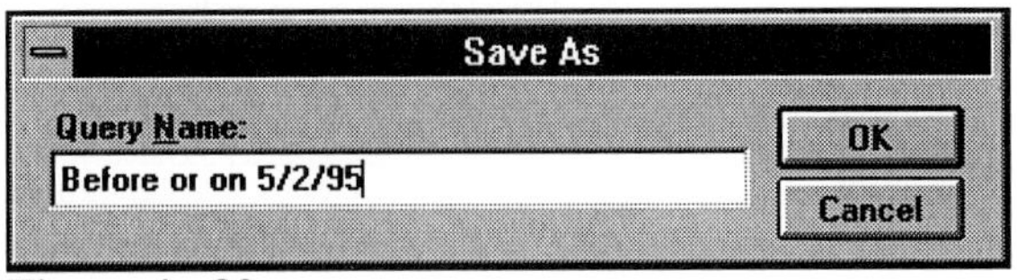

Figure 4 - 30

12. Choose **FILE/Close**.

SUMMARY

In this project we have explored single criterion queries. We practiced opening the Select Query window, selecting the desired fields, sorting by one or more fields, and matching a criterion. The criteria we used were of numerical, text, and date types. We used the inequality symbols for ranges of values. In the next lesson we will use multiple criteria and multiple tables in queries.

KEY TERMS

Criterion
Datasheet View
Design View
Dynaset
Operator
Print Preview
QBE Grid
Query By Example
Select Query
Selector

INDEPENDENT PROJECTS

Independent Project 4.1: The School Newspaper

This Independent Project continues the Newspaper Ad database from Independent Project 3.1. The newspaper's business manager has requested two lists.

The first is a listing of all the Full Page (FP) ads in order of the Date Paid. The Issue Date and the Salesperson ID fields are not important for this list, so those two will be left out of the result. The result of this query should look like Figure 4 - 31.

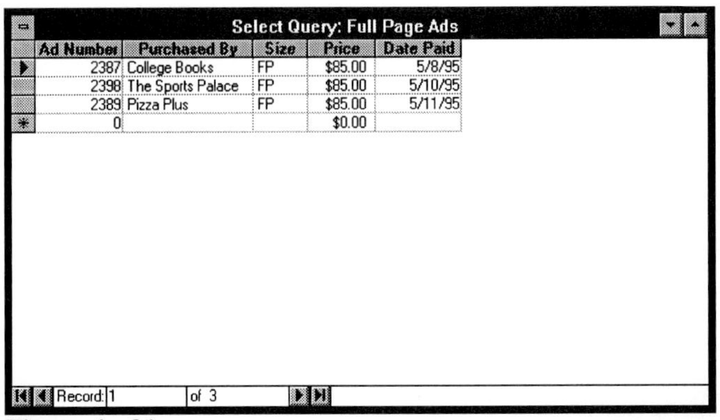

Figure 4 - 31

The second is a list of all ads sold by Leslie Kaples sorted by Price, but it should only include the Ad Number, Purchased By, Price, and Date Paid fields. The result should resemble Figure 4 - 32.

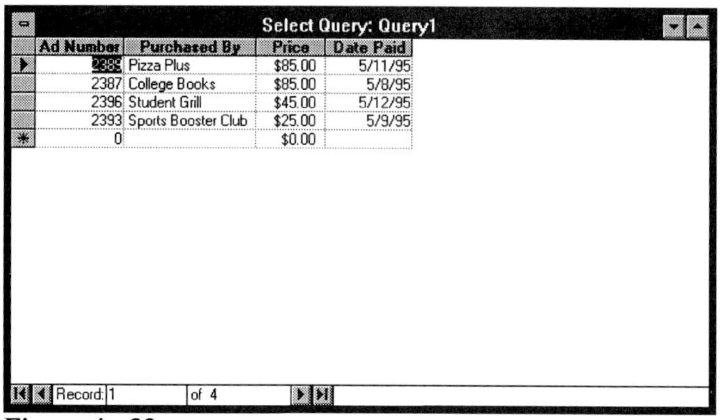

Ad Number	Purchased By	Price	Date Paid
[illegible]	Pizza Plus	$85.00	5/11/95
2387	College Books	$85.00	5/8/95
2396	Student Grill	$45.00	5/12/95
2393	Sports Booster Club	$25.00	5/9/95
0		$0.00	

Figure 4 - 32

1. Run *Access* and maximize its window.
2. Open the **xercise1.mdb** database with **FILE/Open Database** or by clicking the **Open Database** tool on the toolbar, then clicking on the name **xercise1.mdb** and clicking the **OK** button.
3. Click on the **Query** button at the left edge of the database window.
4. Click the **New** button to start a new query.
5. Click the **New Query** button in the New Query dialog box.
6. Click on the name **Ads** in the list of tables and queries in the Add Table dialog box and click the **Add** button.
7. Click **Close** to close the Add Table dialog box.
8. Double-click on the name **Ad Number** in the list of names to include that field in the QBE Grid.
9. Similarly, double-click on **Purchased By**, **Size**, **Price**, and **Date Paid** to include them in the QBE Grid.
10. Click on the **Criteria**: line in the **Size** column and enter: **"FP"** for Full Page.
11. Click the **Datasheet View** button on the toolbar to see the three resulting listings. They still need to be sorted.
12. Click the **Design View** button to return to the query design.
13. Click on the **Sort:** line in the **Date Paid** column. Click on the **drop-down arrow** and pick **Ascending**.
14. Click the **Datasheet View** button on the toolbar to see the three resulting listings in sorted order.
15. Print the result by clicking the **Print** button and clicking **OK** in the Print dialog box.
16. Save the query as **Full Page Ads** by picking **FILE/Save Query As**, entering the name, and clicking the **OK** button.
17. Close the query with **FILE/Close**.
18. To begin the second query, click on the **Query** button at the left edge of the database window if it is not already selected.

19. Click the **New** button to start a new query and click the **New Query** button in the New Query dialog box.
20. Click on the name **Ads** in the list of tables and queries in the Add Table dialog box, click the **Add** button, and click **Close**.
21. Double-click on the **Ad Number** field to include it in the first column of the QBE Grid.
22. Similarly, double-click on **Purchased By**, **Price**, **Date Paid**, and **Salesperson ID**.
23. Press the **END** key so you can see the Salesperson ID column.
24. Click on the **Criteria:** line under Salesperson ID and enter: **"K17"**
25. Since the business manager did not want to see the Salesperson ID, click on the **Show:** box to remove its X.
26. Click on the **Sort:** line in the **Price** column, click on the drop-down arrow, and pick **Descending**.
27. Click the **Datasheet View** button on the toolbar to see the result.
28. Print the result by clicking the **Print** button and clicking **OK** in the Print dialog box.
29. We do not need to save this query, so close it without saving with **FILE/Close**. When the alert box asks about saving, click the **No** button.
30. Close the database with **FILE/Close Database**.
31. If you need to exit from *Access* and/or Windows, do so properly.

Independent Project 4.2: The Book Store

This Independent Project continues the Book Store database from Independent Project 3.2. The owner has requested two lists.

The first is a listing of the books that have fewer than 50 copies in stock. This listing should include the Book Code, Title, Publisher Code, and Quantity in Stock. Since this will be needed repeatedly as a check on books to be reordered, this query will be saved. The result of the first query should look like Figure 4 - 33.

The second is a list of all books sold by Texts and Tomes (code TT12) sorted by Year of Publication and including the Book Code, Title, Author, Year of Publication, and Publisher Code fields. This is a temporary query and will be printed, but not saved. The result should resemble Figure 4 - 34.

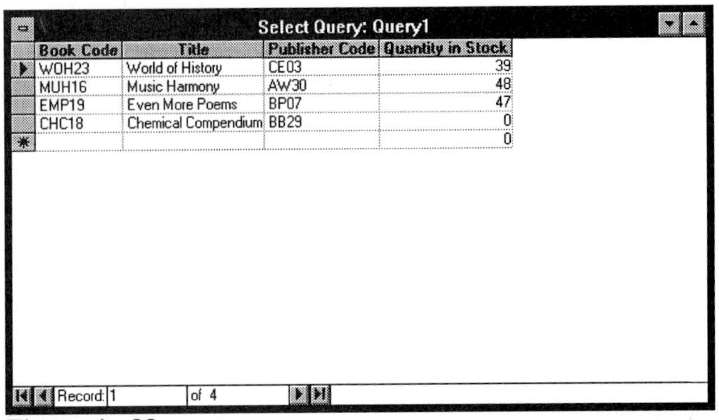

Book Code	Title	Publisher Code	Quantity in Stock
WOH23	World of History	CE03	39
MUH16	Music Harmony	AW30	48
EMP19	Even More Poems	BP07	47
CHC18	Chemical Compendium	BB29	0
			0

Figure 4 - 33

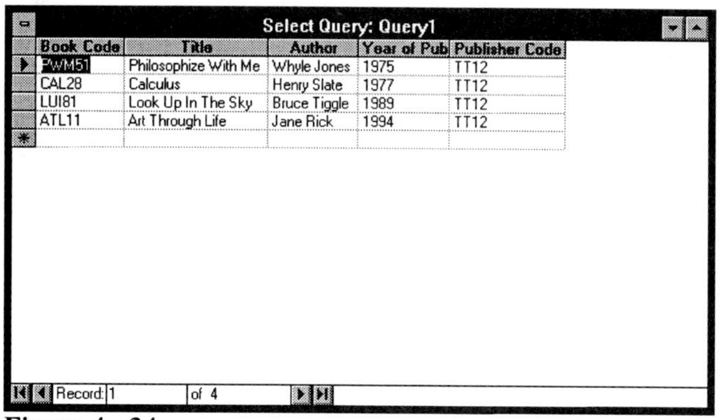

Select Query: Query1

Book Code	Title	Author	Year of Pub	Publisher Code
PWM51	Philosophize With Me	Whyle Jones	1975	TT12
CAL28	Calculus	Henry Slate	1977	TT12
LUI81	Look Up In The Sky	Bruce Tiggle	1989	TT12
ATL11	Art Through Life	Jane Rick	1994	TT12

Record: 1 of 4

Figure 4 - 34

1. Run *Access* and maximize its window.
2. Open the **xercise2.mdb** database with **FILE/Open Database** or by clicking the **Open Database** tool on the toolbar, then clicking on the name **xercise2.mdb** and clicking the **OK** button.
3. Click on the **Query** button at the left edge of the database window.
4. Click the **New** button to start a new query.
5. Click the **New Query** button in the New Query dialog box.
6. Click on the name **Books** in the list of tables and queries in the Add Table dialog box and click the **Add** button.
7. Click **Close** to close the Add Table dialog box.
8. Double-click on the name **Book Code** in the list of names to include that field in the QBE Grid.
9. Similarly, double-click on **Title**, **Publisher Code**, and **Quantity in Stock** to include them in the QBE Grid.
10. Click on the **Criteria**: line in the **Quantity in Stock** column and enter: **<50**
11. Click the **Datasheet View** button on the toolbar to see the four resulting listings (see Figure 4 - 33).
12. Print the result by clicking the **Print** button and clicking **OK** in the Print dialog box.
13. Save the query as **Low Quantities** by picking **FILE/Save Query As**, entering the name, and clicking the **OK** button.
14. Close the query with **FILE/Close**.
15. To begin the second query, click on the **Query** button at the left edge of the database window if it is not already selected.
16. Click the **New** button to start a new query and click the **New Query** button in the New Query dialog box.
17. Click on the name **Books** in the list of tables and queries in the Add Table dialog box, click the **Add** button, and click **Close**.
18. Double-click on the **Book Code** field to include it in the first column of the QBE Grid.
19. Similarly, double-click on **Title**, **Author**, **Year of Publication**, and **Publisher Code**.
20. Press the **END** key so you can see the Publisher Code column.

21. Click on the **Criteria:** line under Publisher Code and enter: **"TT12"**
22. Click on the **Sort:** line in the **Year of Publication** column, click on the drop-down arrow, and pick **Ascending**.
23. Click the **Datasheet View** button on the toolbar to see the result (see Figure 4 - 34).
24. Print the result by clicking the **Print** button and clicking **OK** in the Print dialog box.
25. We do not need to save this query, so close it without saving with **FILE/Close**. When the alert box asks about saving, click the **No** button.
26. Close the database with **FILE/Close Database**.
27. If you need to exit from *Access* and/or Windows, do so properly.

Independent Project 4.3: The Real Estate Office

This Independent Project continues the Real Estate Office database from Independent Project . The office manager has requested three lists.

A client has asked about commercial properties that are on the first floor of a building. This first listing should include the Code, Address, City, State, Zip, Size, Floor, Price, and Available fields and be sorted by date Available. This is a temporary query and will be printed, but not saved. The result of this first query should look like Figure 4 - 35.

Select Query: Query1

Code	Address	City	State	Zip	Size	Floor	Price	Available
MC29	Maple Court	New Canaan	CT	06840	450	1	$125,000.00	5/15/95
RP12	2 Research Park	Stamford	CT	06902	18000	1	$3,400,000.00	6/1/95
RP13	3 Research Park	Stamford	CT	06902	18000	1	$3,400,000.00	6/1/95
ES52	5 Elm St.	Greenwich	CT	06830	4800	1	$72,000.00	6/1/95
RP15	5 Research Park	Stamford	CT	06902	21000	1	$4,100,000.00	8/1/95
RP16	6 Research Park	Stamford	CT	06902	19000	1	$3,900,000.00	10/1/95
					0	0	$0.00	

Record: 1 of 6

Figure 4 - 35

The second is a list of all properties priced below $1,000,000. Include the Code, Address, City, State, Zip, Size, Purchase or Rent, Price, Available, and Agency Code fields. Since this query is a common requirement in the office, it will be saved as well as printed. This dynaset should match Figure 4 - 36.

Select Query: Query1

Code	Address	City	State	Zip	Size	Purc	Price	Available	Agency
ES52	5 Elm St.	Greenwich	CT	06830	4800	R	$72,000.00	6/1/95	SC18
MC29	Maple Court	New Canaan	CT	06840	450	P	$125,000.00	5/15/95	PP15
LW17	1 Lewis Way	Danbury	CT	06810	12000	R	$125,000.00	7/1/95	PP24
GP25	12 Gedney Place	Danbury	CT	06810	8900	R	$105,000.00	7/15/95	SC18
RR19	952 River Rd.	Stamford	CT	06901	3750	R	$49,000.00	9/1/95	PP24
FA28	18 Frost Ave.	Greenwich	CT	06830	3700	R	$52,000.00	8/1/95	RR11
					0		$0.00		

Record: 1 of 6

Figure 4 - 36

The third is a list of all properties that will be available on or before 8/1/95 sorted by date available. Include the Code, Address, City, State, Zip, Size, Purchase or Rent, Price, Available, and Agency Code fields. This one will be printed, but not saved. The result of this third query should resemble Figure 4 - 37.

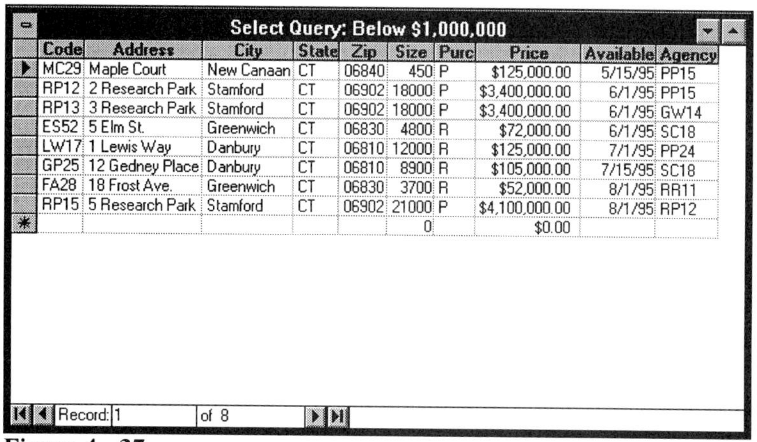
Select Query: Below $1,000,000

Code	Address	City	State	Zip	Size	Purc	Price	Available	Agency
MC29	Maple Court	New Canaan	CT	06840	450	P	$125,000.00	5/15/95	PP15
RP12	2 Research Park	Stamford	CT	06902	18000	P	$3,400,000.00	6/1/95	PP15
RP13	3 Research Park	Stamford	CT	06902	18000	P	$3,400,000.00	6/1/95	GW14
ES52	5 Elm St.	Greenwich	CT	06830	4800	R	$72,000.00	6/1/95	SC18
LW17	1 Lewis Way	Danbury	CT	06810	12000	R	$125,000.00	7/1/95	PP24
GP25	12 Gedney Place	Danbury	CT	06810	8900	R	$105,000.00	7/15/95	SC18
FA28	18 Frost Ave.	Greenwich	CT	06830	3700	R	$52,000.00	8/1/95	RR11
RP15	5 Research Park	Stamford	CT	06902	21000	P	$4,100,000.00	8/1/95	RP12
					0		$0.00		

Record: 1 of 8

Figure 4 - 37

1. Run *Access* and maximize its window.
2. Open the **xercise3.mdb** database.
3. Click on the **Query** button at the left edge of the database window.
4. Begin a new query.
5. Add **Commercial Listings** to the query window and close the Add Table dialog box.
6. Include the **Code**, **Address**, **City**, **State**, **Zip**, **Size**, **Floor**, **Price**, and **Available** fields.
7. Enter the criteria to limit listings to the **first floor** of a building.
8. Include the operator to sort by date **Available** in **Ascending** order.
9. View the resulting listings (see Figure 4 - 35).
10. Print the result.
11. To begin the second query, either clear the grid or modify the existing fields in the QBE Grid.
12. Include the **Code**, **Address**, **City**, **State**, **Zip**, **Size**, **Purchase or Rent**, **Price**, **Available**, and **Agency Code** fields.
13. Enter the criterion for **Price below $1,000,000**. Be careful to type the correct number of zeros and do **not** include the $ or commas.
14. View the result (see Figure 4 - 36).
15. Save the query as **Below $1,000,000**.
16. Print the result.
17. Return to the design.
18. Begin setting up the third query by removing any criteria.
19. See the list of required fields in the paragraph above step 1 and make any adjustments that are necessary.
20. Enter the criterion for date available **on or before 8/1/95**.

21. Set the sort operator for ascending date **Available**.
22. View the result (see Figure 4 - 37).
23. Print the result.
24. We do not need to save this query, so close it without saving.
25. Close the database.
26. If you need to exit from *Access* and/or *Windows*, do so properly.

Independent Project 4.4: The Veterinarian

This Independent Project continues the veterinarian database from Independent Project 3.4. She has requested three lists. Include all fields in each query, print each dynaset, and save each query.

- A list of all dogs.
- All animals weighing less than 20 pounds.
- Any animal born on or before 1/1/92.

Lesson

5 Multiple Criteria and Multi-Table Queries

Objectives

In this lesson you will learn how to:

- Specify multiple criteria for selecting records
- Use additional query operators
- Use wildcard characters in queries
- Join data from two or more tables with a multiple table query

PROJECT DESCRIPTION

In the previous lesson, the queries needed to match only a single value. It is more likely that the data you are seeking must match multiple criteria. For example, you may need all of the CDROMs released before a certain date, that were published by a particular publisher. The date restriction must be matched as well as the restriction on publisher. Additionally, the data you need in the dynaset may reside in two or more tables. With multiple tables you use a query to join the data into a single dynaset.

In this lesson we will run several queries to obtain inventory information. The queries will be based on the CDROM table and use multiple criteria. Then we will query the CDROM table together with various other tables to gather additional information about the orders for CDROMs.

MULTIPLE CRITERIA

There are only two types of queries with multiple criteria: *And Queries* and *Or Queries*. An *And Query* contains two (or more) criteria, both of which must be matched simultaneously. An example would be all of the CDROMs that were released after 5/2/95 **and** are priced below $100. The resulting dynaset would contain only listings that satisfied both conditions.

An *Or Query* will have two or more conditions, any one of which may be matched. All of the CDROMs that were released after 5/2/95 **or** are priced below $100 would be an example. The dynaset for this last example would have some listings released after 5/2/95 no matter what their price, some priced below $100 no matter when they were released, and possibly some records that match both parts of the criteria.

A query with multiple criteria is set up the same way a single criterion query is. Then, in the **Select Query** window two or more examples to be matched are entered in the **Criteria:** section of the QBE Grid. The multiple criteria might be entered in different fields, or within one field. For example, all prices greater than $100 and less than $500 would place both conditions in the Price field whereas all items priced greater than $100 and released after 5/2/95 would put criteria in two different fields.

Just as in English where we call a sentence compound when its two parts are connected by the word and, multiple criteria queries are also called *compound.*

To Query with Multiple Criteria:

- Open the **Query** window in the normal way by clicking the **Query** tab on the left edge of the **Database** window, clicking the **New** button at its top, and choosing the **New Query** button.
- Add the desired table or tables from the **Add Table** dialog box.
- Select the desired fields.
- Enter the first criterion.
- Enter a second criterion.
- Enter any additional criteria.
- View the resulting dynaset.

To Enter Criteria for an And Query:

- Type more than one criterion in the same **Criteria**: row of the QBE Grid.

Activity 5.1: An And Query

We need a list of the expensive CDROMs on which we might be overstocked. Any CDROM that costs more than $100 **and** of which we have more than 50 in stock is possibly overstocked.

1. Open the **Sales** database if it is not already open on the workspace.
2. Click on the **Query** tab at the left edge of the **Database** window.
3. Click the **New** button at the top of the **Database** window.
4. In the **New Query** dialog box, click on the **New Query** button.
5. Pick the **CDROM** table and click the **Add** button to place a list of its fields in the top half of the **Select Query** window (see Figure 5 - 1).

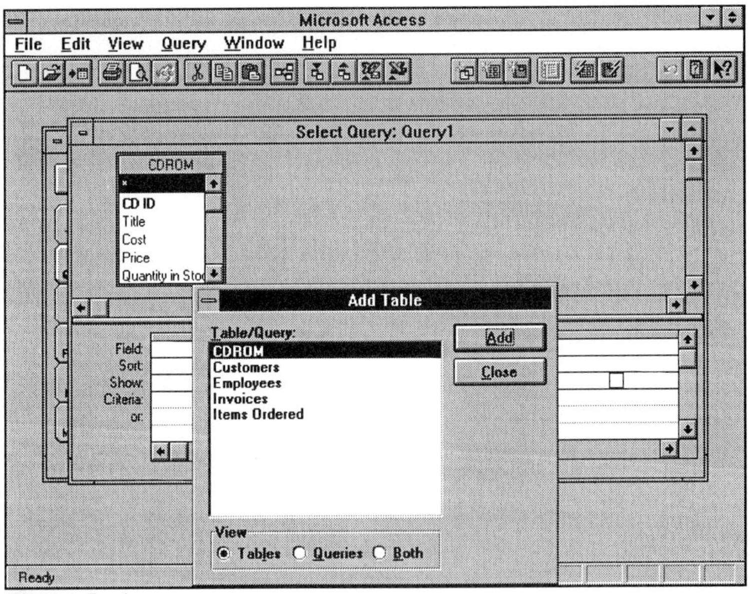

Figure 5 - 1

6. Click the **Close** button to close the **Add Table** dialog box.

7. Double-click the **Title** field in the list of fields to include it in the first column in the QBE Grid.
8. Also double-click the **Cost** and **Quantity In Stock** fields.
9. Click on the **Criteria:** line in the **Cost** column of the QBE Grid and enter: **>100**
10. Click on the **Criteria:** line in the **Quantity In Stock** column and enter: **>50** (Figure 5 - 2).

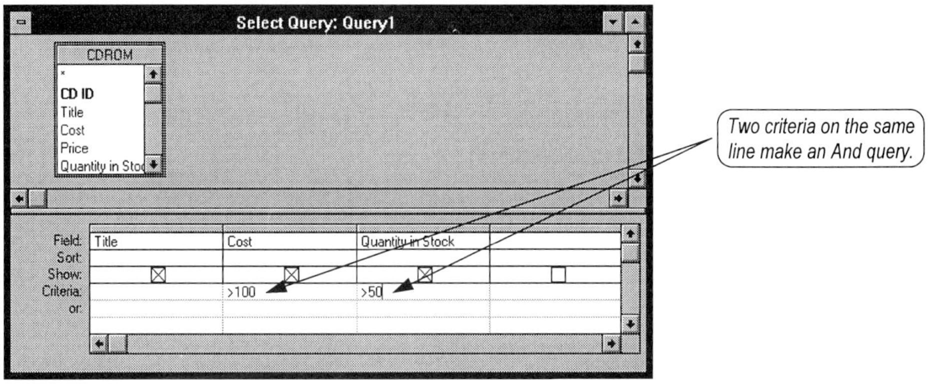

Figure 5 - 2

11. Click the **Datasheet View** button on the toolbar to see the resulting dynaset.

    Each of the two listings has a Cost above $100 as well as a Quantity greater than 50 (see Figure 5 - 3).

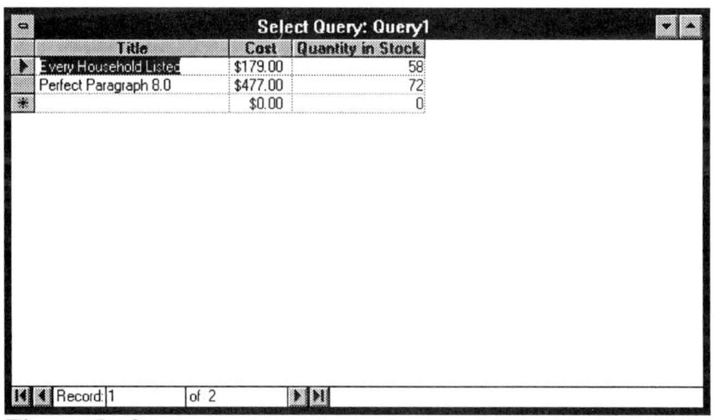

Figure 5 - 3

12. Click the **Design View** button to return to the query design.

To Enter Criteria for an Or Query:

- If the criteria are based on different fields, type the first criterion on the **Criteria:** line and the second criterion on the **or:** line.
- If the criteria are all in the same field, type the first criterion and a space, type the word **or**, type a space and the second criterion.
- For more than two criteria, use additional lines in separate fields, or the word **or** additional times within a single field.

Activity 5.2: A Multiple Field Or Query

Our manager redefines "possibly overstocked" to mean any CDROM that costs more than $100 **or** of which we have more than 50 in stock. We need a new list of the CDROMs on which we may be overstocked. This will be an important query that we will need over and over, thus we will save this query.

1. Delete the **>50** on the **Criteria:** line of the **Quantity In Stock** column.
2. Move down onto the **or:** line of the **Quantity In Stock** column and enter: **>50** (Figure 5 - 4).

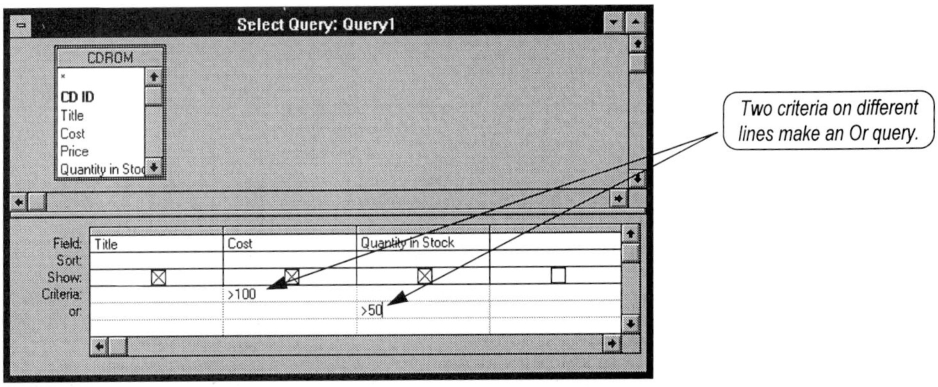

Figure 5 - 4

3. Click the **Datasheet View** button to see the resulting dynaset.

   Of the ten listings (see Figure 5 - 5), four have only a Cost above $100, four have only a Quantity greater than 50, and two have both.

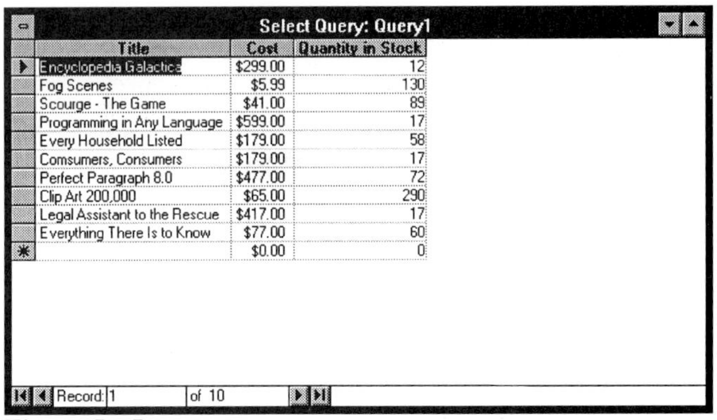

Figure 5 - 5

4. Choose **FILE/Save Query** to begin saving this query design.

   A query can be saved while either the design or the dynaset is showing in the window.
5. Enter the name: **Overstocked** and click **OK**.
6. Print the result by clicking the **Print** button and clicking **OK** in the Print dialog box.
7. Click the **Design View** button to return to the query design.

INCLUDING EVERY FIELD IN THE QBE GRID

Occasionally you need every field from a table included in the QBE Grid. While you could double-click each field, there is a quicker method for selecting all fields.

To Select Every Field Into the QBE Grid:

- Double-click the header that contains the table name at the top of the list of fields in the upper section of the query window. All of the names will be highlighted.
- Move the mouse on top of any one of the names, hold down (do not click) the mouse button, and drag that name to the **Field**: line of the QBE Grid. When you release the mouse button, all fields will be installed.
- As *Access* usually does not scroll the QBE Grid to show you the active field when you use this technique, press the **HOME** key to move to the first field.

Activity 5.3: Including All Fields

Our manager also asks for a listing of all of the data on CDROMs numbered C01, E04, or L01. Since this query is based on the same CDROM table we do not need to begin all over, but the currently selected fields and criteria are not what we need. Therefore, we will again use Clear Grid to start a new design based on the same table. Since we need all data on the three CDROMs, we will include all fields in the QBE Grid.

1. Choose **EDIT/Clear Grid**.
2. Double-click on the table name **CDROM** at the top of the list of fields in the upper section of the window to select all of the fields.

   All of the field names in the list will be highlighted (see Figure 5 - 6).

Double-click on the table name to select all fields.

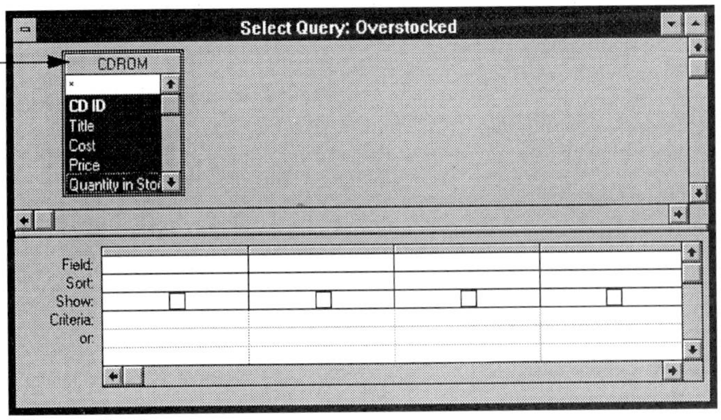

Figure 5 - 6

3. Move the mouse on top of any one name in the highlighted list, hold down the mouse button, and drag that name down to the **Field:** line of the first column in the QBE Grid. Release the mouse button.

   *The highlighted field is **Notes**, but it is not currently showing in the window.*

4. Press the **HOME** key to move the highlight onto the first field, **CD ID** (see Figure 5 - 7).

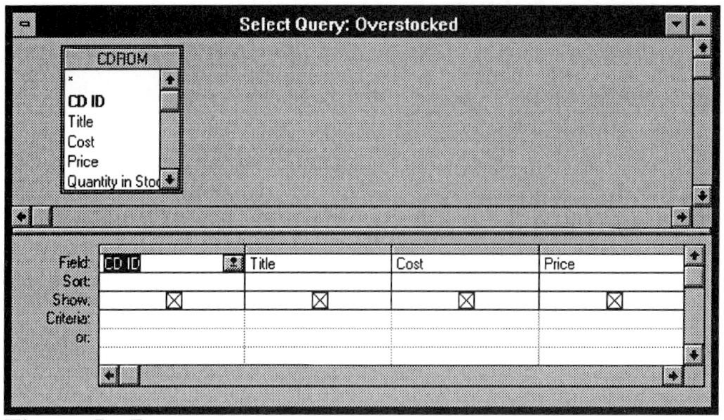

Figure 5 - 7

ADDITIONAL QUERY OPERATORS

An *operator* in a query is a symbol, word, or group of words that specify the range of values to be matched. We have already used the operators =, >, and <, as well as some combinations of those. Additional operators are listed in Table 5 - 1.

Operator	Example
between __ and __	between #4/1/95# and #4/30/95#
or	"C01" or "E04"
not	not "Windows"
null	null

Table 5 - 1

Activity 5.4: A Single Field Or Query

Our manager asked for all data on CDROMs numbered C01, E04, or L01. Since these ID numbers need to be specified in the same field, we can use the **or** operator rather than separate **or:** lines.

1. Click on the **Criteria:** line in the **CD ID** column.

   If you were too close to the left edge of the QBE Grid, the entire ***Criteria****: line may have been highlighted. If so, click again closer to the center of the column on the* ***Criteria****: line so the cursor is a blinking vertical line.*

2. Type: **"C01" or "E04" or "L01"**

   Be careful that you type zeros in the above criterion. Also, you can widen the column in the QBE Grid by dragging the line at the right edge of the selector bar for the desired column, just like changing a column width in a table (Figure 5 - 8).

3. Click the **Datasheet View** button to see the resulting dynaset.

   The three ID numbers should be listed in the dynaset (Figure 5 - 9).

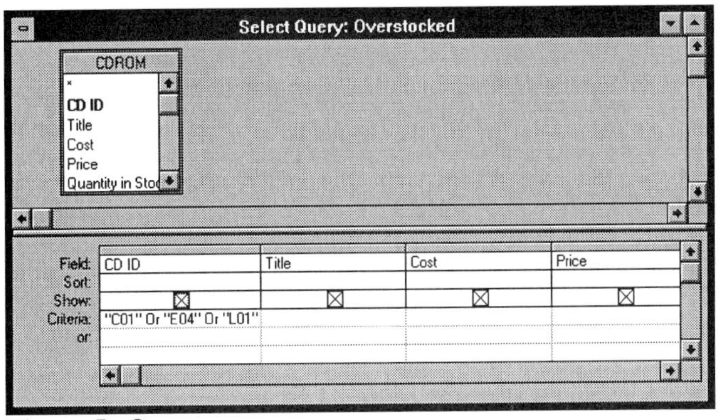

Figure 5 - 8

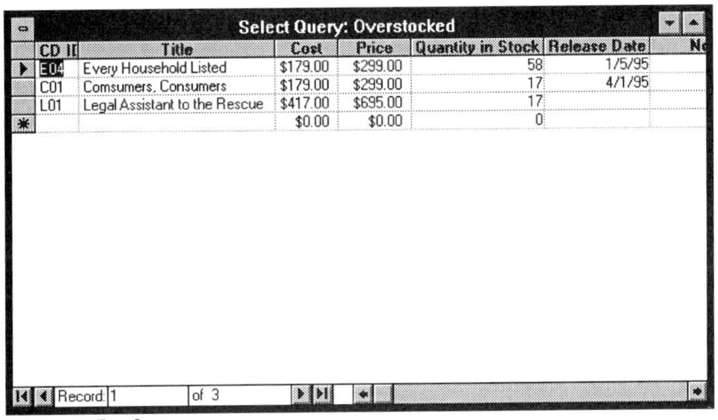

Figure 5 - 9

4. Print the result by clicking the **Print** button and clicking **OK** in the Print dialog box.
5. Click the **Design View** button to return to the query design.

THE BETWEEN OPERATOR

When you need the data entries that fall between a starting and an ending value, use the **between** operator. While in English *between* often means between but not equal to the given values, in *Access* the specified end points will be included as well.

To specify a criterion using between:

- On the **Criteria**: line in the QBE Grid type the word **between** and a space, then the beginning value and a space, the word **and** and a space, and finally the ending value.

Activity 5.5: Using the Between Operator

We need a list of all of the CDROMs released between 2/15/95 and 4/30/95.

1. Erase the previous criterion in the **CD ID** column.
2. Move to the **Release Date** column.

   On the **Criteria**: line enter: **between 2/15/95 and 4/30/95** (Figure 5 - 10).

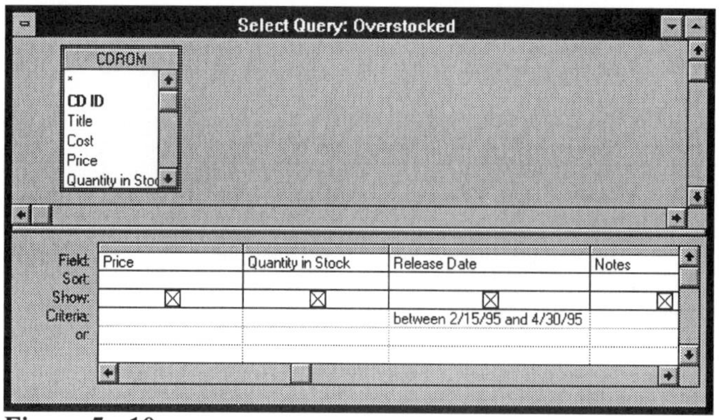

Figure 5 - 10

3. Click the **Datasheet View** button to see the resulting dynaset.

   The five dates in the dynaset should be between or on the starting and ending dates (see Figure 5 - 11).

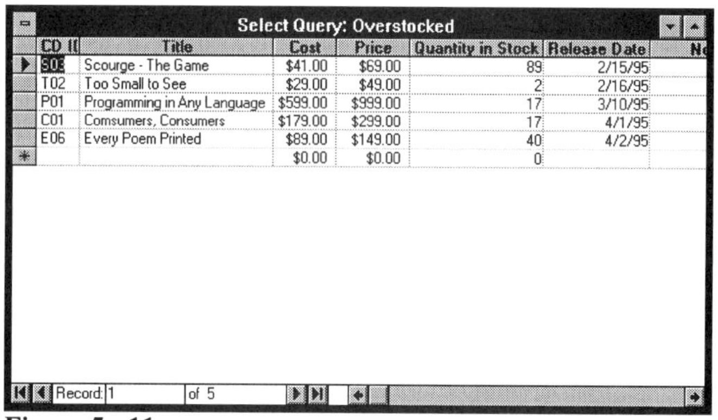

CD ID	Title	Cost	Price	Quantity in Stock	Release Date
S03	Scourge - The Game	$41.00	$69.00	89	2/15/95
T02	Too Small to See	$29.00	$49.00	2	2/16/95
P01	Programming in Any Language	$599.00	$999.00	17	3/10/95
C01	Comsumers, Consumers	$179.00	$299.00	17	4/1/95
E06	Every Poem Printed	$89.00	$149.00	40	4/2/95
		$0.00	$0.00	0	

Figure 5 - 11

4. Print the result by clicking the **Print** button and clicking **OK** in the Print dialog box.
5. Click the **Design View** button to return to the query design.

THE NOT OPERATOR

Surprisingly often in queries, you know exactly what you do not want. To query for all entries that do not match a value, use the **not** operator.

To use the not operator:

- On the Criteria: line in the QBE Grid type the word **not** and a space, followed by the value to be excluded.

Activity 5.6: The Not Operator

1. Erase the previous criterion.

   *A quick way to erase a long criterion is to move up one line by pressing the **UP ARROW** key and back down onto the **Criterion**: line with the **DOWN ARROW** key. That move highlights the entire set of characters. Then press the **DELETE** key to erase the highlighted criterion.*

2. Move to the **Criteria:** line in the **Notes** column.
3. Enter: **not "Windows"** (see Figure 5 - 12).

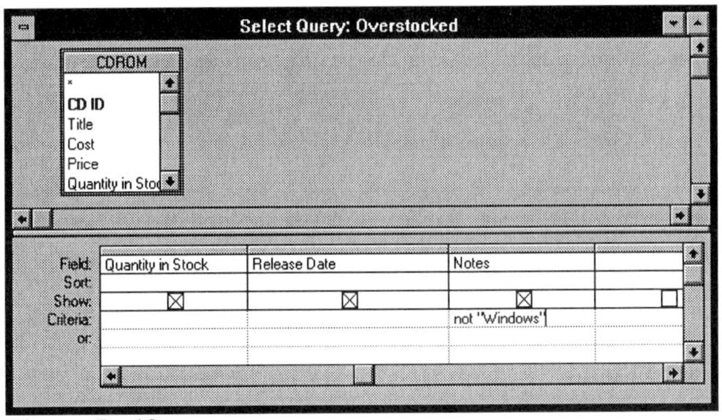

Figure 5 - 12

4. Click the **Datasheet View** button to see the resulting dynaset.

   The eight listings in the dynaset (see Figure 5 - 13) will contain a variety of Notes that are not Windows, although one has "Windows - B&W." Since Windows - B&W is not exactly Windows, it matches our criterion, too. Shortly we will see how to eliminate this entry that includes the word Windows, even though it's not exactly the same.

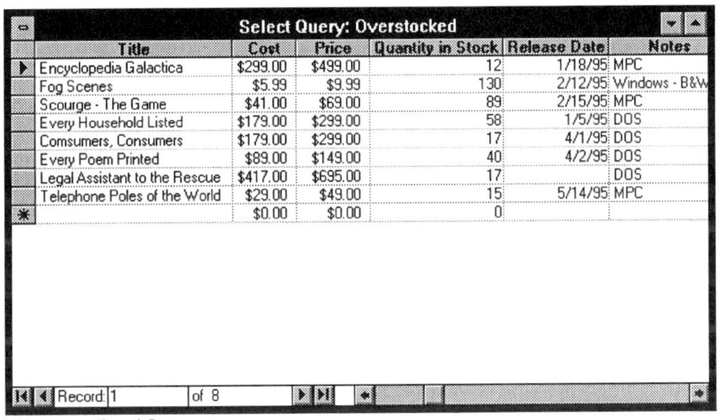

Title	Cost	Price	Quantity in Stock	Release Date	Notes
Encyclopedia Galactica	$299.00	$499.00	12	1/18/95	MPC
Fog Scenes	$5.99	$9.99	130	2/12/95	Windows - B&W
Scourge - The Game	$41.00	$69.00	89	2/15/95	MPC
Every Household Listed	$179.00	$299.00	58	1/5/95	DOS
Comsumers, Consumers	$179.00	$299.00	17	4/1/95	DOS
Every Poem Printed	$89.00	$149.00	40	4/2/95	DOS
Legal Assistant to the Rescue	$417.00	$695.00	17		DOS
Telephone Poles of the World	$29.00	$49.00	15	5/14/95	MPC
	$0.00	$0.00	0		

Figure 5 - 13

5. Print the result by clicking the **Print** button and clicking **OK** in the Print dialog box.
6. Click the **Design View** button to return to the query design.

THE NULL OPERATOR

Every time we need a set of records we type the value to be matched. In the columns where we do not type a value, there is no restriction on the data. What if we needed the records where there was no entry in that field, that is, where the field was empty?

We cannot leave the **Criterion**: line empty since that means no restriction. The solution is the operator **null**. Null means empty.

To use the null operator:

- On the **Criteria**: line in the QBE Grid type the word **null** in the desired column. Actually the operator is **Is Null**, but *Access* will always fill in the **Is** for you.

Activity 5.7: The Null Operator

We need a list of those CDROMs that do not yet have a Release Date filled in.

1. Erase the previous criterion.
2. Move to the **Criterion**: line of the **Release Date** column and enter: **null** (see Figure 5 - 14).

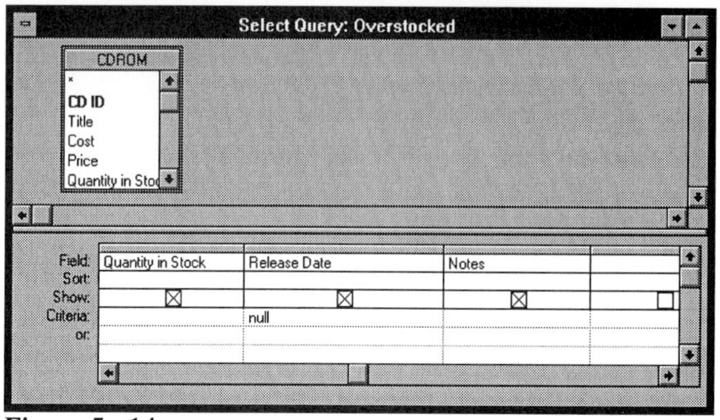

Figure 5 - 14

3. Click the **Datasheet View** button to see the resulting dynaset.

   The two listings in the dynaset will have empty **Release Date** *fields (see Figure 5 - 15).*

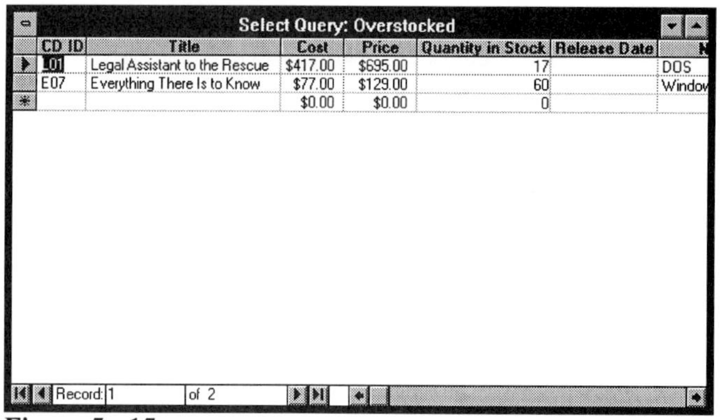

Figure 5 - 15

4. Click the **Design View** button to return to the query design.

WILD CARDS

Earlier, we queried for the records that did not have "Windows" in the Notes field. While most listings in the dynaset contained completely different entries, one had the entry "Windows - B&W." A portion of the entry matched, but not the whole entry. How do we match portions of entries?

Wild card characters allow you to match a portion of the entry in a field. The wild card characters are * and ?. The * represents any number of characters from no characters to the maximum. Thus, "**Windows***" would represent any entry that begins with the characters "Windows" including just Windows with no more characters and Windows followed by any other set of characters. "***Windows***" would stand for any entry that contains "Windows" anywhere within it, for the wild cards stand for possible characters in front of Windows and after Windows.

The **?** represents exactly one character, no more and no less. As an example, 5/?/95 would represent any single-digit day in May of 1995. 5/??/95 would represent the two-digit days. To represent any day in May of 1995, use the asterisk as in 5/*/95.

When you use a wild card in a criterion, the word "like" must begin the entry. Thus, the two examples with Windows and May of 1995 would really be entered as **like "*Windows*"** and **like "5/*/95"**. As with the word Is when we used Null, *Access* will automatically fill in the word **like** for you. Also, when you use a wild card with a date, that is the only time the date will not be surrounded by pound signs; quotation marks are used instead.

To use wild cards in a query:

- Open the query in the normal way.
- Select fields as usual.
- Fill in criteria that include one or more wild card characters.

Activity 5.8: Using Wild Cards in the Notes Field

We need listings of every CDROM that has **Windows** anywhere within the Notes field.

1. Erase the previous criterion.
2. Move to the **Criterion**: line of the **Notes** column, and enter: **like "*Windows*"** (see Figure 5 - 16).

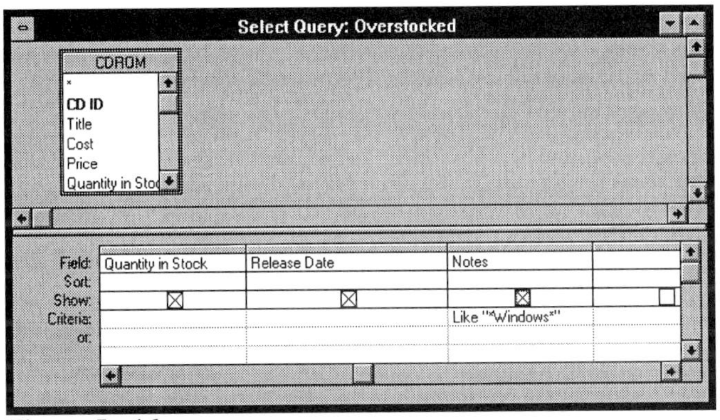

Figure 5 - 16

3. Click the **Datasheet View** button to see the resulting dynaset.

   The eight listings (see Figure 5 - 17) in the dynaset will have "Windows" somewhere within the ***Notes*** *field.*

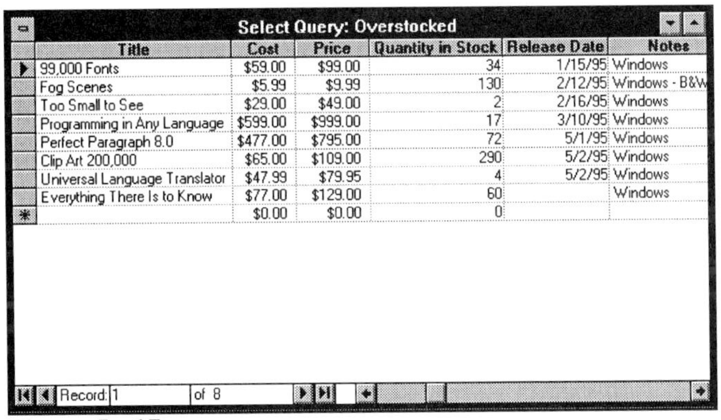

Select Query: Overstocked

Title	Cost	Price	Quantity in Stock	Release Date	Notes
99,000 Fonts	$59.00	$99.00	34	1/15/95	Windows
Fog Scenes	$5.99	$9.99	130	2/12/95	Windows - B&W
Too Small to See	$29.00	$49.00	2	2/16/95	Windows
Programming in Any Language	$599.00	$999.00	17	3/10/95	Windows
Perfect Paragraph 8.0	$477.00	$795.00	72	5/1/95	Windows
Clip Art 200,000	$65.00	$109.00	290	5/2/95	Windows
Universal Language Translator	$47.99	$79.95	4	5/2/95	Windows
Everything There Is to Know	$77.00	$129.00	60		Windows
	$0.00	$0.00	0		

Record: 1 of 8

Figure 5 - 17

4. Print the result by clicking the **Print** button and clicking **OK** in the Print dialog box.
5. Click the **Design View** button to return to the query design.

Activity 5.9: Using Wild Cards in the TITLE Field

We need to see the listings of each CDROM that has the word **every** anywhere within its title. Since we only need to see the data, we will not save this query when we are finished.

1. Erase the previous criterion.
2. Move to the **Criteria:** line of the **Title** column, and enter: **like "*every*"** (Figure 5 - 18).

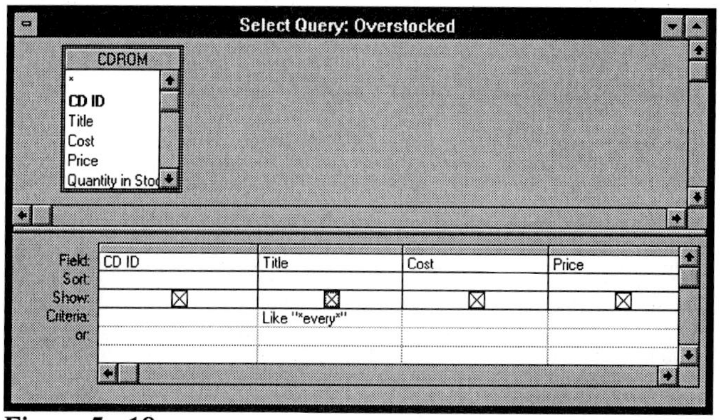

Figure 5 - 18

3. Click the **Datasheet View** button to see the resulting dynaset.

   Each of the four listings in the dynaset will have "every" somewhere within its title Figure 5 - 19).

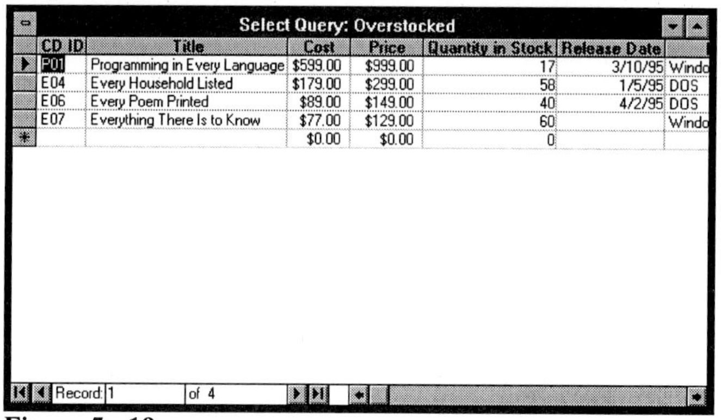

Figure 5 - 19

4. Print the result by clicking the **Print** button and clicking **OK** in the Print dialog box.
5. Click the **Design View** button to return to the query design.
6. Choose **FILE/Close**. When asked about saving, click the **No** button.

   *The **Database** window should be the active window again.*

MULTIPLE TABLE QUERIES

The best design for the majority of databases is to have multiple tables holding the data. For the reasons given in Lesson 3, it is usually the only way to handle the data efficiently. Yet with a multi-table design, reports and calculations will often need to access data from more than one table at a time. To join the data from multiple tables you use a *join* query.

A join query is merely a select query with more than one table in the upper section of the query window. When you install more than one table in the query window, you must then *link* the tables by showing *Access* which field (or fields) in one table is the same as a field in another table. Every table included in the query must be linked to some other table. If you do not establish the link between two tables, each record in the first table will be joined with every record in the second table. Without a link, two tables with 1,000 records each would produce a dynaset with 1,000,000 listings!

Access 2.0 will often guess what the link is and automatically connect the two matching fields if they have the same name and one of them is a Primary Key. This is still another reason for a careful and consistent design and assigning primary keys. Should *Access* guess correctly, you have no more to do. Should it guess incorrectly, however, you must click the mouse on the incorrect link line that *Access* drew, press the **DELETE** key to erase it, and properly link the tables yourself.

When you include more than one table in the upper section of the **Query** window and properly link the tables, you may place fields from each table in the QBE Grid. Of course, you may sort, enter criteria, and do all the normal activities we have performed with single tables when you employ multiple table queries.

To join data from multiple tables through a query:

- Open the **Query** window and choose the first table.
- Choose the second table.
- Choose any additional tables, then close the **Add Table** dialog box.
- Establish the link between tables by clicking on the common field in the first table and dragging from that field onto the matching field in the second table.
- Link any additional tables.
- Pick the desired fields for the QBE Grid.
- Enter any values to be matched on the **Criteria:** line in the column that would contain those values.
- Include any sorting operators.
- Click the **Datasheet View** button  to see the resulting join as a dynaset.

Activity 5.10: Joining Multiple Tables with a Query

We need a dynaset with the names of the employees who sold each invoice. Since the invoice data is in the Invoices table with only the Employee ID to represent the salesperson, and the employees' names are in the Employees table, we must join the needed fields from the two tables. The common field in each of the two tables is Employee ID.

1. Open the **Sales** database if it is not already open on the workspace.
2. Click on the **Query** tab at the left edge of the **Database** window.
3. Click the **New** button at the top of the **Database** window.
4. In the **New Query** dialog box, click on the **New Query** button.

5. Pick the **Employees** table and click the **Add** button to place a list of its fields in the top half of the **Select Query** window.
6. Pick the **Invoices** table and click the **Add** button to place a list of its fields next to Employees.

   Access will connect the common field in each table for you since Employee ID is the primary key in Employees, and a field with the same name exists in Invoices. This is the correct link (see Figure 5 - 20).

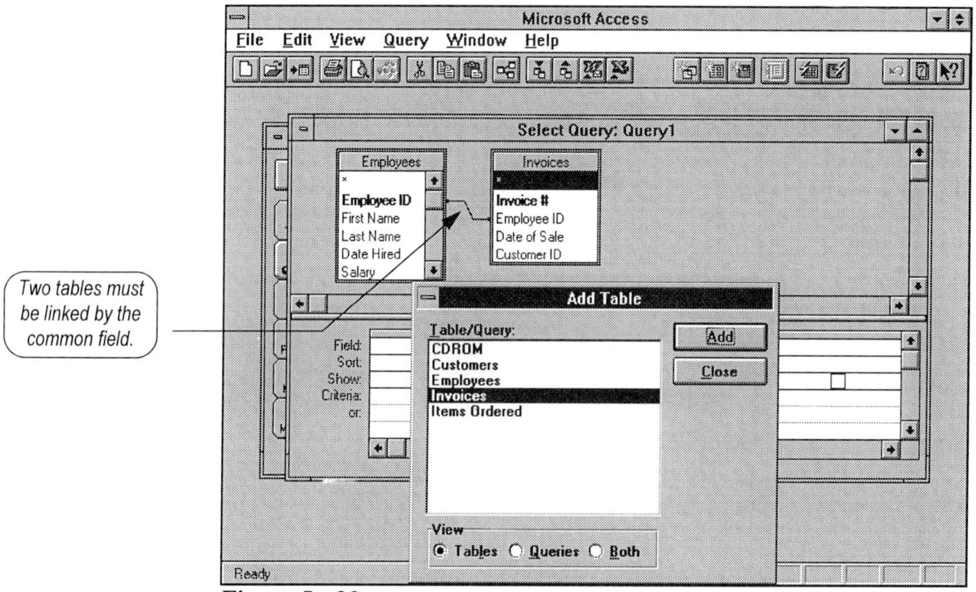

Figure 5 - 20

7. Click the **Close** button to close the **Add Table** dialog box.
8. Double-click **First Name** in the Employees table list to include it in the QBE Grid.
9. Double-click **Last Name**.
10. Double-click the gray title bar of the Invoices table list to highlight all of its fields.
11. Move the mouse on top of any one of the field names and drag that name down to the third column of the QBE Grid to install all four fields from Invoices (see Figure 5 - 21).

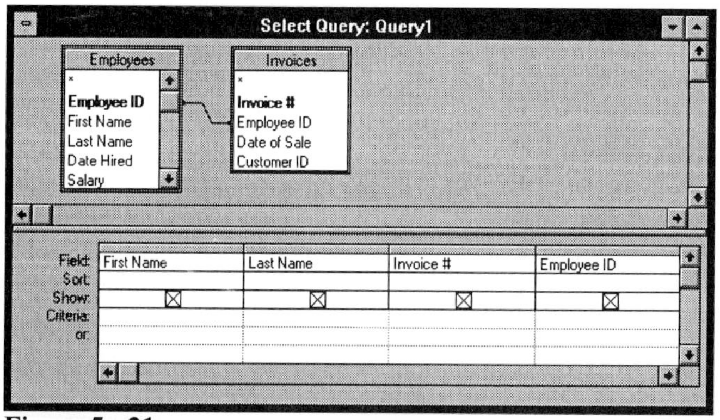

Figure 5 - 21

12. Click the **Datasheet View** button to see the result.

    The two sales people Daphne Green and George Jeffers are matched to the invoices they sold. Notice that the Employee ID matches the name for each invoice (see Figure 5 - 22).

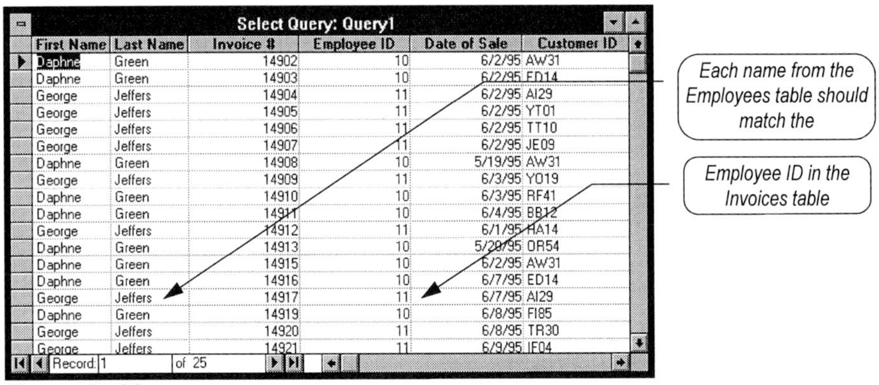

Figure 5 - 22

Also notice the Customer ID number for each invoice. Who is the customer? The next query will join the customer names to this listing by matching the Customer IDs to the Customers table.

13. Print the result by clicking the **Print** button and clicking **OK** in the Print dialog box.
14. Return to the design by clicking the **Design View** button.

Activity 5.11: Joining a Third Table into the Query

We would like the names of the customers who bought the items on each invoice. We still need all of the previous data from the Employees and Invoices tables, but want to add the customer names from the Customers table. So we need a third table, the Customers table. When finished, we will save this query with the name **Employees Sales to Customers** as we would probably need these results frequently.

1. Choose **QUERY/Add Table** in the menu or click the **Add Table** button on the toolbar.
2. Double click on **Customers** in the Add Table dialog box, then close it.

   *Again Access figures out that the Primary Key **Customer ID** matches the field of the same name in Invoices, and draws the link line. This line is also correct (Figure 5 - 23).*

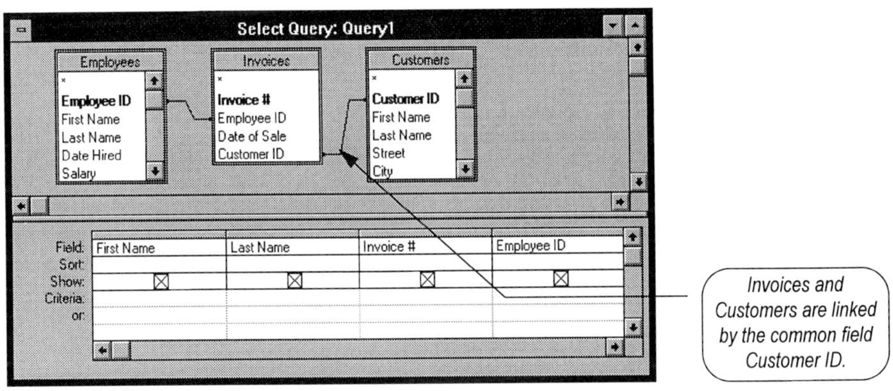

Figure 5 - 23

3. Maximize the **Select Query** window.
4. Click on the **selector bar** at the top of the **Employee ID** field in the QBE Grid to select the whole column.
5. Press the **DELETE** key to remove that column.
6. Similarly, click the **selector** above **Customer ID**, and press **DELETE** to remove that column.

7. In the **Customers** field list, double-click the **First Name** and **Last Name** fields to include them in the QBE Grid (Figure 5 - 24).

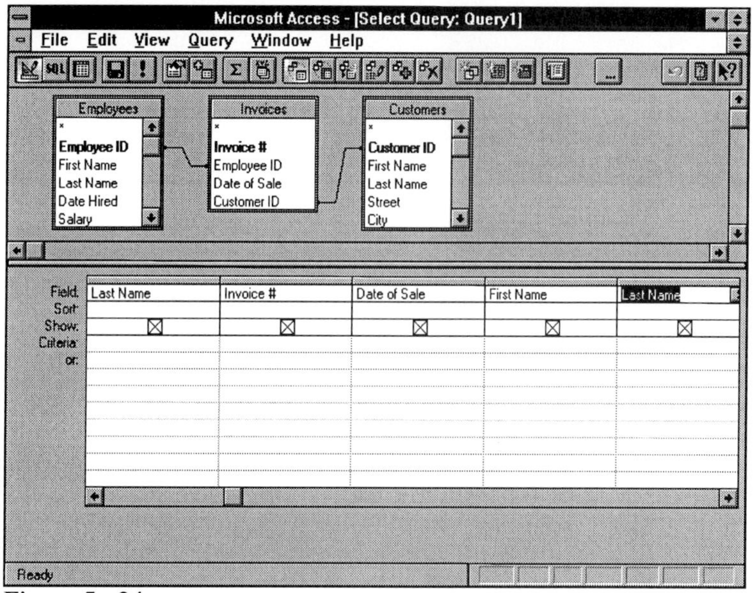

Figure 5 - 24

You will probably need to scroll to the right to see the last field.

8. Click the **Datasheet View** button to see the result.

This dynaset joins data from three tables. Notice some of the customers' names occur multiple times (Figure 5 - 25). This is the very redundancy we eliminated with separate tables. We have instructed the computer to temporarily show the redundant names.

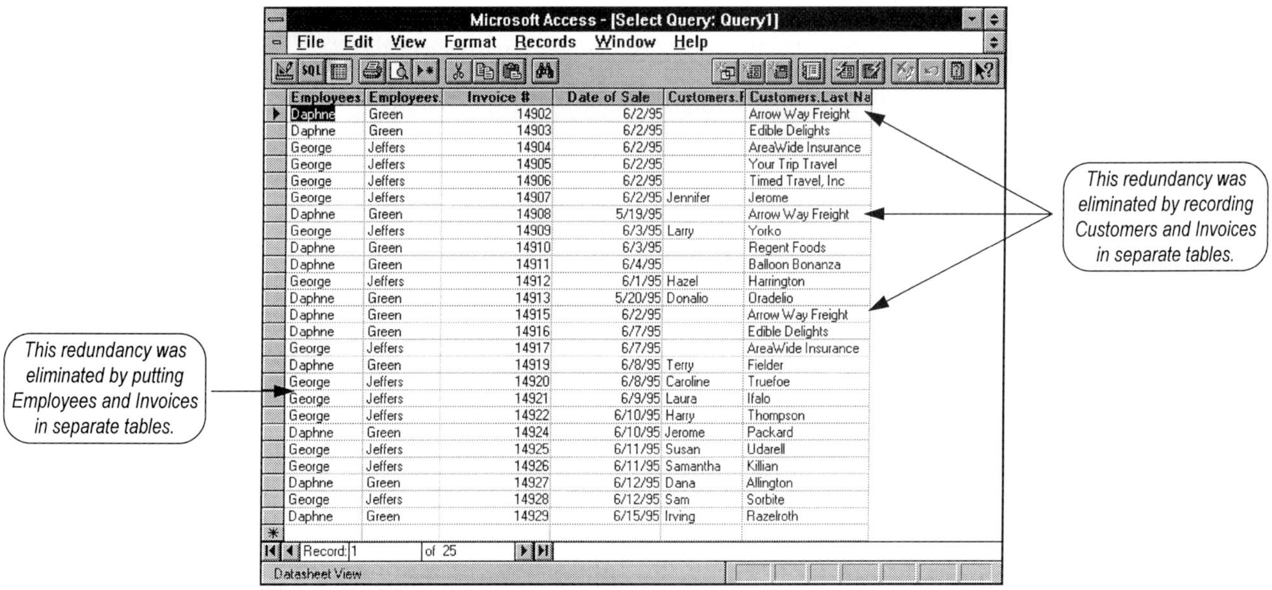

Figure 5 - 25

8. Choose **FILE/Save Query As** to save this query.

9. Type the name **Employees Sales to Customers** in the **Save As** dialog box and click **OK**.
10. Print the result by clicking the **Print** button and clicking **OK** in the Print dialog box.
11. Close the query with **FILE/Close**.

Activity 5.12: A Second Multiple Table Query

We need a dynaset with the items sold on each invoice. The **Invoices** table does not contain that data since we could not predict how many items a customer would purchase. The items on each invoice are listed in the Items Ordered table. We will join Invoices and Items Ordered.

1. Open the **Sales** database if it is not already open on the workspace.
2. Click on the **Query** tab at the left edge of the **Database** window.
3. Click the **New** button at the top of the **Database** window.
4. In the **New Query** dialog box, click on the **New Query** button.
5. Pick the **Invoices** table and click the **Add** button to place a list of its fields in the top half of the **Select Query** window.
6. Pick the **Items Ordered** table and click the **Add** button to place a list of its fields next to Invoices.

   Access will connect the common field in each table for you since Invoice # is the primary key in Invoices and one of the primary keys in Items Ordered. The primary keys are displayed in bold letters in the field list (see Figure 5 - 26).

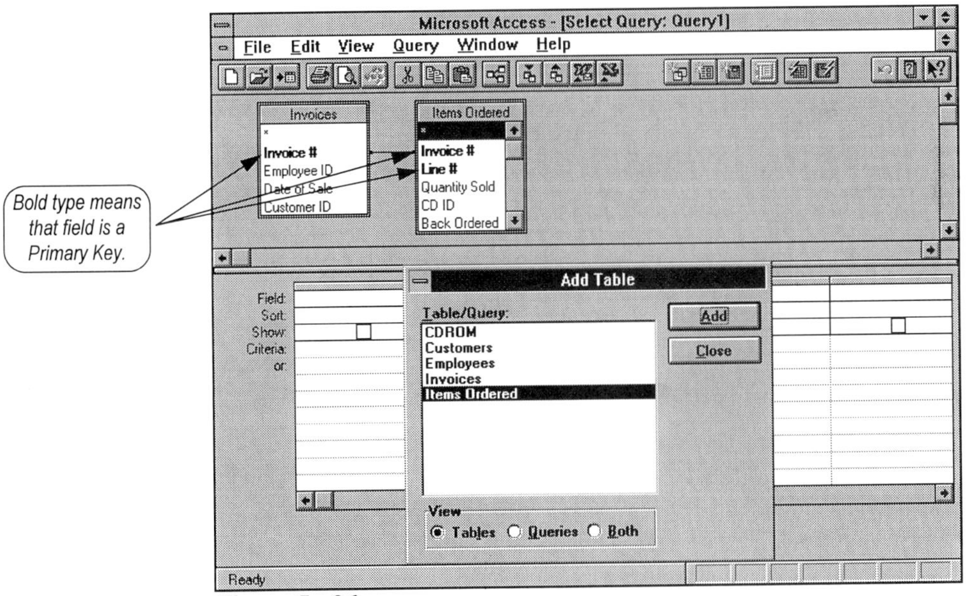

Figure 5 - 26

7. Click the **Close** button to close the **Add Table** dialog box.
8. Double-click **Invoice #** in the Invoices table list to include it in the QBE Grid.
9. Double-click **Date of Sale**.
10. From the Items Ordered field list, double-click the **Line #** field.
11. Also double-click the **Quantity Sold** and the **CD ID** fields (see Figure 5 - 27).

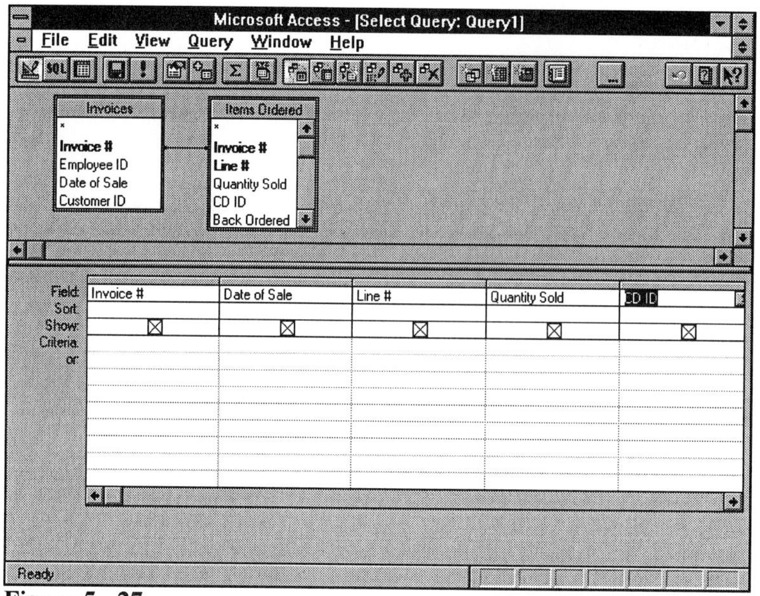

Figure 5 - 27

12. Click the **Datasheet View** button to see the result.

    Notice that this dynaset shows the invoice numbers multiple times (see Figure 5 - 28), once for each item ordered on that invoice. This redundancy was avoided in the tables by designing separate tables.

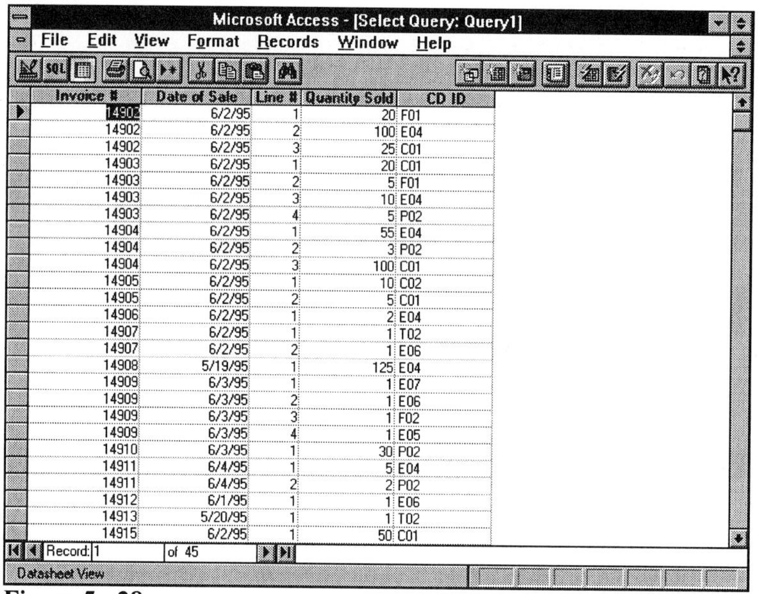

Invoice #	Date of Sale	Line #	Quantity Sold	CD ID
14902	6/2/95	1	20	F01
14902	6/2/95	2	100	E04
14902	6/2/95	3	25	C01
14903	6/2/95	1	20	C01
14903	6/2/95	2	5	F01
14903	6/2/95	3	10	E04
14903	6/2/95	4	5	P02
14904	6/2/95	1	55	E04
14904	6/2/95	2	3	P02
14904	6/2/95	3	100	C01
14905	6/2/95	1	10	C02
14905	6/2/95	2	5	C01
14906	6/2/95	1	2	E04
14907	6/2/95	1	1	T02
14907	6/2/95	2	1	E06
14908	5/19/95	1	125	E04
14909	6/3/95	1	1	E07
14909	6/3/95	2	1	E06
14909	6/3/95	3	1	F02
14909	6/3/95	4	1	E05
14910	6/3/95	1	30	P02
14911	6/4/95	1	5	E04
14911	6/4/95	2	2	P02
14912	6/1/95	1	1	E06
14913	5/20/95	1	1	T02
14915	6/2/95	1	50	C01

Figure 5 - 28

13. Choose **FILE/Save Query As** to save this query.
14. Type the name **Invoice Items** in the **Save As** dialog box and click **OK**.
15. Print the result by clicking the **Print** button and clicking **OK** in the Print dialog box.
16. Close the query with **FILE/Close**.

ALTERING A QUERY

A saved query can be opened in design mode and altered to suit a new set of requirements.

Activity 5.13: Joining a Third Table into the Existing Invoice Items Query

We would like the names of the products ordered on each invoice. We still need all of the previous data from the Invoices and Items Ordered tables, but want to add the CDROM names from the CDROM table. So we need a third table, the CDROM table.

This amended query will be an improvement on the old design, so we will save it with the same name to replace that old design.

1. Click on the **Query** tab at the left edge of the **Database** window.
2. Click on **Invoice Items** to highlight that name.
3. Click the **Design** button at the top of the **Database** window.
4. Choose **QUERY/Add Table** in the menu or click the **Add Table** button on the toolbar.
5. Click on **CDROM** in the **Add Table** dialog box and click the **Add** button (see Figure 5 - 29), then close the dialog box.

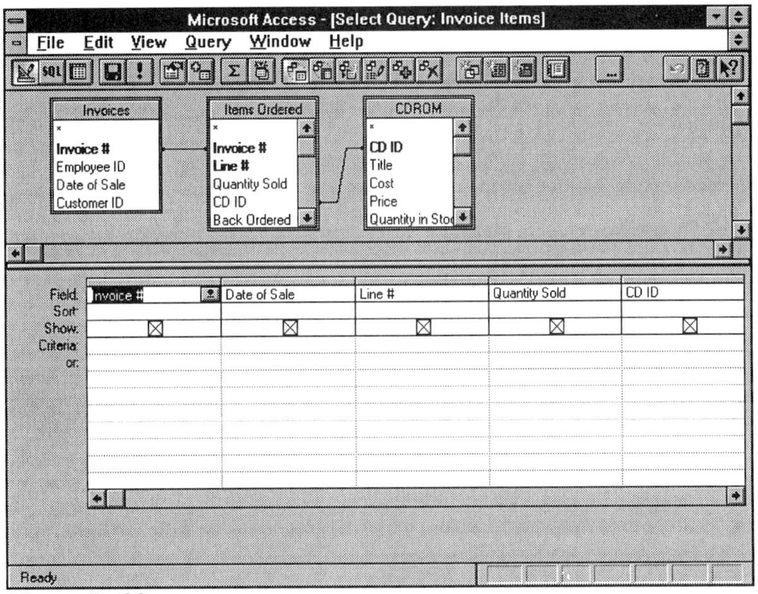

Figure 5 - 29

*Access figures out that the primary key **CD ID** matches the field of the same name in CDROM, and draws the link line for you (see Figure 5 - 29).*

6. Maximize the **Select Query** window if it is not already maximized.
7. Click on the **selector bar** at the top of the **CD ID** field in the QBE Grid to select the whole column.
8. Press the **DELETE** key to remove that column.
9. In the **CDROM** field list, double-click the **Title** and **Price** fields to include them in the QBE Grid.

   You may not be able to see Price in the sixth column off the right edge of the screen, but it is there. You could scroll to the right with the scroll bar to see it.

10. Click the **Datasheet View** button to see the result (see Figure 5 - 30).

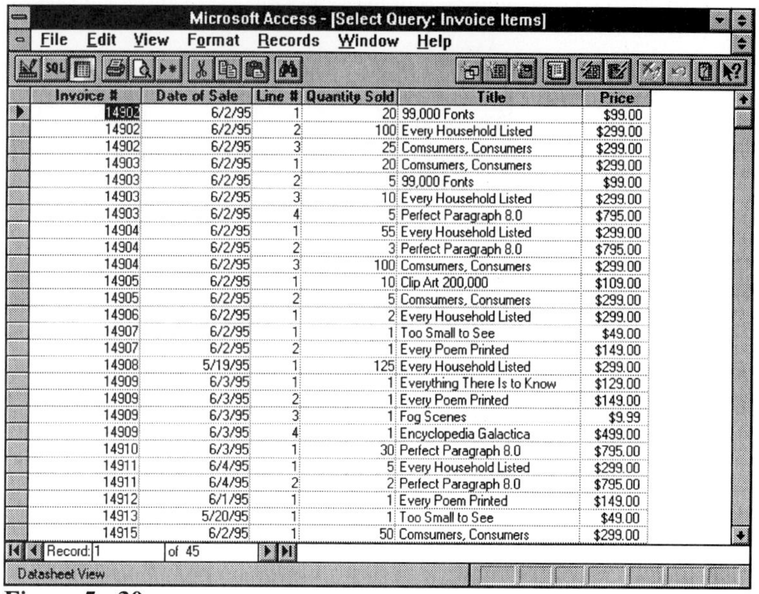

Invoice #	Date of Sale	Line #	Quantity Sold	Title	Price
14902	6/2/95	1	20	99,000 Fonts	$99.00
14902	6/2/95	2	100	Every Household Listed	$299.00
14902	6/2/95	3	25	Comsumers, Consumers	$299.00
14903	6/2/95	1	20	Comsumers, Consumers	$299.00
14903	6/2/95	2	5	99,000 Fonts	$99.00
14903	6/2/95	3	10	Every Household Listed	$299.00
14903	6/2/95	4	5	Perfect Paragraph 8.0	$795.00
14904	6/2/95	1	55	Every Household Listed	$299.00
14904	6/2/95	2	3	Perfect Paragraph 8.0	$795.00
14904	6/2/95	3	100	Comsumers, Consumers	$299.00
14905	6/2/95	1	10	Clip Art 200,000	$109.00
14905	6/2/95	2	5	Comsumers, Consumers	$299.00
14906	6/2/95	1	2	Every Household Listed	$299.00
14907	6/2/95	1	1	Too Small to See	$49.00
14907	6/2/95	2	1	Every Poem Printed	$149.00
14908	5/19/95	1	125	Every Household Listed	$299.00
14909	6/3/95	1	1	Everything There Is to Know	$129.00
14909	6/3/95	2	1	Every Poem Printed	$149.00
14909	6/3/95	3	1	Fog Scenes	$9.99
14909	6/3/95	4	1	Encyclopedia Galactica	$499.00
14910	6/3/95	1	30	Perfect Paragraph 8.0	$795.00
14911	6/4/95	1	5	Every Household Listed	$299.00
14911	6/4/95	2	2	Perfect Paragraph 8.0	$795.00
14912	6/1/95	1	1	Every Poem Printed	$149.00
14913	5/20/95	1	1	Too Small to See	$49.00
14915	6/2/95	1	50	Comsumers, Consumers	$299.00

Figure 5 - 30

This dynaset joins data from three tables. This time the redundancy occurs in the Titles and Prices of the CDROMs.

11. Choose **FILE/Save Query** to save this query with the same name and replace the old design.
12. Print the result by clicking the **Print** button and clicking **OK** in the Print dialog box.
13. Return to the design by clicking the **Design View** button.

    How could we add the Customers' names to this result? How about the Employees' names?

14. Close the query with **FILE/Close**.

SUMMARY

In this project we have used multiple criteria and multiple table queries. We used multiple criteria for *And queries* and *Or queries*. We also used the *between*, *or*, *not*, and *null* operators, as well as wild card characters in queries. The multiple table queries joined data from more than one table into a single dynaset. This was achieved by linking the common field in one table to the matching field in the second table.

In the next lesson we will design reports and labels for both tables and queries. The final lesson will explore calculating with queries, as well as Action Queries, which can alter the data throughout a table.

KEY TERMS

And Query	Link	Wild Card
Compound	Operator	
Join	Or Query	

INDEPENDENT PROJECTS

Independent Project 5.1: The School Newspaper

This Independent Project continues working with the Newspaper Ad database from Independent Project 4.1. The newspaper's editor needs a list of any companies with "sport" in their names to get ready for the Home Coming issue. The list should include all fields. Also, the business manager wants a listing of where the sales force lives, together with the businesses to whom they are selling ads. It should include the Purchased By field from the Ads table, as well as the First Name, Last Name, and Room fields from the Sales Force table. The two tables will need to be linked by their common field, Salesperson ID.

The first query result should look like Figure 5 - 31. The second will correspond to Figure 5 - 32.

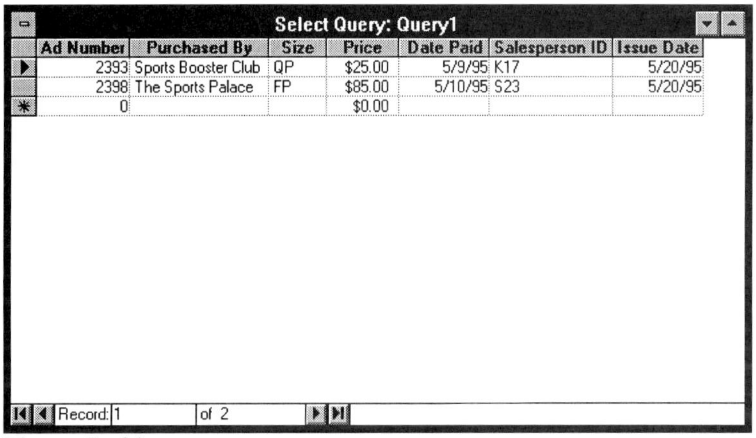

Select Query: Query1

Ad Number	Purchased By	Size	Price	Date Paid	Salesperson ID	Issue Date
2393	Sports Booster Club	QP	$25.00	5/9/95	K17	5/20/95
2398	The Sports Palace	FP	$85.00	5/10/95	S23	5/20/95
0			$0.00			

Record: 1 of 2

Figure 5 - 31

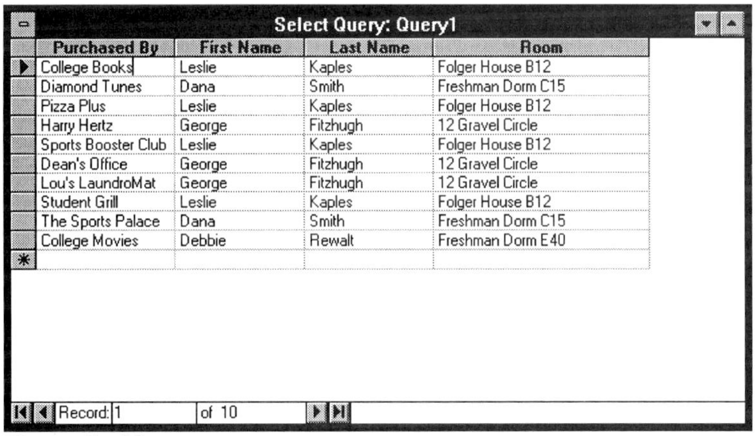

Select Query: Query1

Purchased By	First Name	Last Name	Room
College Books	Leslie	Kaples	Folger House B12
Diamond Tunes	Dana	Smith	Freshman Dorm C15
Pizza Plus	Leslie	Kaples	Folger House B12
Harry Hertz	George	Fitzhugh	12 Gravel Circle
Sports Booster Club	Leslie	Kaples	Folger House B12
Dean's Office	George	Fitzhugh	12 Gravel Circle
Lou's LaundroMat	George	Fitzhugh	12 Gravel Circle
Student Grill	Leslie	Kaples	Folger House B12
The Sports Palace	Dana	Smith	Freshman Dorm C15
College Movies	Debbie	Rewalt	Freshman Dorm E40

Record: 1 of 10

Figure 5 - 32

1. Run *Access* and maximize its window.
2. Open the **xercise1.mdb** database with **FILE/Open Database** or by clicking the **Open Database** tool on the toolbar, then clicking on the name **xercise1.mdb** and clicking the **OK** button.

3. Click on the **Query** button at the left edge of the database window.
4. Click the **New** button to start a new query.
5. Click the **New Query** button in the New Query dialog box.
6. Click on the name **Ads** in the list of tables and queries in the Add Table dialog box and click the **Add** button.
7. Click **Close** to close the Add Table dialog box.
8. Double-click on the name **Ads** in the gray box at the top of the list of names to select all fields.
9. Move the mouse on top of any name in the highlighted list, hold down the mouse button, and drag that name down to the Field: line of the first column in the QBE Grid. When you release the mouse button, the entire set of field names will be installed.
10. Press the **HOME** key to jump to the first column.
11. Click on the **Criteria:** line in the **Purchased By** column and enter: **like "*Sport*"**
12. Click the **Datasheet View** button on the toolbar to see the resulting listings (see Figure 5 - 31).
13. Print the result by clicking the **Print** button and clicking **OK** in the Print dialog box.
14. Click the **Design View** button to return to the query design. You do not need to save this query, so we will build the second query from here.
15. Clear the current selection of fields from the QBE Grid with **EDIT/Clear Grid**.
16. To add the Sales Force table, either click the **Add Table** button on the toolbar or pick **QUERY/Add Table**.
17. Click on the name **Sales Force** in the Add Table list and click the **Add** button. Access should automatically link the two tables by the common field Salesperson ID.
18. Click **Close** to close the Add Table dialog box.
19. Double-click on the name **Purchased By** in the Ads table field list to include it in the QBE Grid.
20. Double-click on **First Name**, then **Last Name**, and finally **Room** in the Sales Force field list.
21. Click the **Datasheet View** button on the toolbar to see the resulting listings (see Figure 5 - 32).
22. Print the result by clicking the **Print** button and clicking **OK** in the Print dialog box.
23. Save the query as **Company vs Room** by picking **FILE/Save Query As**, entering the name, and clicking the **OK** button. Do not type a period in the save name as periods are not legal.
24. Close the query with **FILE/Close**.
25. Close the database with **FILE/Close Database**.
26. If you need to exit from *Access* and/or Windows, do so properly.

Independent Project 5.2: The Book Store

This Independent Project continues working with the Book Store database from Independent Project 4.2. The owner needs a list of books that are priced below $30 and that have between 50 and 100 in stock. It should include all fields. Since this is a one time request, you will print, but not save, this query. She also wants a complete listing of publisher's Name, Title, Author's name, and Year of Publication. It should be sorted by publisher's name. The two tables, Publishers and Books, will need to be linked by their common field, Publisher Code. As this listing may be required repeatedly, this one will be saved.

The first query result should look like Figure 5 - 33. The second will correspond to Figure 5 - 34.

	Book Code	Title	Author	Year of Pub	Publisher Code	Cost	Price	Quantity in Stock
▶	POG17	The Physics of Glass	Kate Rice	1993	BP07	$4.75	$7.95	80
	LUI81	Look Up In The Sky	Bruce Tiggle	1989	TT12	$17.00	$28.95	63
	ATL11	Art Through Life	Jane Rick	1994	TT12	$13.50	$22.95	86
	MOR47	Modern Russian	Igora Bylov	1990	CE03	$17.00	$28.50	59
*						$0.00	$0.00	0

Figure 5 - 33

	Name	Title	Author	Year of Pub
▶	Atlantic Works	Music Harmony	Eliza Smith	1986
	Atlantic Works	Music Composition	Eliza Smith	1985
	Books Plus	Even More Poems	Sina Grant	1976
	Books Plus	The Physics of Glass	Kate Rice	1993
	Bulky Books	Chemical Compendium		1995
	College Editions	Economically Correct	Lester Dane	1974
	College Editions	Modern Russian	Igora Bylov	1990
	College Editions	World of History	James Dyce	1988
	Texts and Tomes	Philosophize With Me	Whyle Jones	1975
	Texts and Tomes	Art Through Life	Jane Rick	1994
	Texts and Tomes	Calculus	Henry Slate	1977
	Texts and Tomes	Look Up In The Sky	Bruce Tiggle	1989
*				

Figure 5 - 34

1. Run *Access* and maximize its window.
2. Open the **xercise2.mdb** database with **FILE/Open Database** or by clicking the **Open Database** tool on the toolbar, then clicking on the name **xercise2.mdb** and clicking the **OK** button.
3. Click on the **Query** button at the left edge of the database window.
4. Click the **New** button to start a new query.
5. Click the **New Query** button in the New Query dialog box.
6. Click on the name **Books** in the list of tables and queries in the Add Table dialog box and click the **Add** button.
7. Click **Close** to close the Add Table dialog box.
8. Double-click on the name **Books** in the gray box at the top of the list of names to select all fields.
9. Move the mouse on top of any name in the highlighted list, hold down the mouse button, and drag that name down to the Field: line of the first column in the QBE Grid. When you release the mouse button, the entire set of field names will be installed.
10. Press the **END** key to jump to the last column.
11. Click on the **Criteria:** line in the **Price** column and enter: **<30**

12. Click on the **Criteria:** line in the **Quantity in Stock** column and enter: **between 50 and 100**
13. Click the **Datasheet View** button on the toolbar.
14. **Maximize** the window so you can see the four resulting listings (see Figure 5 - 33).
15. Print the result by clicking the **Print** button and clicking **OK** in the Print dialog box.
16. Click the **Design View** button to return to the query design. You do not need to save this query, so we will build the second query from the current one.
17. Clear the current selection of fields from the QBE Grid with **EDIT/Clear Grid**.
18. To add the Publishers table, either click the **Add Table** button on the toolbar or pick **QUERY/Add Table**.
19. Click on the name **Publishers** in the Add Table list and click the **Add** button. *Access* should automatically link the two tables by the common field Publisher Code.
20. Click **Close** to close the Add Table dialog box.
21. Double-click on the field **Name** in the Publishers table field list to include it in the QBE Grid.
22. Double-click on **Title**, then **Author**, and finally **Year of Publication** in the Books field list.
23. Click on the **Sort:** line in the **Name** column, click the **drop-down** arrow to open the list of sort operators, and click on **Ascending**.
24. Click the **Datasheet View** button on the toolbar to see the resulting listings (see Figure 5 - 34).
25. Print the result by clicking the **Print** button and clicking **OK** in the Print dialog box.
26. Save the query as **Publishers' Books** by picking **FILE/Save Query As**, entering the name, and clicking the **OK** button.
27. Close the query with **FILE/Close**.
28. Close the database with **FILE/Close Database**.
29. If you need to exit from *Access* and/or Windows, do so properly.

Independent Project 5.3: The Real Estate Office

This Independent Project continues working with the Real Estate Office database from the earlier lessons. The office manager needs a list of commercial properties that are larger than 4000 square feet in size and priced below $150,000. It should include all fields. Since this is a one time request, you will print, but not save, this query. He also wants a complete listing of properties by Agency name. The Agency Name, Phone 1, and Fax fields from the Agencies table should be included, as well as Address, City, Size, Available, and Agent fields from Commercial Listings. It should be sorted by Agency Name. The two tables, Agencies and Commercial Listings, will need to be linked by their common field, Agency Code. As this listing would be needed continually, this one will be saved and printed.

The first query result should look like Figure 5 - 35. The second will correspond to Figure 5 - 36.

Code	Address	City	State	Zip	Size	Floor	Purc	Price	Available	Agency	Agent
ES52	5 Elm St.	Greenwich	CT	06830	4800	1	R	$72,000.00	6/1/95	SC18	Brown
LW17	1 Lewis Way	Danbury	CT	06810	12000	2	R	$125,000.00	7/1/95	PP24	Smith
GP25	12 Gedney Place	Danbury	CT	06810	8900	3	R	$105,000.00	7/15/95	SC18	Equat
					0	0		$0.00			

Figure 5 - 35

Agency Name	Phone 1	Fax	Address	City	Size	Available	Agent
George Winkle	972-9538	972-9625	3 Research Park	Stamford	18000	6/1/95	Purcell
Priceless Properties	359-1111	359-1212	2 Research Park	Stamford	18000	6/1/95	Ruth
Priceless Properties	359-1111	359-1212	Maple Court	New Canaan	450	5/15/95	Green
Profitable Properties	748-3471	748-0102	952 River Rd.	Stamford	3750	9/1/95	Smith
Profitable Properties	748-3471	748-0102	1 Lewis Way	Danbury	12000	7/1/95	Smith
Regal Real Estate	359-0050	359-0055	18 Frost Ave.	Greenwich	3700	8/1/95	Funchall
Right Properties	748-9410	748-9411	6 Research Park	Stamford	19000	10/1/95	Williams
Right Properties	748-9410	748-9411	5 Research Park	Stamford	21000	8/1/95	Williams
Smith and Cross	661-2831	661-2001	12 Gedney Place	Danbury	8900	7/15/95	Equat
Smith and Cross	661-2831	661-2001	5 Elm St.	Greenwich	4800	6/1/95	Brown
					0		

Figure 5 - 36

1. Run *Access* and maximize its window.
2. Open the **xercise3.mdb** database.
3. Click on the **Query** button at the left edge of the database window.
4. Begin a new query.
5. Add **Commercial Listings** to the query window and close the Add Table dialog box.
6. Double-click on the name **Commercial Listings** to select all fields and drag any single name down to the Field: line to install all fields into the QBE Grid.
7. Move to the **Size** column.
8. Enter the criteria for **Size larger than 4000** square feet and **Price below $150,000**.
9. View the resulting listings (see Figure 5 - 35).
10. Print the result.
11. Return to the query design. You do not need to save this query.
12. Clear the QBE Grid.
13. Add the **Agencies** table to the top section of the query window. Access should automatically link the two tables by the common field Agency Code.

!

NOTE: *If Access does not link the two tables, you must have typed a different name for the Agency Code field in the Commercial Listings table. To establish the link between tables yourself, click on the field that represents Agency Code in Commercial Listings and drag from that name onto Agency Code in the Agencies table. The normal link line will be drawn and you will be ready to continue.*

14. Place the **Agency Name**, **Phone 1**, and **Fax** fields from the Agencies table into the QBE Grid.
15. Include **Address**, **City**, **Size**, **Available**, and **Agent** from the Commercial Listings table.
16. Sort in Ascending order by **Agency Name**.
17. View the resulting listings (see Figure 5 - 36).
18. Save the query as **Properties by Agency**.

19. Print the result.
20. Close the query.
21. Close the database.
22. If you need to exit from *Access* and/or Windows, do so properly.

Independent Project 5.4: The Veterinarian

This Independent Project continues working with the veterinarian database from the earlier lessons. She needs the following two lists. Include all fields, print the resulting dynaset, and save each query.

- A list of dogs that weigh less than 50 pounds.
- A list of animals with "er" anywhere within their name.

She also needs a listing of the owners with their pets. Include the fields named below, print the resulting dynaset, and save the query.

- A list that includes Name, Area Code, and Phone from the owners table and the name, type of animal, and date of last visit from the pets table.

  ***NOTE**: If Access does not automatically link the two tables, you must have typed a different name for the Owner Code field in the pets table. To establish the link between tables yourself, click on the field that represents Owner Code in Pet Owners and drag from that name onto the owners code field in the pets table. The normal link line will be drawn and you will be ready to continue.*

Lesson 6

Reports

Objectives

In this lesson you will learn how to:

- Design a report with the **Report Wizard**
- Preview a report design
- Modify a report design
- Print a report

PROJECT DESCRIPTION

While working on the screen is ideal for editing and viewing a table's data, often a paper print-out is required to share the data with others. A typical business needs dozens of standard and special purpose reports to review such activities as sales, inventory, accounts receivable, and customer distribution, to mention just a few topics. In this lesson we will see how to design and print two different types of reports, as well as mailing labels.

The first report will print a list of customers who have outstanding balances, as shown in Figure 6 - 1. This report is a *Tabular* Design.

Outstanding Balances

19-Dec-94

Cust ID	First Name	Last Name	Area Code	Phone	Credit Limit	Balance
PA34	Jerome	Packard	608	828-551	$100.00	$49.00
JE09	Jennifer	Jerome	603	446-802	$100.00	$59.10
TR30	Caroline	Truefoe	706	860-297	$200.00	$129.00
AW31		Arrow Way Freight	404	873-490	$5,000.00	$562.00
YT01		Your Trip Travel	719	380-921	$3,000.00	$593.40
RF41		Regent Foods	704	523-610	$5,000.00	$1,982.00
						$3,374.50

Figure 6 - 1

The second report will be a *Groups/Totals* design and will print the customers in groups by state as illustrated in Figure 6 - 2.

Customers by State

Monday, December 19, 1994

State	Cust ID	First Name	Last Name	City	Zip	Credit Limit
CA						
	AI29		AreaWide Insurance	Nevada City	95959	$10,000.00
	TH92	Harry	Thompson	Irvine	92714	$500.00
	UD20	Susan	Udarell	San Jose	95112	$100.00
						$10,600.00
CO						
	ED14		Edible Delights	Loveland	80538	$5,000.00
	YT01		Your Trip Travel	Colorado Springs	80915	$3,000.00
						$8,000.00
FL						
	OR54	Donalio	Oradelio	Boca Raton	33433	$0.00

Figure 6 - 2

The third report will produce *Mailing Labels* for the complete customer list as illustrated in Figure 6 - 3.

Laura Ifalo 4529 Garrett Ave. Peabody, MA 01960	Jennifer Jerome 82 Marlow Ln. Marlow, NH 03456	Samantha Killian 89 Harvard Place South Plainfield, NJ 07090
Timed Travel, Inc 1000 Flying Cloud Drive New York, NY 10118	Dana Allington 89 Canter Rd. Astoria, NY 11103	Regent Foods 6990 Industrial Blvd. Charlotte, NC 28273
ArrowWay Freight 2395 E. Third Ave. Atlanta, GA 30308	Caroline Truefoe 10204 Elm Rd. Martinez, GA 30907	Donalio Oradelio 90 South Main Boca Raton, FL 33433
Jerome Packard Saleno Court Middleton, WI 53562	Irving Razelroth 12 Skyway Jefferson, SD 57038	Hazel Harrington 12093 Brighton Dr. Morton Grove, IL 60053

Figure 6 - 3

DESIGNING A REPORT

The two steps in producing a designed report are to create the design, and then print the report. While this is somewhat more involved than just clicking the print button on the toolbar as we have done previously, a designed report offers far more flexibility. A report design can place fields anywhere on the page, not just in the row and column format of a table. You may select which fields you want included in the design and leave out unneeded fields. Computed results can be included, both as grand totals at the end of the report, and on each line to calculate results for each listing like a percentage of the total. Once a design is created, it can be saved and used over and over again.

A report may be designed for either a table or a query. A single table report would be limited to the fields within that one table along with any calculations that could be directly computed from its data. It would print all of the records in the table. A query can, of course, join data from two or more tables, so that a report could include a more comprehensive range of data. Since a query can restrict the included listings as well, a report designed around a query would print only the records that matched the query's criteria.

The report itself will usually have a *header* (see Figure 6 - 4) at the beginning (the head) of a report to introduce the overall report and a *footer* (see Figure 6 - 4) at the end (the foot) of the report to include any summary results. The report header normally contains the title of the report, and may also have a date or other introductory information. The report footer often has final results like grand totals.

Each page can also have a header and footer (see Figure 6 - 4). The page header is usually where the column headings belong. The page footer typically contains the page number.

Each header or footer is placed in its own section in the design and is separated from the preceding section by a gray bar (see the right side of Figure 6 - 4). Since a typical report will have a Report Header, Page Header, Page Footer, and Report Footer, there will be several sections.

The section for the fields that will print each listing from the table or query is the *Detail* section, another section separated with a gray bar (see Figure 6 - 4 and Figure 6 - 15). Each section bar has its name on it with an arrow pointing downward toward the section contents.

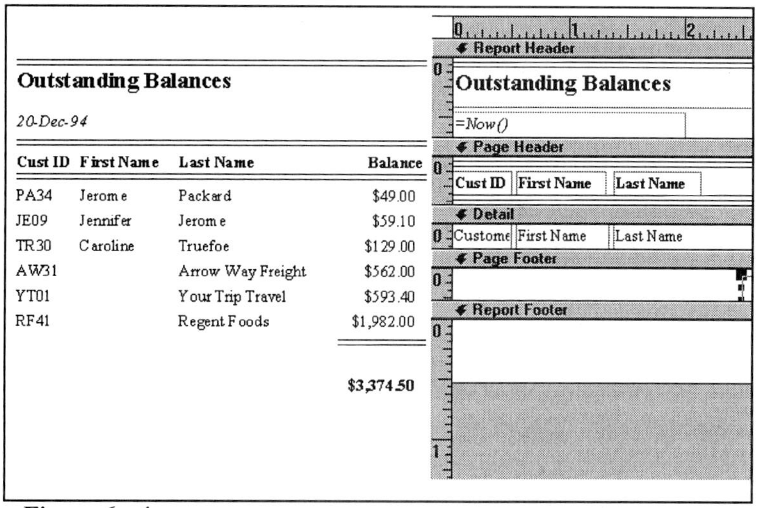

Figure 6 - 4

THE REPORT WIZARD

While it would be possible to design a report by selecting and placing each individual item onto the layout yourself, that would be very tedious. A typical report design will have thirty or forty items that must be carefully placed and lined up with one another. A much easier solution is to employ the *Report Wizard*. The *Report Wizard* asks a sequence of questions as to how you want the design to look, and then produces the design for you. This eliminates the tedium, yet allows considerable flexibility. Once the *Report Wizard* is finished producing the report design, you may, of course, alter the design in any way desired in the **Report** window.

The Report Wizard has several different basic designs from which to select (see Figure 6 - 8). We will explore three common designs: Tabular, Groups/Totals, and Mailing Label.

To design a Tabular report with the *Report Wizard*:

- If you will be producing the report from a query, prepare and save the query.
- Click the **Report** tab at the left edge of the **Database** window.
- Click the **New** button at the top of the **Database** window.

- From the list in the **New Report** dialog box, pick the table or query that is the basis for the report.
- Click the **Report Wizard** button to have the *Wizard* do most of the work for you. (The **Blank Report** button allows you to create and place each item one by one onto the report design yourself, a tedious job at best and normally one to be avoided.)
- Pick **Tabular** as the report type from the list presented by the *Report Wizard* (Figure 6 - 8).
- Select the fields you need on the report from the list the *Wizard* presents.
- Pick any fields by which to sort the report.
- Choose the style for the report, the page orientation, and any extra spacing between lines.
- Enter the title for the report and decide whether to preview the report or go directly to the design to make modifications.

Activity 6.1: The Query to be Used in a Tabular Report

Management needs to review a list of those customers who have an Outstanding Balance. The report should be sorted by the size of the balance. The required fields are Customer ID, First Name, Last Name, Area Code, Phone number, Credit Limit, and Outstanding Balance. The whole table contains customers who both do and don't have an outstanding balance, so we first need to query to select only those customers who have a balance.

1. The Sales database should be open.
2. Click the **Query** tab at the left edge of the **Database** window.
3. Click the **New** button at the top of the **Database** window.
4. Click the **New Query** button in the **New Query** dialog box.
5. Click on **Customers** in the list of tables and click the **Add** button. Then close the **Add Table** dialog box.
6. Double-click each of the required fields in the following order: **Customer ID, First Name, Last Name, Area Code, Phone, Credit Limit,** and **Outstanding Balance**.
7. Press the **LEFT ARROW** key so you can see the last two fields in the QBE Grid.
8. Click on the **Criteria:** line in the **Outstanding Balance** column and enter: **>0** (Figure 6 - 5).

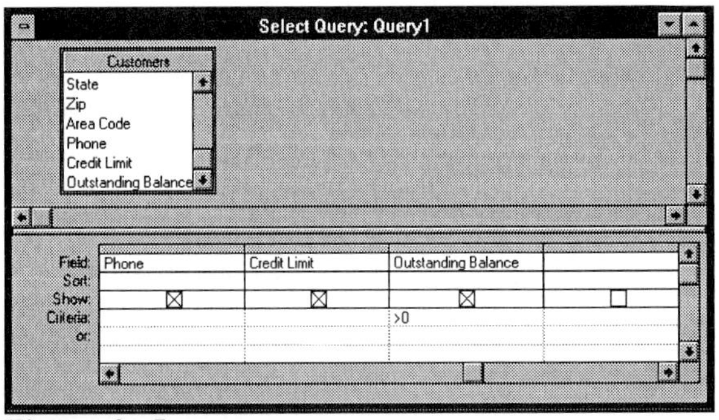

Figure 6 - 5

9. Click the **Datasheet View** button  on the toolbar to visually check the result.

   There should be six records with outstanding balances (see Figure 6 - 6*).*

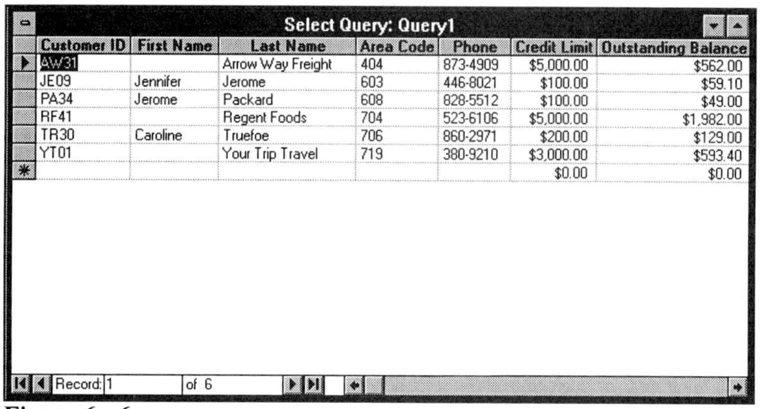

Figure 6 - 6

10. Pick **FILE/Save Query As**.
11. Enter the name **Outstanding Balances** and click the **OK** button.
12. Close the query with **FILE/Close**.

Activity 6.2: A Tabular Report

Now that we have the desired records with outstanding balances, we can create the report. The source of the data for the report will be the **Outstanding Balances** query, and we will use the *Report Wizard* to design a Tabular report. The report will be sorted by size of balance.

1. Click the **Report** tab at the left edge of the database window.
2. Click the **New** button at the top of the database window.
3. Click the drop-down arrow to open the list of tables and queries in the **New Report** dialog box and click on **Outstanding Balances** (see Figure 6 - 7).

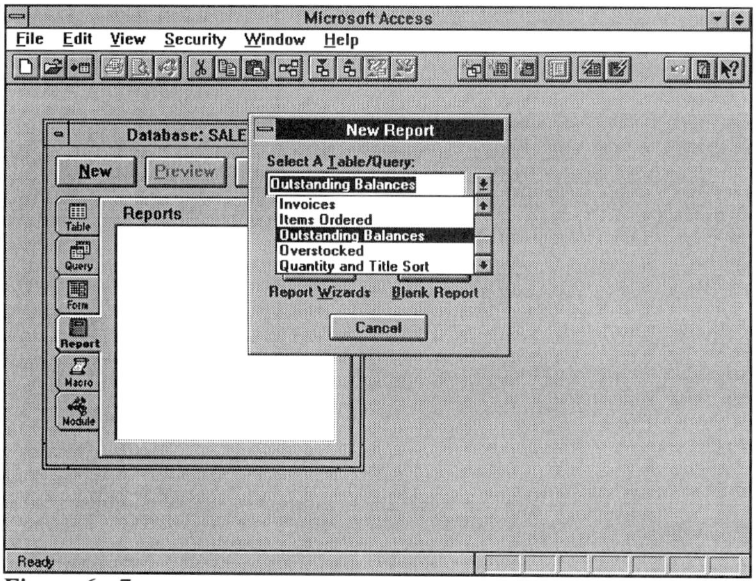

Figure 6 - 7

Be careful not to double-click on the table name as the first click would select the table, and the second click would click the button underneath.

4. Click the **Report Wizards** button.
5. Pick **Tabular** as the type of report design from the list presented by the *Report Wizard* (see Figure 6 - 8).

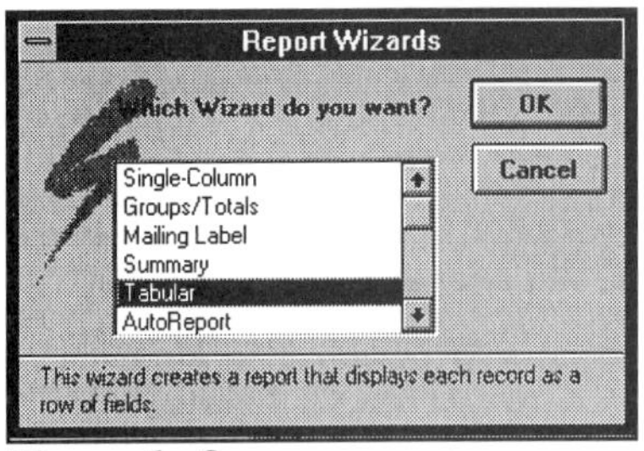

Figure 6 - 8

*The **Tabular Report Wizard** dialog box appears with the list of fields from which to select (see Figure 6 - 9). To pick individual fields in any order, click on the name of the field in the Available fields list and click the **single arrowhead** button that points to the right. To include all fields click the **double arrowhead** button that points to the right. The arrowheads pointing to the left will bring one or all of the fields back so you can reselect.*

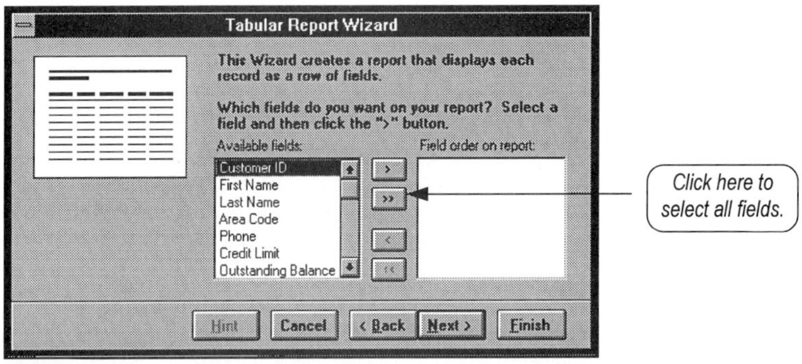

Figure 6 - 9

6. Since we already selected the required fields in the query, we want all of the fields, so click the **double arrowhead** button that points to the right (see Figure 6 - 9).
7. Click the **Next** > button.

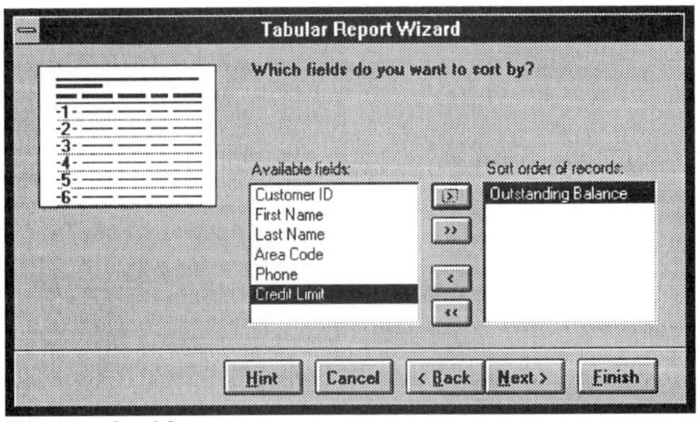

Figure 6 - 10

The next question is by which fields, if any, do you wish to sort the listings (see Figure 6 - 10). Again, select a field and use the arrowhead button to send it into the ***Sort order of records****: column. You may select up to six fields by which to sort.*

8. Click on **Outstanding Balance** to highlight it and click the **single arrowhead** button to transfer it to the **Sort order of records:** column (see Figure 6 - 10).
9. Click the **Next** > button.

What style *is the next question (see Figure 6 - 11). We will use Executive as the look for our report. Landscape is correct for the Orientation, but we will change the additional Line spacing to 0.*

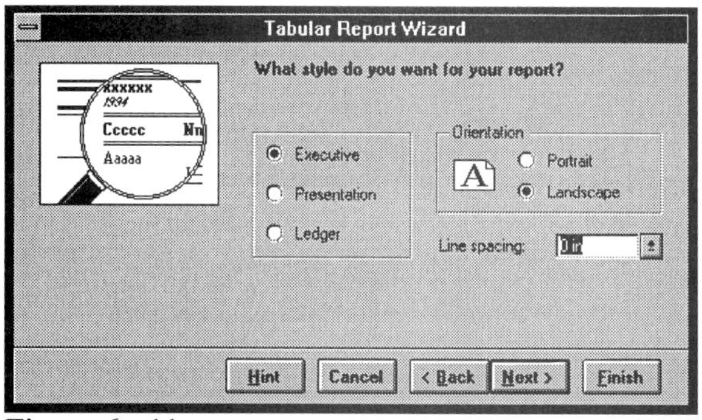

Figure 6 - 11

10. Click on the arrow for the drop-down list for **Line spacing:** and click on **0 in** (Figure 6 - 11).
11. Click the **Next** > button.

The final set of questions (notice the finish flag in Figure 6 - 12) asks for a title for the report, whether the fields should all be squeezed onto a single page, whether you want the Cue Cards opened automatically, and whether to go to preview mode or design mode.

Figure 6 - 12

12. The query name **Outstanding Balances** is perfect as a title for this report and we want none of the other options, so click **See the report with data in it** and then the **Finish** button (see Figure 6 - 12).

The progress can be monitored on the Status Bar as the Wizard puts the design together. The Wizard completes the design and moves to the Print Preview screen so you can see the result (see Figure 6 - 13).

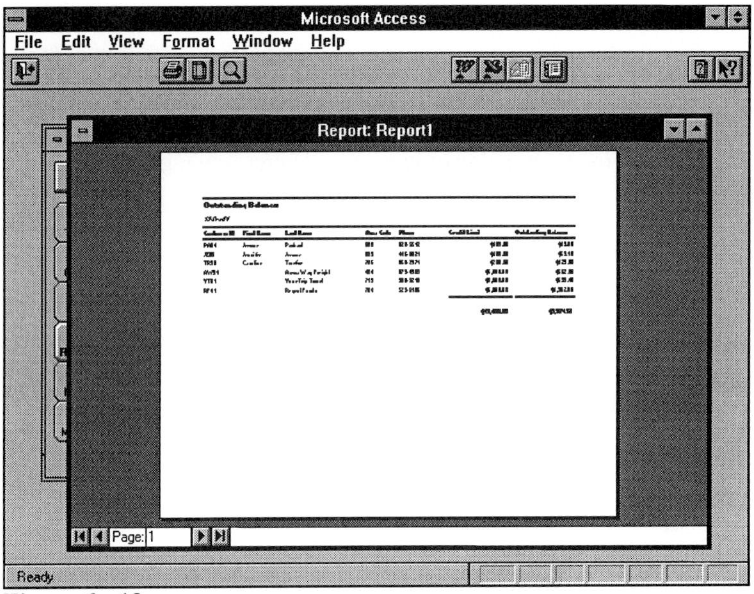

Figure 6 - 13

13. Save this design before anything can happen to it by picking **FILE/Save As**, entering the name **Outstanding Balances** as the Report Name, and clicking **OK**.
14. Maximize the **Preview** window.
15. If the overall page is not showing as in Figure 6 - 13, click the **Zoom** button on the toolbar or click anywhere on the white page.
16. To zoom in on the last two columns, move the mouse pointer (the magnifying glass) so it is on top of the right end of the upper double ruled line, and click the mouse.

    The Outstanding Balances should be in sorted order with a total at the bottom of the column (see Figure 6 - 14). That total is useful. However, the total for the Credit Limit is not, so we will remove it from the design.

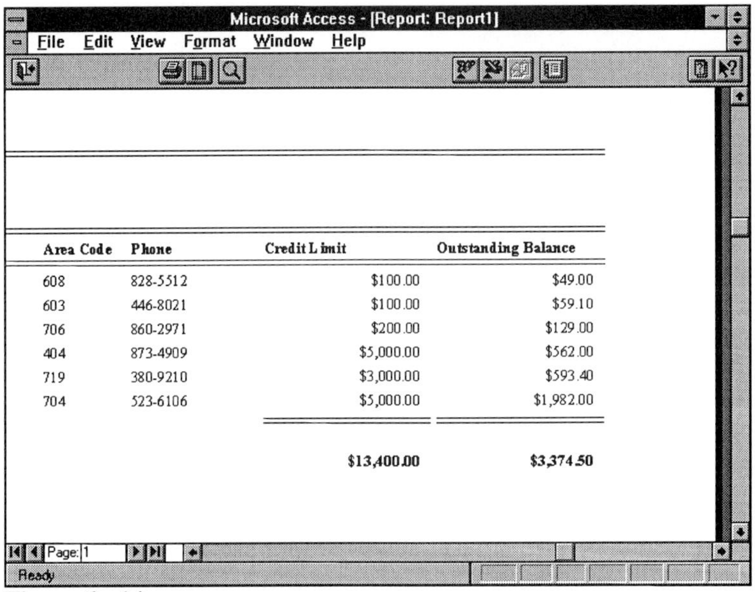

Figure 6 - 14

17. Click the **Close Window** button  on the toolbar.

    The report design screen appears (see Figure 6 - 15). This is the design the Wizard worked out for you. An additional toolbar named the Toolbox probably also appeared on the desktop. The Toolbox is used to place additional items onto the report design.

18. Click on the Toolbox button  on the toolbar to remove the Toolbox from the report design screen.

    If you will be continuing on to the next section, leave the design on the screen.

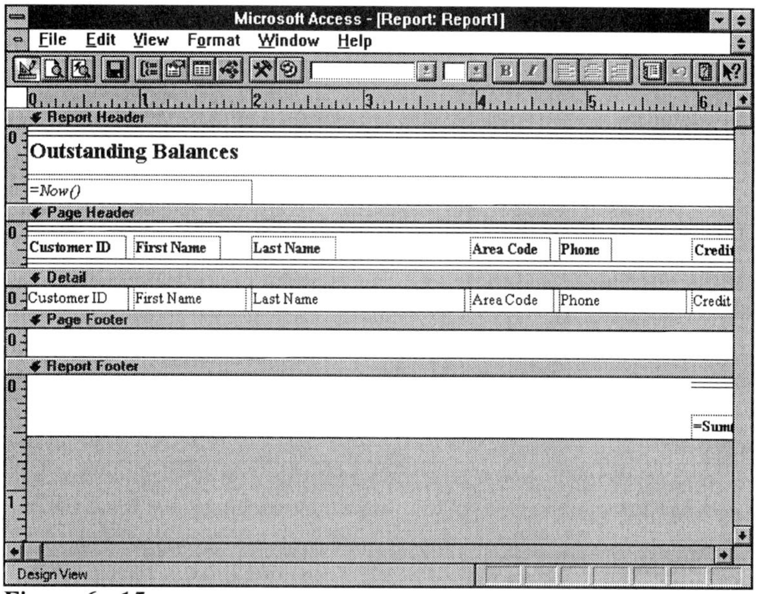

Figure 6 - 15

CHANGING A REPORT DESIGN

Any changes to a report design are performed in the Report window (Figure 6 - 15). The existing design is divided into the sections that were discussed earlier, namely the Report Header, Page Header, Detail section, Page Footer, and Report Footer. Each section begins with the gray bar and extends downward to the next section bar.

Each item included in the design is a *control*. The field controls and label controls are shown as boxes. The ruling line controls are the drawn lines.

The design can be changed by altering the controls and sections. Clicking on a control will produce *handles* at each corner and the middle of each side. The top left handle is the **move handle**. The others are **sizing** handles (see Figure 6 - 16).

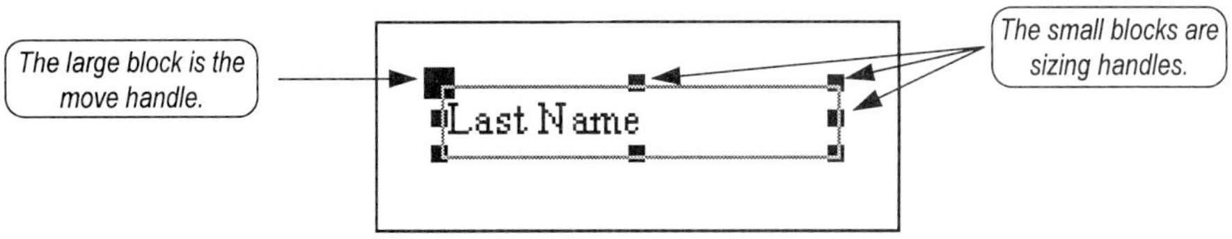

Figure 6 - 16

To change the existing controls on a report design:

- Select the control by clicking on it.

- Move it by dragging its **move handle** to a new position on the design.
- Delete it by pressing the **DELETE** key.
- Resize it by dragging a **sizing handle** until the control is the appropriate size.

Activity 6.3: Changing the Tabular Report Design

We need to delete the total for the Credit Limit and the two ruling lines above that control.

1. If the report design is not already on the screen, click on the **Report Tab**, click on the name **Outstanding Balance** in the list of reports, and click the **Design** button at the top of the database window.
2. Click the **rightward pointing arrow** button at the right end of the lower scroll bar until you can see the right edge of the report design as in Figure 6 - 17.

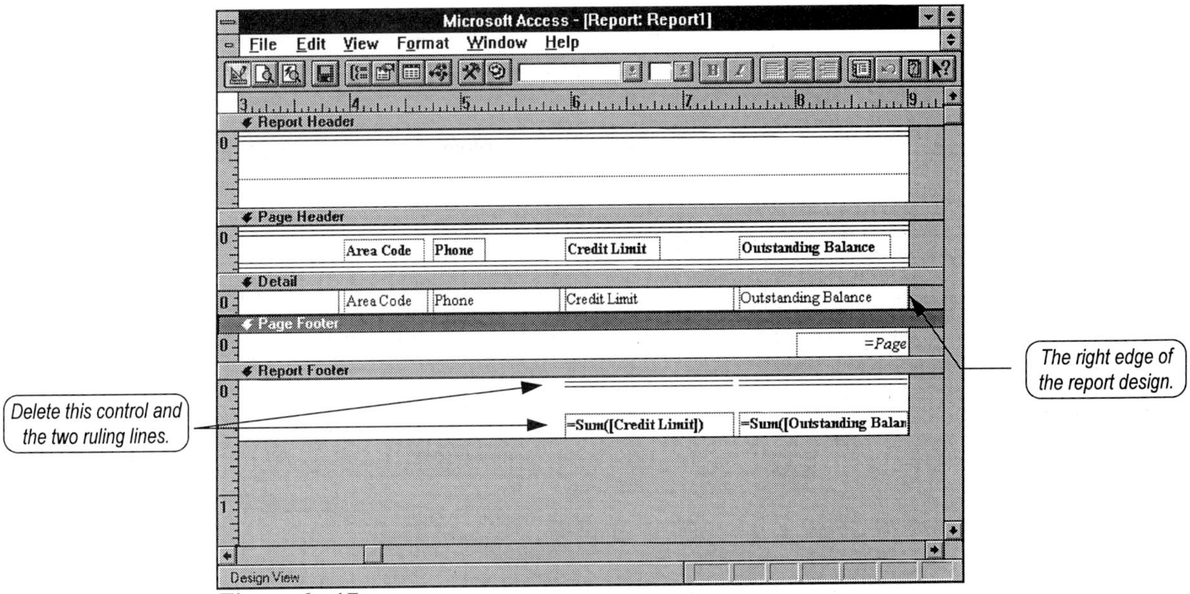

Figure 6 - 17

*If you clicked too many times, you may have scrolled past the **Credit Limit** control. If so, click the **left arrow** to scroll back a little so you can see it.*

3. At the very bottom of the report design, click on the control that contains **=Sum([Credit Limit])** to select it.

   Handles will appear on the control.

4. Press the **DELETE** key.

   The control will disappear from the design (see Figure 6 - 18).

5. Click on either one of the lines that is directly above where the control used to be. When handles appear on the line, press **DELETE**.

   The line will disappear.

6. Similarly click on and delete the remaining line.

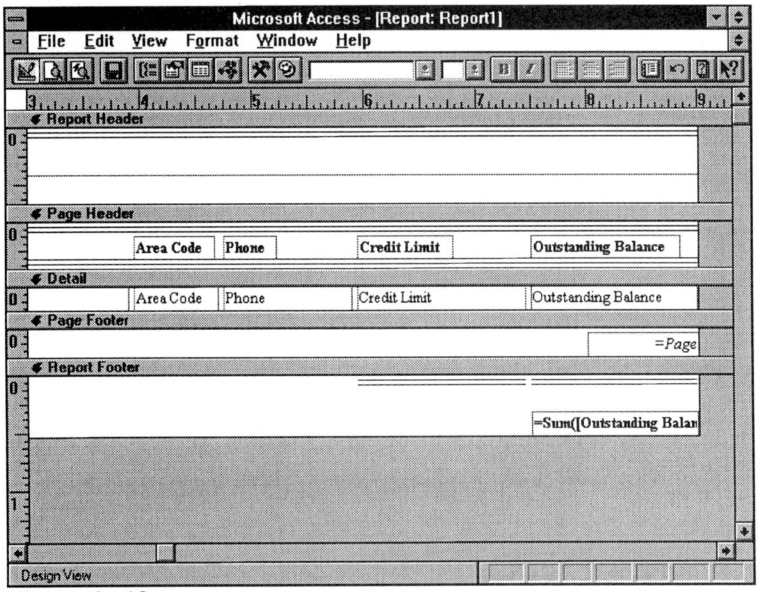

Figure 6 - 18

7. Click the **Print Preview** button on the toolbar.

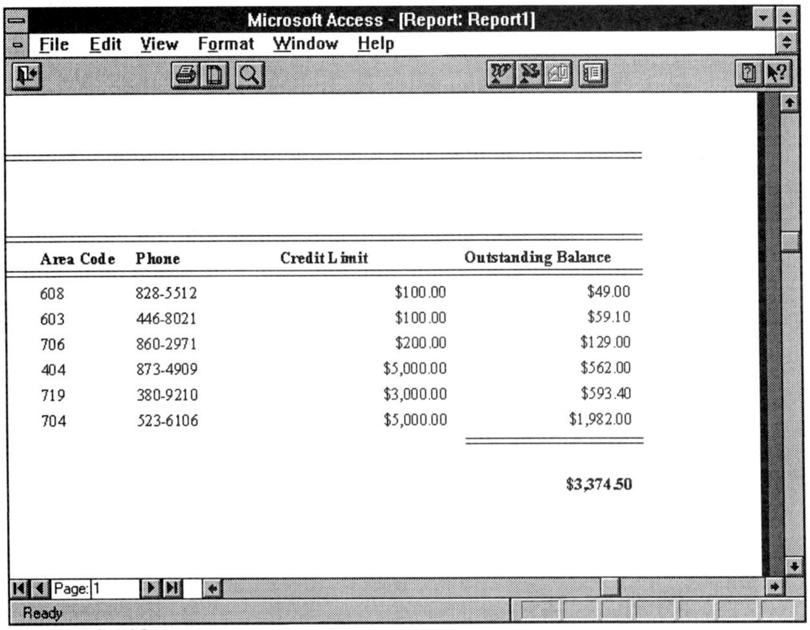

Figure 6 - 19

The preview should no longer show a total for Credit Limit (see Figure 6 - 19).

8. Save the modified design with **FILE/Save**.
9. Print the report by clicking the **Print** button on the toolbar and clicking **OK** in the dialog box.
10. Close the report design with **FILE/Close**.

DESIGNING A GROUPS/TOTALS REPORT

Often a report will need to be *grouped* on the entries in one or more fields. *Grouped* means that all the records with one particular value in a field are assembled into a cluster, and each additional value in that field is placed in a separate gathering. Each group is then separated from the next and given a header section to introduce the group and a footer section to conclude the group. The header would typically contain the name of the group and the footer often holds subtotals for the group.

To design a Groups/Totals report with the Report Wizard:

- Click the **Report** tab at the left edge of the **Database** window.
- Click the **New** button at the top of the **Database** window.
- From the list in the **New Report** dialog box, pick the desired table or query on which to report.
- Click the **Report Wizards** button to have the *Wizard* do most of the work for you.
- Pick **Groups/Totals** from the list of report types presented by the Report Wizard.
- Select the fields you need on the report from the list the *Wizard* presents.
- Choose any fields by which to group the report.
- Pick the fields by which to sort within each grouping.
- Choose the style for the report, the page orientation, and any extra spacing between lines.
- Enter the title for the report and decide whether to preview the report or go directly to the design to make modifications.

Activity 6.4: A Group/Totals Report

Management would like a report that shows which states the various customers come from. The report should list their Customer ID, First Name, Last Name, City, State, Zip Code, and Credit Limit. The report should be grouped by state and sorted alphabetically by customer name within each state. Since the report will include every listing, we will base the report on the data table itself rather than a query.

1. Click the **Report** tab at the left edge of the **Database** window.
2. Click the **New** button at the top of the **Database** window.
3. Click the drop-down arrow to open the list of tables and queries in the **New Report** dialog box. Pick **Customers** and click the **Report Wizards** button.
4. Pick **Groups/Totals** as the type of report and click the **OK** button.
5. In the list of Available fields, click on **Customer ID** and click the **single arrowhead** button that points to the right to transfer it to the Field Order on Report list (see Figure 6 - 20).

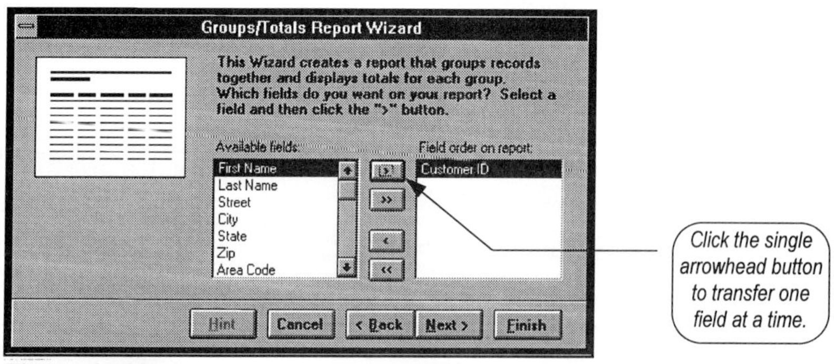

Figure 6 - 20

6. Click on **First Name** in the Available fields list and click the **single arrowhead** button to transfer it to the Field Order on Report list.
7. Click on **Last Name** and click the **single arrowhead** button.
8. Similarly, click on **City**, then **State**, then **Zip**, then **Credit Limit**, clicking the **single arrowhead** button each time (see Figure 6 - 21).

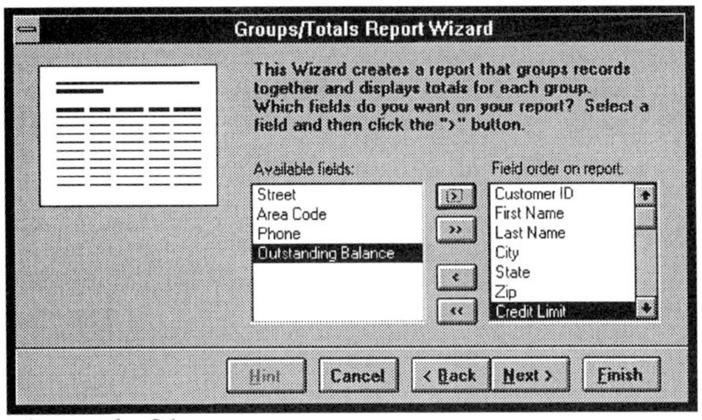

Figure 6 - 21

9. Click the **Next** > button.

   *The next question is by which fields, if any, do you wish to group the listings. Select a field and use the **arrowhead** button to send it into the **Group records by**: column. You may select up to four fields by which to group.*

10. Click on **State** to highlight it and click the **single arrowhead** button to transfer it to the **Group records by:** column (see Figure 6 - 22).

Figure 6 - 22

11. Click the **Next** > button.

    *The next question for a Groups/Totals report is how to do the grouping. You may group by the first letter only, which would create an alphabetical grouping of all As, Bs, etc. Other options are the first two letters, three letters, four letters, or five letters. The usual choice is **Normal** which means that the entire entry must be the same for two data items to be in the same group. We want Normal.*

    Since we want Normal grouping and that is already chosen (see Figure 6 - 23), click the **Next** > button without changing anything.

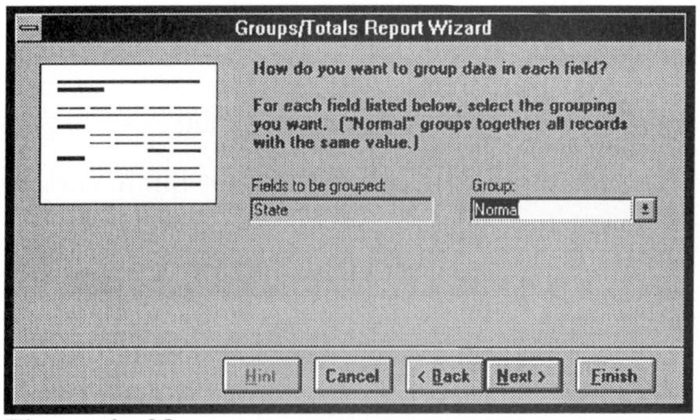

Figure 6 - 23

The report needs to be sorted in name order. We will sort by Last Name. Then, should any two or more customers have the same last name, we will sort secondarily by their First Name.

12. Click on **Last Name** to highlight it and click the **single arrowhead** button to transfer it to the **Sort order of records:** column.
13. Similarly, click on **First Name** to highlight it and click the **single arrowhead** button to transfer it to the **Sort order of records:** column (see Figure 6 - 24).

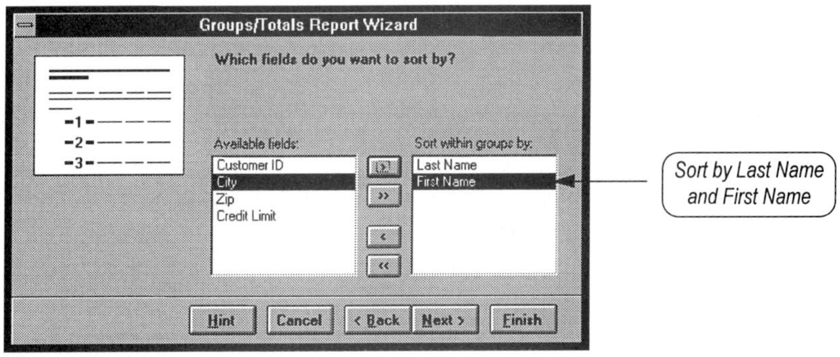

Figure 6 - 24

14. Click the **Next** > button.
15. For style we will use Executive, and Landscape is correct for the Orientation. Click on the arrow for the drop-down list for **Line spacing:** and click on **0 in** (see Figure 6 - 25).

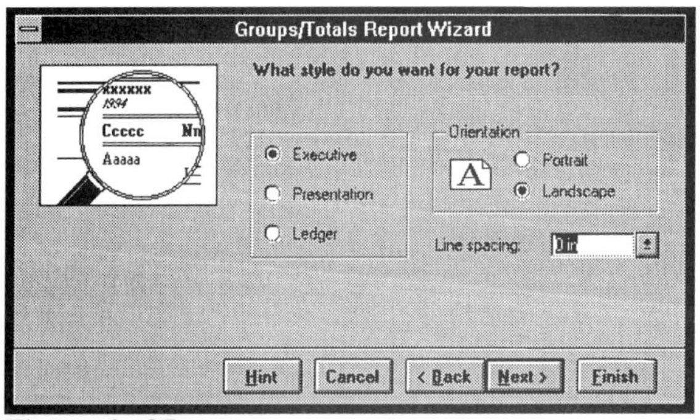

Figure 6 - 25

16. Click the **Next** > button.
17. For the title enter: **Customers by State**

18. Uncheck **Calculate percentages of the total**. Leave **See all the fields on one page** and **Open Cue Cards...** unchecked (see Figure 6 - 26).

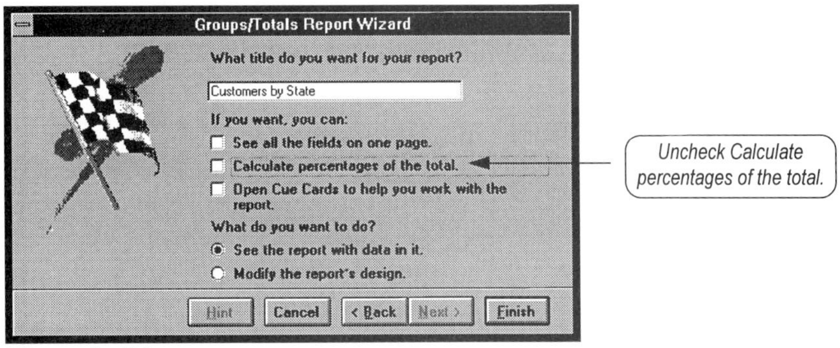

Figure 6 - 26

19. We want to **See the report with data in it**, so click that option and click the **Finish** button.

    The progress can be monitored on the Status Bar as the Wizard puts the design together. When complete, the Wizard displays the Print Preview screen so you can see the result (see Figure 6 - 27).

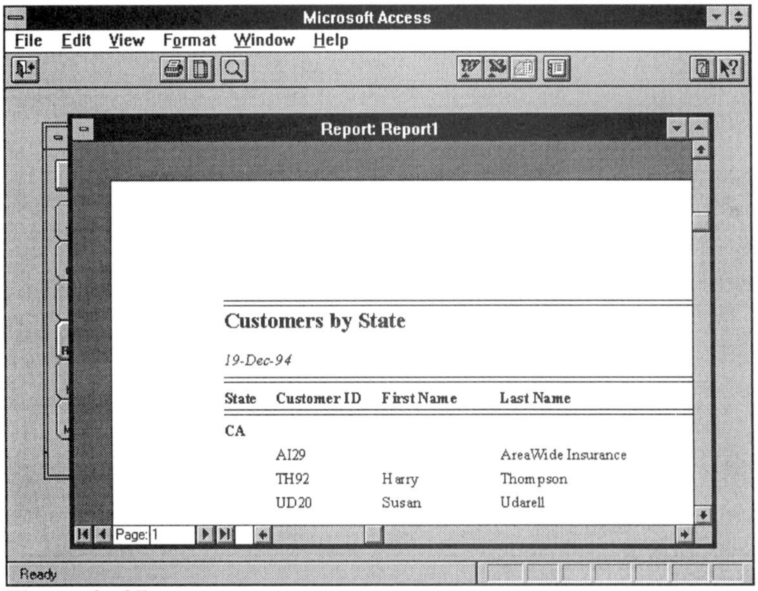

Figure 6 - 27

20. Save this design before anything can happen to it by picking **FILE/Save As**, entering the name **Customers by State** as the Report Name, and clicking **OK**.
21. Maximize the **Preview** window.

    Notice the groups for each state with the customer names in alphabetical order within each group (see Figure 6 - 27). CA, the first state in the report, is one line above the actual listings. CA is the group header.

22. If the overall page is not showing, click the **Zoom** button  on the toolbar or click anywhere on the white page.

23. If the overall page is not showing, click the **Zoom** button on the toolbar or click anywhere on the white page.
24. Click the magnifying glass pointer on the top right corner of the page to see the right side of the report.

    Notice the subtotals for Credit Limit (see Figure 6 - 28). The sub-totals are the footers for the groups.

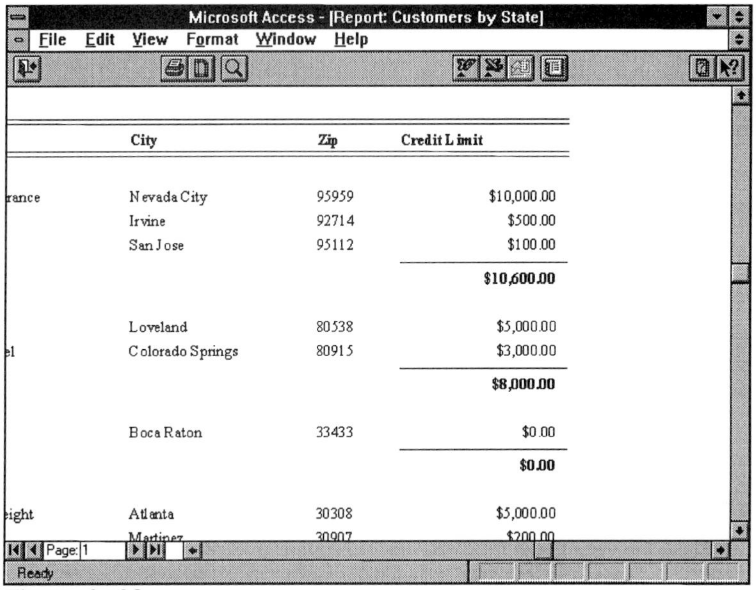

Figure 6 - 28

25. Click the **Close Window** button on the toolbar.

    *The report design screen appears (see Figure 6 - 29). Notice the **State Header** and **State Footer**, which are the group header and group footer sections.*

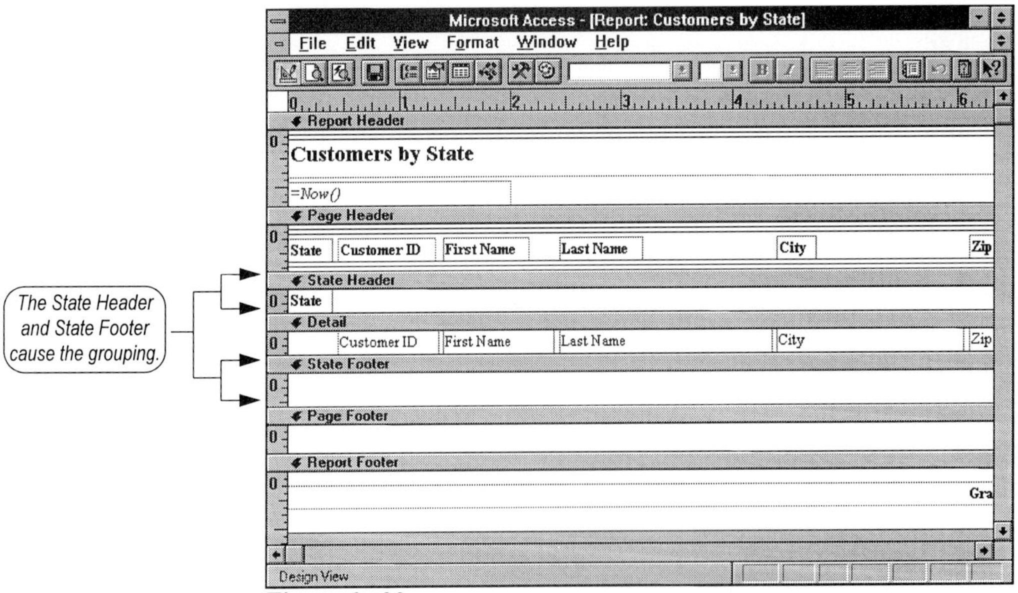

Figure 6 - 29

CHANGING THE FORMATTING OF CONTROLS

Any changes to the appearance of an item on the report is called *formatting*. The formatting of several items on our Groups/Totals report should be changed to improve its appearance and make it more readable.

While alterations to the font, size, bold, italics, or alignment can be made with the toolbar buttons, additional changes must be made in the *Properties List*. The *Properties List* is the complete collection of settings for a control.

To change the formatting of controls on a report design:

- Select the desired control by clicking on it.
- Click the toolbar buttons for font, size, bold, italic, or alignment.
- For additional formatting, open the Properties List by clicking the **Properties** button on the toolbar or with **VIEW/Properties** and change its settings.

Activity 6.5: Formatting the Report Design

We will increase the size of the characters in the title and center it on the page. Also, the state name should stand out better, so we will increase its size, too. The Customer ID will be changed to italics. Finally, the date will be changed to show the day of week and a spelled out month.

1. Click on the main title **Customers by State** to select that control.

   Handles will appear on each corner and side as in Figure 6 - 30.

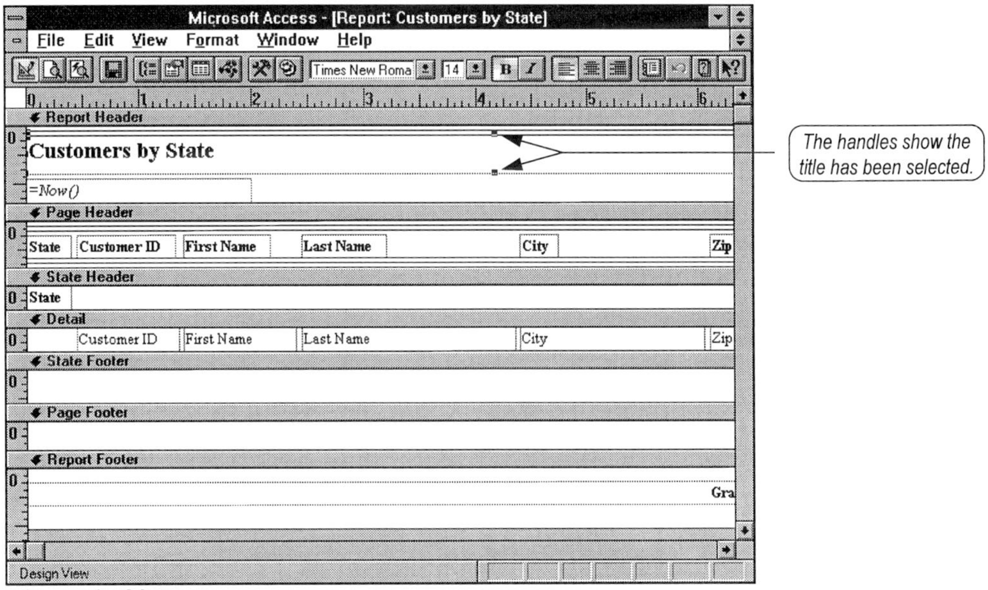

Figure 6 - 30

2. Click the drop-down arrow for the **Font Size** on the toolbar and choose **20**.
3. Click the **Center Align Text** button on the toolbar to center the title on the page.

   The title will be repositioned in the center of the page (Figure 6 - 31).

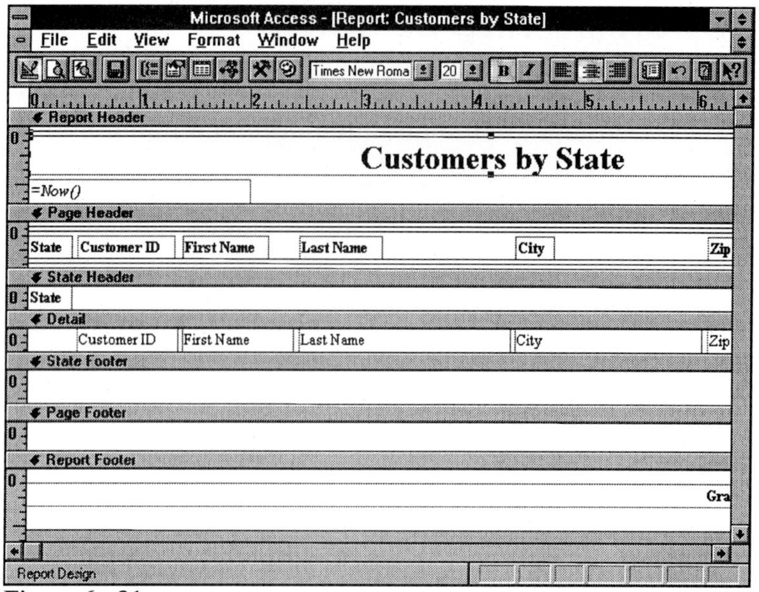

Figure 6 - 31

4. Click on the **State** control in the **State Header** (see Figure 6 - 32). This is not the State control in the Page Header; that control represents the label at the top of the column.

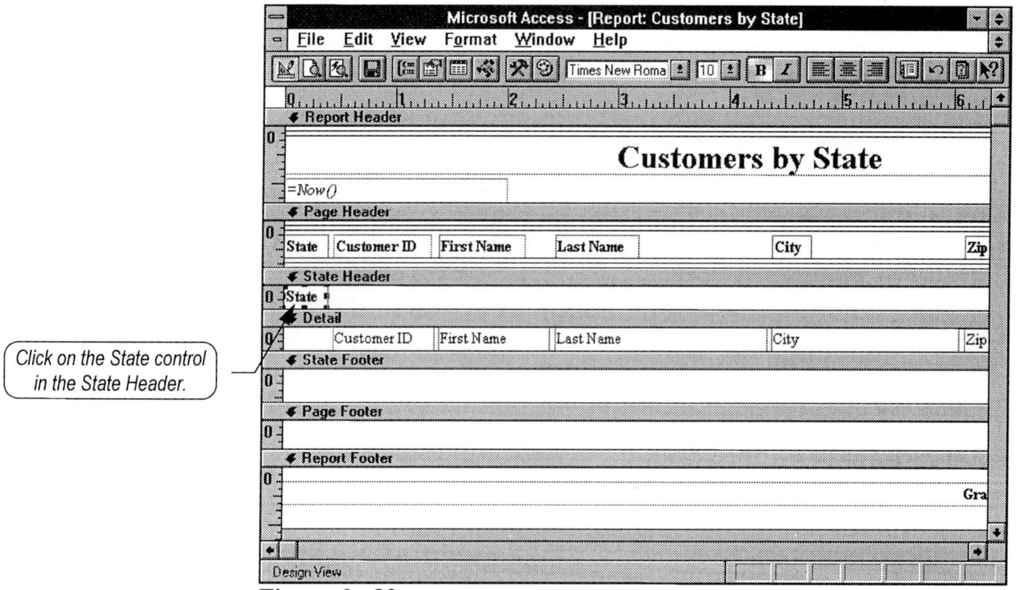

Figure 6 - 32

5. Open the list of font sizes [8] and click on **14**.
6. Click on the **Customer ID** control in the Detail section.
7. Click the **Italics** button [*I*] on the toolbar.
8. Click on the date control in the **Report Header**. This control shows =***Now()*** which is *Access'* way of getting the date right **now**.
9. Click the **Properties** button on the toolbar to open the Properties List (Figure 6 - 33).

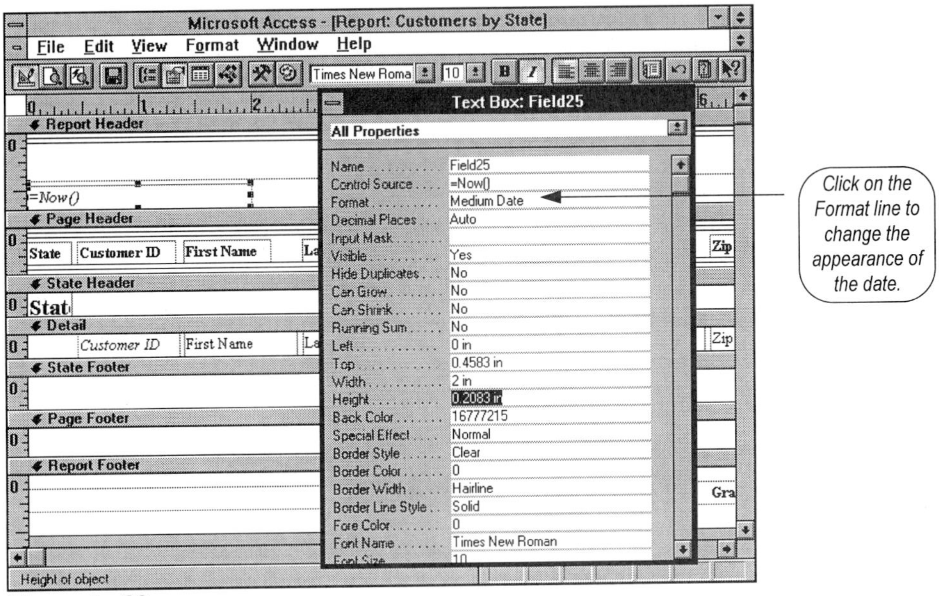

Figure 6 - 33

10. In the top section of the dialog box, click on the drop-down arrow and choose **All Properties**.
11. On the third line of the named properties it says **Format**. Click on the white text box to the right of **Format**, and click the drop-down arrow that appears.
12. In the drop-down list, click on **Long Date** (see Figure 6 - 34). You may need to scroll upward or downward to find **Long Date**.

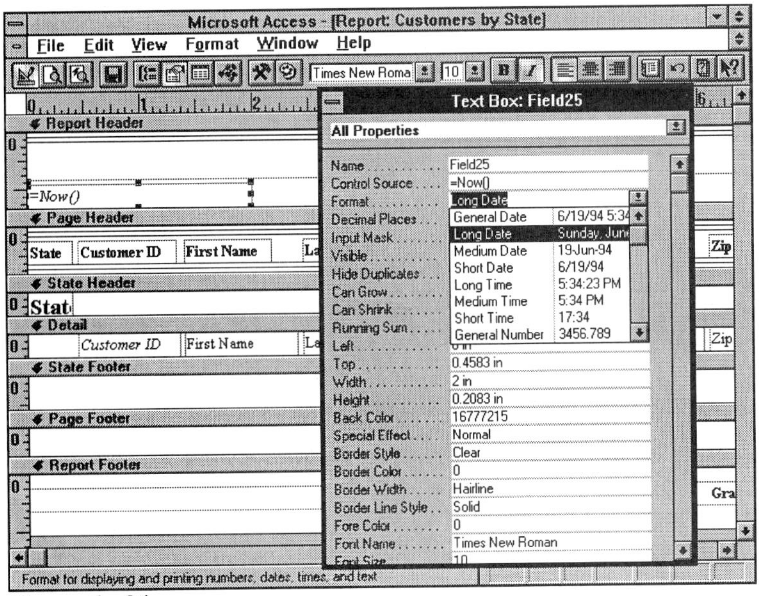

Figure 6 - 34

13. Click the **Properties** button [button] on the toolbar to close the Properties List.
14. Click the **Print Preview** button [button] on the toolbar to view the changes.

The title should be larger and centered, the state should be larger, the Customer ID should be in italics, and the date should be spelled out (see Figure 6 - 35). You may need to scroll around to see each change.

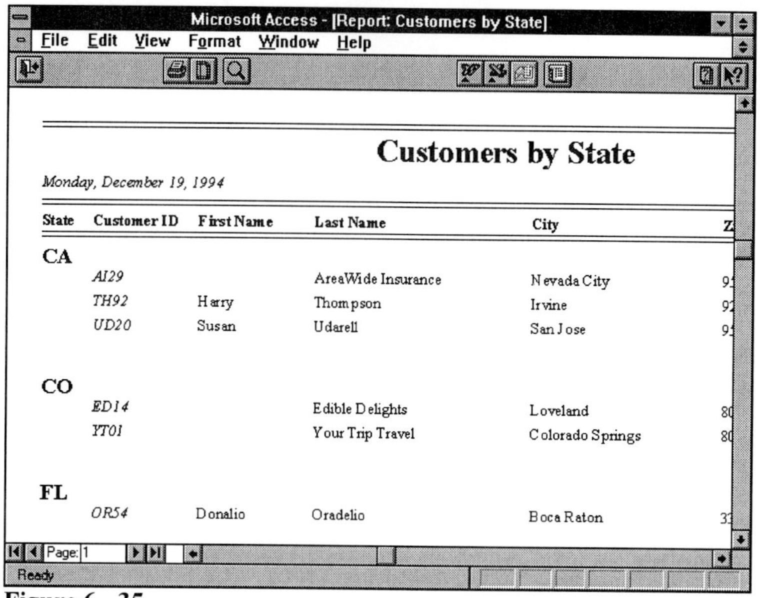

Figure 6 - 35

15. Print the report by clicking the **Print** button on the toolbar and clicking **OK** in the dialog box.
16. Save the changed design with **FILE/Save**.
17. Close the design with **FILE/Close**.

DESIGNING MAILING LABELS

A mailing label design is another common type of report. The *Report Wizard* has a choice for labels, too.

To design a mailing label report with the *Report Wizard*:

- Click the **Report** tab at the left edge of the **Database** window.
- Click the **New** button at the top of the **Database** window.
- From the list in the **New Report** dialog box, pick the desired table or query on which to report.
- Click the **Report Wizards** button to have the wizard do most of the work for you.
- Pick **Mailing Label** as the type of report from the list presented by the *Report Wizard.*
- Choose the contents for each line of the label design by clicking the field and punctuation buttons in the **Mailing Label Wizard** dialog box.
- Pick any fields by which to sort the report.
- Choose sheet or continuous labels, then the Avery label dimensions and number of labels across.
- Set the font, size, weight, and color.
- Choose to either see the labels as they will print, or to move directly to the design window.

Activity 6.6: Mailing Labels

A mailing will be sent to all customers, so we need a set of mailing labels. These will be regular mailing labels with First and Last Name on the top line, Street on the second line, and City-State-Zip on the third line. They should be sorted into zip code order, then by name within each zip code.

1. Click the **Report** tab at the left edge of the **Database** window.
2. Click the **New** button at the top of the **Database** window.
3. Click on **Customers** in the list of tables and queries in the *New Report* dialog box, then click the **Report Wizards** button.
4. Pick **Mailing Label** as the type of report and click the **OK** button.
5. To begin the first line, click on **First Name** in the *Available fields*: list and click the **arrowhead** button that points to the right to transfer it to the Label appearance box (see Figure 6 - 36).

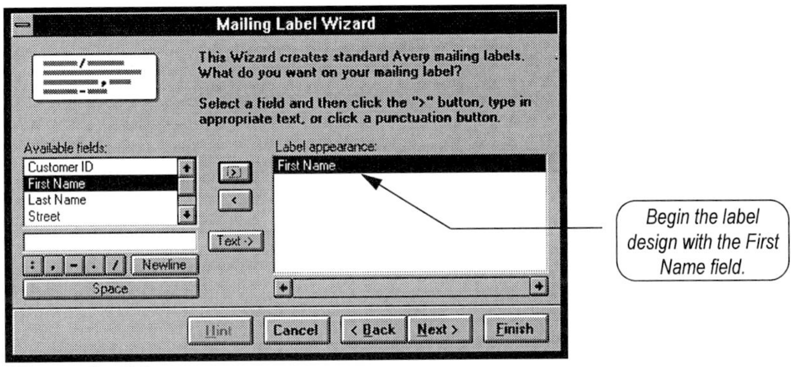

Figure 6 - 36

6. Click the **Space** button (do not type a space) to place a space between the first and last names.

   Spaces will show as tiny dots in the Label appearance box.

7. Click on **Last Name** and click the **arrowhead** button that points to the right to transfer it to the Label appearance box (see Figure 6 - 37).

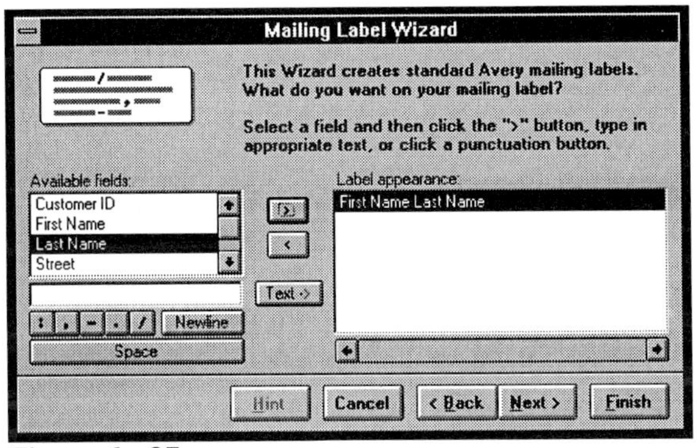

Figure 6 - 37

That completes the top line of the mailing label, so we're ready to begin the second line.

8. Click the **Newline** button to begin the second line.

9. Click on **Street** and click the **arrowhead** button to transfer it to the Label appearance box.

   Street is the only field on the second line.

10. Click the **Newline** button to begin the third line.
11. Click on **City** and click the **arrowhead** button.
12. Click the **comma** button for the comma to separate city from state.
13. Click the **Space** button.
14. Click on **State** and click the **arrowhead** button.
15. Click the **Space** button twice to separate State from Zip with two spaces.
16. Click on **Zip** and click the **arrowhead** button (see Figure 6 - 38).

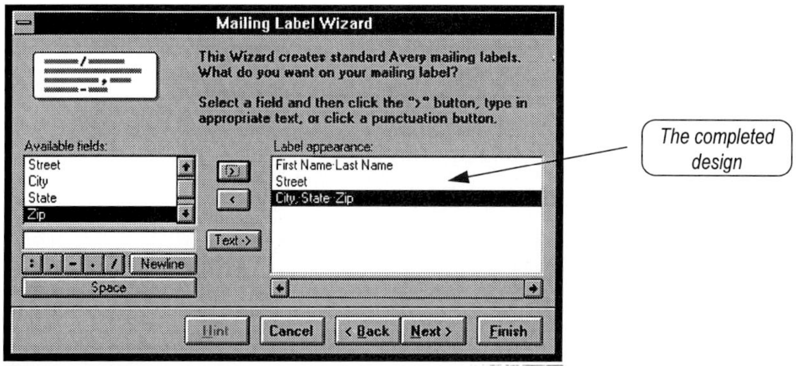

Figure 6 - 38

17. Click the **Next** > button.

   The Wizard asks for the fields by which to sort (see Figure 6 - 39). The Post Office prefers zip code order so we will sort by Zip. For people in the same zip code, we will select Last Name as the second most important field for sorting.

18. Click on **Zip** to highlight it and click the **single arrowhead button** to transfer it to the **Sort order:** column.
19. Similarly, click on **Last Name** to highlight it and click the **single arrowhead** button to transfer it to the **Sort order:** column (see Figure 6 - 39).

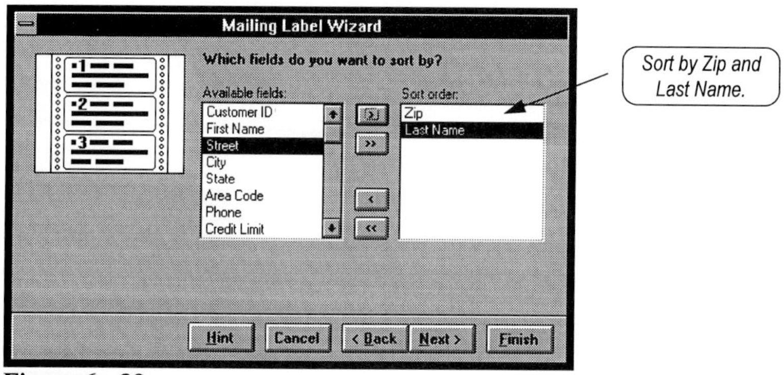

Figure 6 - 39

20. Click the **Next** > button.

*There are several different varieties of labels listed in the **What label size do you want?** dialog box (Figure 6 - 40). If you will be printing to a laser printer or on plain paper rather than gummed labels, click on **Sheet feed** in the **Label Type** box and pick **Avery number 5160**. If you will be printing to strips of labels in a dot matrix printer, click on **Continuous** for **Label Type** and pick **4145** as the Avery number. If you are not sure, ask your instructor which to select.*

21. Click on **Sheet feed** in the **Label Type** box and pick **Avery number 5160**. Unit of Measure should remain **English** (see Figure 6 - 40).

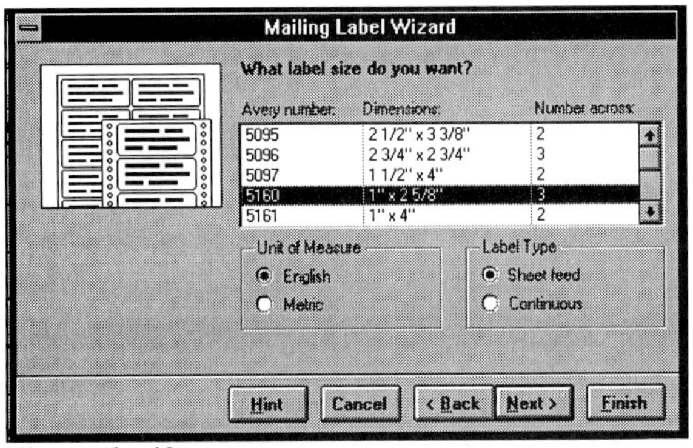

Figure 6 - 40

Avery 5160 is the standard size for three across and ten down labels on sheets that go in a laser printer.

22. Click the **Next** > button.

23. Set the Font name: to **Arial**, the Font size: to **8**, the Font weight: to **Normal**, and the Text color: to **Black**. Do not check Italic or Underline (see Figure 6 - 41).

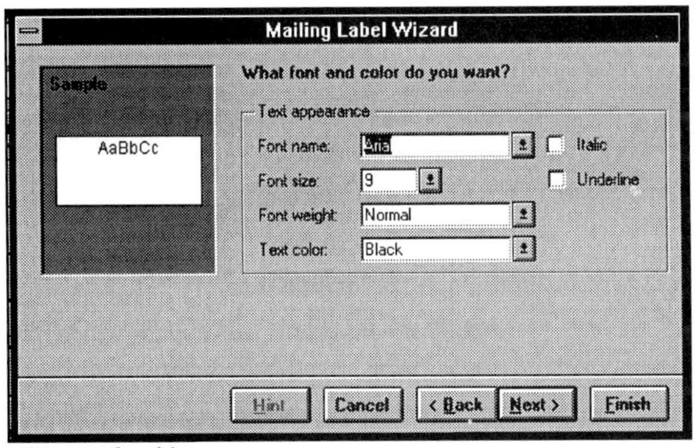

Figure 6 - 41

24. Click the **Next** > button.

25. We want to **See the mailing labels as they will look printed**, so click that option and click the **Finish** button. Do not check the Cue Cards box (see Figure 6 - 42).

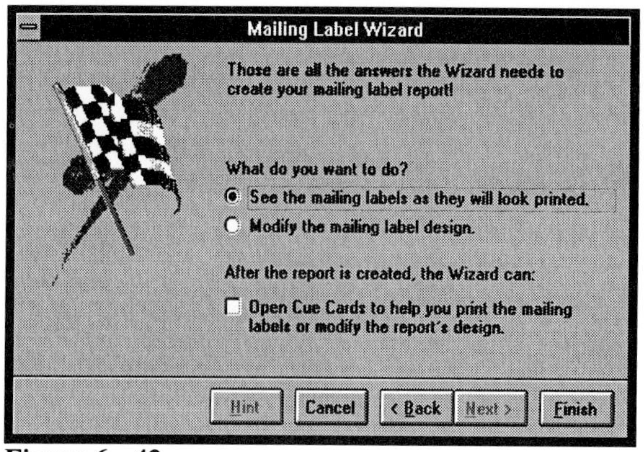

Figure 6 - 42

The progress can be monitored on the Status Bar as the Wizard puts the design together. The Wizard completes the design and moves to the Print Preview screen (see Figure 6 - 43).

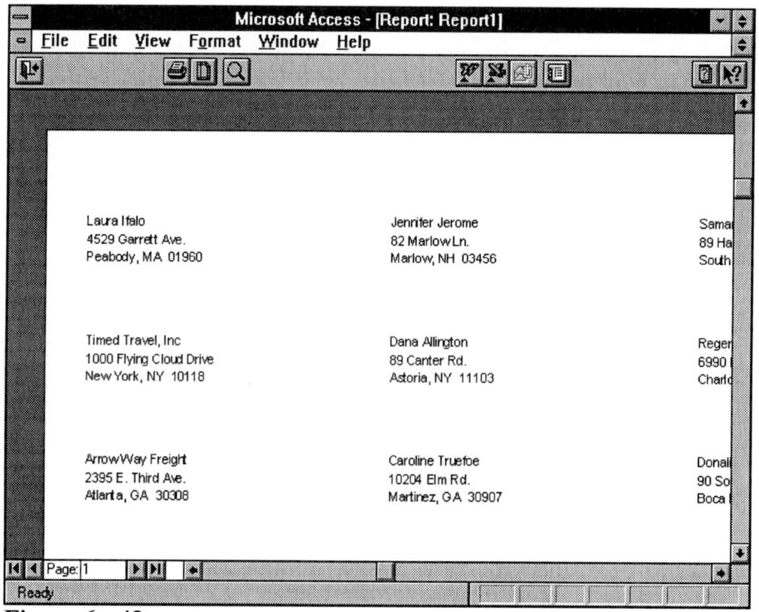

Figure 6 - 43

26. Save this design by picking **FILE/Save As**, entering **Customer Mailing Labels** as the Report Name, and clicking **OK**.
27. Maximize the Preview window.

    Notice that the labels are three across and in zip code order (see Figure 6 - 43).
28. Click anywhere on the white page to see the overall page (see Figure 6 - 44).
29. Print the report by clicking the **Print** button  on the toolbar and clicking **OK** in the dialog box.
30. Close the design with **FILE/Close**.

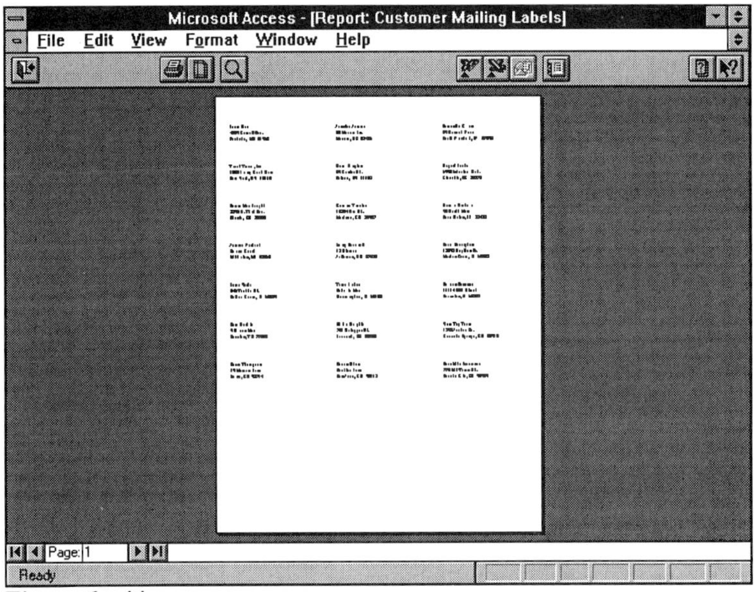

Figure 6 - 44

SUMMARY

In this Project, we have produced three different types of reports based on the data in the Customers table. The Tabular report contained listings from a query that selected only customers with an outstanding balance. It included totals in the report footer. We customized the design by removing one of the two totals. The second design was a Groups/Totals report for the customers grouped by state. We changed the formatting on some of its controls. The third design was for mailing labels, which were sorted by zip code.

In the final lesson we will see how to calculate with queries and how to alter the data in a table with the Action Queries.

KEY TERMS

Control
Detail Section
Footer
Formatting
Grouped
Groups/Totals Report
Handle
Header
Mailing Label Report
Properties List
Report Wizard
Tabular Report

INDEPENDENT PROJECTS

Independent Project 6.1: The School Newspaper

This Independent Project continues working with the Newspaper Ad database from Independent Project 5.1. The newspaper's business manager requires a report of the sales of ads grouped by the salespersons. The name of the salesperson, Ad Number, Price, and Purchased By fields are needed. Since that data resides in two separate tables, you will need to prepare a query to join the data from Sales Force and Ads first.

The top portion of the finished report should resemble Figure 6 - 45.

ADVERTISEMENT SALES

02-Jan-95

Last Name	First Name	Ad Number	Price	Purchased By
Fitzhugh	**George**			
		2395	$25.00	Lou's LaundroMat
		2394	$15.00	Dean's Office
		2391	$15.00	Harry Hertz
			$55.00	
			12.22%	
Kaples	**Leslie**			
		2396	$45.00	Student Grill
		2393	$25.00	Sports Booster Club
		2389	$85.00	Pizza Plus
		2387	$85.00	College Books
			$240.00	
			53.33%	

Figure 6 - 45

1. Run *Access* and maximize its window.
2. Open the **xercise1.mdb** database with **FILE/Open Database** or by clicking the **Open Database** tool on the toolbar, then clicking on the name **xercise1.mdb** and clicking the **OK** button.
3. Click on the **Query** button at the left edge of the database window.
4. Click the **New** button to start a new query.
5. Click the **New Query** button in the New Query dialog box.
6. Click on **Ads** in the list of tables and click the **Add** button.
7. Click on **Sales Force** in the list of tables and click the **Add** button. Access should link the two tables by the Salesperson ID field automatically.
8. Close the Add Table dialog box.
9. Double-click the **Last Name** field in the Sales Force table to add it to the QBE Grid.
10. Similarly, double-click on **First Name**, **Ad Number**, **Price**, and **Purchased By**.
11. Maximize the query window.
12. View the results by clicking the **Datasheet View** button to verify the query design.
13. Save the query by choosing **FILE/Save Query As**, entering the name **Sales**, and clicking the **OK** button.
14. Close the query with **FILE/Close**.
15. Begin creating the report by clicking on the **Report** tab at the left edge of the database window.
16. Click the **New** button.
17. Open the list of tables and queries by clicking the drop-down arrow and, remembering to carefully click just once, choose **Sales**.
18. Click on the **Report Wizards** button.
19. In the list of report types, click on **Groups/Totals** and click the **OK** button.

20. In the first Groups/Totals Report Wizard dialog box, click on the button with the **double arrow head pointing to the right** to include all fields from the query and click the **Next** button.
21. In the **Which fields do you want to group by?** dialog box, click on the button with the **single arrow head pointing to the right** to include only **Last Name**. Click **Next**.
22. You want **Normal** grouping, so make no changes in the **How do you want to group data in each field?** dialog box. Just click **Next**.
23. For **Which fields do you want to sort by?** pick no fields and click **Next**.
24. For **What style...** pick **Executive**, **Portrait**, and **0 in.** of extra Line spacing. Click **Next**.
25. Type the title **ADVERTISEMENT SALES**, leave the **X** on Calculate percentages, and do not check the other two options.
26. You want to **See the report with data in it**, so click on that option and click the **Finish** button.
27. Maximize the report window.
28. Totaling the Ad Numbers makes no sense, so you should remove that sum and percentage. To begin, click the **Close Window** tool to switch to the report design.
29. In the **Last Name Footer** section, click on the **=[Total_Ad Number]/[Grand Total]** control. Probably only about half of the name actually shows.
30. Press the **DELETE** key to remove that control.
31. Similarly, click on the **=Sum([Ad Number])** control in the Last Name Footer section and press **DELETE** to remove it.
32. Also click on the **line** immediately above the two controls you just removed and press **DELETE**.
33. Click on the **=Sum ([Ad Number])** control in the Report Footer and press **DELETE** to remove it.
34. Click on each of the **two lines** above where the =Sum([Ad Number]) control used to be and press **DELETE** to remove each of them.
35. Click on the title, **ADVERTISEMENT SALES**, and click the **Center-Align Text** tool.
36. Click the **Print Preview** button to examine the new results (see Figure 6 - 45).
37. Save the report by picking **FILE/Save As**, typing the name **Advertisement Sales**, and clicking the **OK** button.
38. Print the report by clicking the **Print** button on the toolbar and clicking **OK** in the Print dialog box.
39. Close the report with **FILE/Close**.
40. Close the database with **FILE/Close Database**.
41. If you need to exit from *Access* and/or Windows, do so properly.

Independent Project 6.2: The Book Store

This Independent Project continues working with the Book Store database from the earlier lessons. The owner has requested a report that lists the publisher, fax number, book titles, and cost for every book. Since that data resides in two separate tables, you will need to prepare a query to join the data from Publishers and Books first.

The top portion of the finished report should resemble Figure 6 - 46.

BOOKS BY PUBLISHER

Monday, January 9, 1995

Name	Area Code	Fax	Title	Cost
Atlantic Works	403	436-7440		
			Music Composition	$19.50
			Music Harmony	$19.50
Books Plus	205	430-7190		
			Even More Poems	$12.60
			The Physics of Glass	$4.75
Bulky Books	408	559-0018		
			Chemical Compendium	$34.50

Figure 6 - 46

1. Run *Access* and maximize its window.
2. Open the **xercise2.mdb** database with **FILE/Open Database** or by clicking the **Open Database** tool on the toolbar, then clicking on the name **xercise2.mdb** and clicking the **OK** button.
3. Click on the **Query** button at the left edge of the database window.
4. Click the **New** button to start a new query.
5. Click the **New Query** button in the New Query dialog box.
6. Click on **Publishers** in the list of tables and click the **Add** button.
7. Click on **Books** in the list of tables and click the **Add** button. Access should link the two tables by the Publisher Code field automatically.
8. Close the Add Table dialog box.
9. Double-click the **Name** field in the Publishers table to add it to the QBE Grid.
10. Similarly, double-click on **Area Code**, **Fax**, **Title**, and **Cost**.
11. Maximize the query window.
12. View the results by clicking the **Datasheet View** button to verify the query design.
13. Save the query by choosing **FILE/Save Query As**, entering the name **Publishers and Books**, and clicking the **OK** button.
14. Close the query with **FILE/Close**.
15. Begin creating the report by clicking on the **Report** tab at the left edge of the database window.
16. Click the **New** button.
17. Open the list of tables and queries by clicking the drop-down arrow and, remembering to carefully click just once, choose **Publishers and Books**. Click on the **Report Wizards** button.
18. In the list of report types, click on **Groups/Totals** and click the **OK** button.
19. In the first Groups/Totals Report Wizard dialog box, click on the button with the **double arrow head pointing to the right** to include all fields from the query and click the **Next** button.

20. In the **Which fields do you want to group by?** dialog box, click on the button with the **single arrow head pointing to the right** to include only **Name**. Click **Next**.
21. You want **Normal** grouping, so make no changes in the **How do you want to group data in each field?** dialog box. Just click **Next**.
22. For **Which fields do you want to sort by?**, pick **Title** and click the **single arrow head pointing to the right**. Click **Next**.
23. For **What style...**, pick **Executive**, **Portrait**, and **0 in.** of extra Line spacing. Click **Next**.
24. In the next dialog box type the title **BOOKS BY PUBLISHER**, remove the **X** on Calculate percentages, and do not check the other two options.
25. You want to **See the report with data in it**, so click on that option and click the **Finish** button.
26. Maximize the report window.
27. Scroll to the right edge of the report by clicking the scroll bar arrow.
28. Totaling the Costs makes no sense, so you should remove both the Grand Total and subtotals, as well as the ruling lines. To begin, click the **Close Window** tool to switch to the design.
29. Scroll to the right edge of the report design, then, in the **Name Footer** section, click on the **=Sum([Cost])** control.
30. Press the **DELETE** key to remove that control.
31. Similarly, click on the **short horizontal line** control immediately above where the =Sum([Cost]) control used to be and press **DELETE** to remove it.
32. Scroll to the bottom of the report design, and click on the **=Sum([Cost])** control in the **Report Footer** section. Press the **DELETE** key to remove that control.
33. Click on the **Grand Total label** control and press **DELETE** to remove it.
34. Also click on each of the **two short lines** immediately above the control you just removed and press **DELETE** for each.
35. Click on the **date** control in the **Report Header**.
36. Click the **Properties** button on the toolbar to open the Properties List.
37. In the top section of the dialog box, click on the drop-down arrow and choose **All Properties**.
38. On the third line of the named properties it says **Format**. Click on the white text box to the right of **Format**, and click the drop-down arrow that appears.
39. In the drop-down list, scroll upward to find **Long Date** and click on it.
40. Click the **Properties** button on the toolbar to close the Properties List.
41. Click the **Italics** button on the toolbar to remove italics from the date and click the **Bold** button to make the date bold.
42. Click the **Print Preview** button to examine the new results (see Figure 6 - 46).
43. Save the report by picking **FILE/Save As**, typing the name **Publishers and Books**, and clicking the **OK** button.
44. Print the report by clicking the **Print** button on the toolbar and clicking **OK** in the Print dialog box.
45. Close the report with **FILE/Close**.
46. Close the database with **FILE/Close Database**.
47. If you need to exit from *Access* and/or Windows, do so properly.

Independent Project 6.3: The Real Estate Office

This Independent Project continues working with the Real Estate Office database from the earlier lessons. The owner has requested a report that lists the commercial properties grouped by agency. From the Agencies table you should include the Agency Name and Phone 1. From the Commercial Listings table include the Agent, Address, City, and Price. Since that data resides in two separate tables, you will need to prepare a query to join the data first.

The top portion of the finished report should resemble Figure 6 - 47.

Agency Listings

16-Jan-95

Agency Name	Phone 1	Agent	Address	City	Price
George Winkle	*972-9538*				
		Purcell	3 Research Park	Stamford	$3,400,000.00
Priceless Properties	*359-1111*				
		Green	Maple Court	New Canaan	$125,000.00
		Ruth	2 Research Park	Stamford	$3,400,000.00
Profitable Properties	*748-3471*				
		Smith	952 River Rd.	Stamford	$49,000.00
			1 Lewis Way	Danbury	$125,000.00

Figure 6 - 47

1. Run *Access* and maximize its window.
2. Open the **xercise3.mdb** database.
3. Begin a new query.
4. Add **Agencies** and then **Commercial Listings** to the top section of the query window.
5. Close the Add Table dialog box.

!

NOTE*: Access should have linked the two tables by Agency Code, but, if not, click on the Agency Code field in Agencies and drag across to the matching field in Commercial Listings to link the two tables by hand.*

6. Add **Agency Name** and **Phone 1** from Agencies to the QBE Grid.
7. Similarly, add **Agent**, **Address**, **City**, and **Price** from Commercial Listings to the QBE Grid.
8. Maximize the query window.
9. View the results to verify the query design.
10. Save the query as **Agency Listings**.
11. Close the query.
12. Begin creating the report by clicking on the **Report** tab at the left edge of the database window.
13. Use the **Agency Listings** query as the basis of the report.

14. Let the **Report Wizard** design a **Groups/Totals** report.
15. Include all fields from the query without changing the order.
16. Group by **Agency Name**.
17. Use **Normal** grouping.
18. Sort by **Agent**.
19. Use **Executive** style, **Landscape** orientation, and **0 in.** of extra Line spacing.
20. Use the title **Agency Listings** and eliminate all options. You want to **See the report with data in it**.
21. Maximize the report window.
22. Scroll to the right edge of the report. Totaling the Prices makes no sense for real estate properties, so you should remove both the Grand Total and sub-totals, as well as their ruling lines from the design.
23. Close the preview window to switch to the report design.
24. Scroll to the right edge of the report design and delete the =**Sum([Price])** control from the **Agency Name Footer**.
25. Similarly, delete the **short horizontal line** control from the **Agency Name Footer**.
26. Scroll to the bottom of the report design and delete the =**Sum([Price])** control from the **Report Footer** section.
27. Delete the **Grand Total label** control.
28. Delete each of the **two short lines** from the **Report Footer** section.
29. In the **Report Header** change the title, **Agency Listings**, to **20 point** characters and center it.
30. In the Agency Name Header, change the **Phone 1** field control to **italics** instead of bold.
31. Select the **Agent** field control in the **Detail section** and open the Properties List.
32. Change the **Hide Duplicates** property to **Yes** so the agents' names will not repeat on successive lines.
33. Close the Properties List.
34. Remove italics from the **date**.
35. Examine the new results with print preview (see Figure 6 - 47).
36. Save the report with the name **Agency Listings**.
37. Print the report.
38. Close the report.
39. Close the database.
40. If you need to exit from *Access* and/or Windows, do so properly.

Independent Project 6.4: The Veterinarian

This Independent Project continues working with the veterinarian database from the earlier lessons. She has requested a report that lists the pets grouped by owner. She hands you a sample of what the report should look like (see Figure 6 - 48). Since that data resides in two separate tables, you will need to prepare a query to join the data first. Create the query and save it, then create the report, save the report design, and print the report.

Owners and Pets

Tuesday, January 17, 1995

Owner Name	Area Code	Phone	Pet Name	Type	Date of Last Visit
Albert Smith	**203**	**359-4181**			
			Runner	horse	2/1/95
			Wild Thing	dog	4/20/95
			Fifi	cat	2/20/95
			Homer	dog	2/1/95
Dan Wilson	**203**	**972-3571**			
			Wilhelm	horse	1/15/95
			Spot	dog	2/1/95
Mureen Utley	**203**	**359-8152**			
			Kuddles	cat	3/8/95
			George	dog	1/15/95
			Fluffy	cat	3/8/95

Figure 6 - 48

Lessons 7 Calculations and Action Queries

Objectives

In this lesson you will learn how to:

- Perform calculations in queries
- Calculate summary results with queries
- Query a query
- Group a summary result
- Perform an update query
- Carry out a delete query

PROJECT DESCRIPTION

Besides the capability of selecting matching records and sorting those results, queries can also perform calculations on the data in one or more tables. The calculated results can be anything from a simple arithmetic operation like **Sale Amount** + **Tax** or **Commission Rate** * **Total Sale** to more complicated calculations. Summary calculations are also possible like **Average Price** or **Sum of the Salaries**.

Yet another type of query, the *Action Query*, can alter the data in a table. One type of Action Query is the *Delete Query*. It can delete groups of records from a table. Another type is the *Update Query* which can replace or update the entries in many or all records.

In the first part of this lesson we will calculate several sets of results from the CDROM table. The simple calculations will first produce a list of inventory values (see Figure 7 - 3), and then a price list for a 25% off sale (see Figure 7 - 7). In the second part we will calculate summary results including the average price of a CDROM and the total inventory value. The third part of this lesson will use grouping within a summary calculation, where we will calculate the minimum and maximum price for each type of CDROM (see Figure 7 - 15). In the last part we will use action queries to change the data in the CDROM table. We will lower all prices by 7%, and then delete the out-of-date CDROMs.

CALCULATIONS IN QUERIES

To perform calculations with queries, set up the query with the required table in the top of the **Query** window and the desired fields in the QBE Grid. Then, create a new field in the QBE Grid by typing on the **Field**: line the name you want it to have in the resulting dynaset followed by a colon and the desired calculation. The value in a field can be included in a calculation by enclosing the field name between square brackets. For example, the values in the Price field would be included in a calculation as **[Price]**.

Suppose you needed to calculate a 10% commission based on the amount in a field named Sale Amount, and wanted to name the result Commission. You would enter on the **Field**: line in a new column of the QBE Grid: **Commission:[Sale Amount]*0.10**. To create a calculation for Total Cost where the field containing the amount of the sale is named Sale Amount and the field holding the shipping expense is named Shipping, type on the **Field**: line of the QBE Grid: **Total Cost:[Sale Amount]+[Shipping]**.

To set up a Calculation Query:

- Click the **Query** tab on the left edge of the **Database** window.
- Click the **New** button at the top of the **Database** window.
- Choose the **New Query** button.
- Add the desired table (or tables) from the **Add Table** dialog box.
- Select any regular fields you will need to see in addition to the calculated result.
- Create the calculation in a new column in the QBE Grid.
- View the resulting dynaset.

Activity 7.1: A Calculation Query for Inventory Value

Your manager asks you to calculate the inventory value of the CDROMs currently in stock. Since inventory value is calculated as **Cost*Quantity in Stock**, we need to create a calculated field with that formula in a query. After we have the calculated values, we will sort the list from largest inventory value to smallest.

1. The **Sales** database should be open.
2. Click on the **Query** tab.
3. Click the **New** button at the top of the **Database** window.
4. In the **New Query** dialog box, click on the **New Query** button.
5. Since we are interested in the CDROM table, pick **CDROM** and click the **Add** button.
6. CDROM is the only table we need to calculate Inventory Value, so click the **Close** button to close the **Add Table** dialog box.
7. Double-click on the **Title** field in the list of fields to include it as the first field in the QBE Grid.
8. Press **TAB** to jump to the second column.
9. Type: **Inventory Value:[Cost]*[Quantity in Stock]** to create the calculation (Figure 7 - 1).

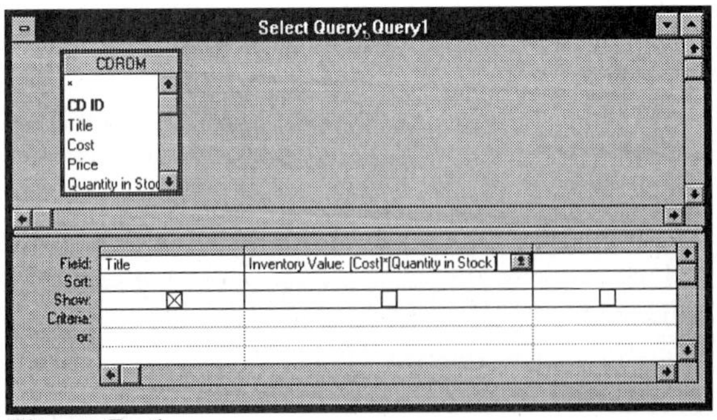

Figure 7 - 1

*Although the **Show**: box is not currently checked, Access will check it for you automatically.*

10. So you can see the entire entry, move the mouse pointer on top of the right edge of the **selector bar**, and drag it further to the right to widen the calculated column in the QBE Grid.

11. Click the **Datasheet View** button on the toolbar to see the resulting dynaset (Figure 7 - 2).

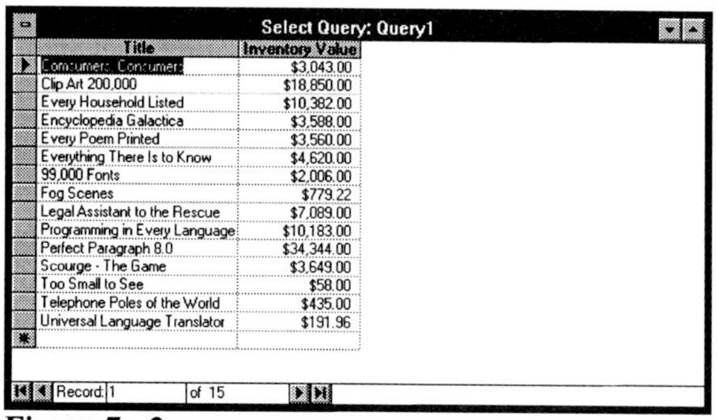

Select Query: Query1

Title	Inventory Value
Comsumers, Consumers	$3,043.00
Clip Art 200,000	$18,850.00
Every Household Listed	$10,382.00
Encyclopedia Galactica	$3,588.00
Every Poem Printed	$3,560.00
Everything There Is to Know	$4,620.00
99,000 Fonts	$2,006.00
Fog Scenes	$779.22
Legal Assistant to the Rescue	$7,089.00
Programming in Every Language	$10,183.00
Perfect Paragraph 8.0	$34,344.00
Scourge - The Game	$3,649.00
Too Small to See	$58.00
Telephone Poles of the World	$435.00
Universal Language Translator	$191.96

Record: 1 of 15

Figure 7 - 2

Each product should be listed together with its calculated inventory value, but they are not in order of inventory value.

12. Return to the query design by clicking the **Design View** button on the toolbar.
13. Click the mouse on the **Sort:** line of the **Inventory Value:** column.
14. Click the drop-down arrow to open the list of sort operators and pick **Descending**.
15. Click the **Datasheet View** button on the toolbar to see the resulting dynaset (see Figure 7 - 3).

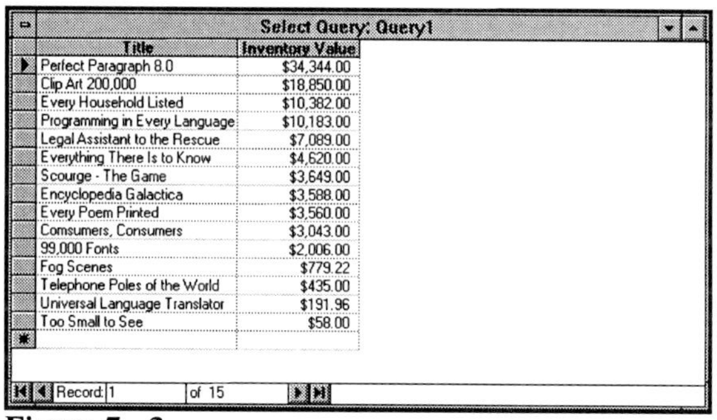

Select Query: Query1

Title	Inventory Value
Perfect Paragraph 8.0	$34,344.00
Clip Art 200,000	$18,850.00
Every Household Listed	$10,382.00
Programming in Every Language	$10,183.00
Legal Assistant to the Rescue	$7,089.00
Everything There Is to Know	$4,620.00
Scourge - The Game	$3,649.00
Encyclopedia Galactica	$3,588.00
Every Poem Printed	$3,560.00
Comsumers, Consumers	$3,043.00
99,000 Fonts	$2,006.00
Fog Scenes	$779.22
Telephone Poles of the World	$435.00
Universal Language Translator	$191.96
Too Small to See	$58.00

Record: 1 of 15

Figure 7 - 3

The product with the largest inventory value should be on top.

16. Pick **FILE/Save Query As**, enter the name: **Inventory Value**, and click **OK** to save this query.
17. Click the **Print** button on the toolbar and click **OK**.
18. Click the **Design View** button to return to the query design.

Activity 7.2: Calculating Discounted Prices

The company decides to run a holiday 25% off sale. You need to calculate the new, reduced prices. If you take 25% off, that leaves 75% of the regular price. Thus, the calculation is Price*0.75.

Since CDROM is already in the **Query** window, we will merely modify the current query. This is a one-time sale, and so it does not need to be saved.

1. Return to the query design by clicking the **Design View** button on the toolbar.

2. Click on the **selector bar** at the top of the **Inventory Value** column.
3. Press **DELETE** to remove everything in that column.
4. Double-click on **Price** in the list of fields to include it in the second column of the QBE Grid.
5. On the **Field**: line of the empty third column type: **Discounted Price:[Price]*0.75** to create the calculation.
6. Widen the field so you can see the entire entry as in Figure 7 - 4.

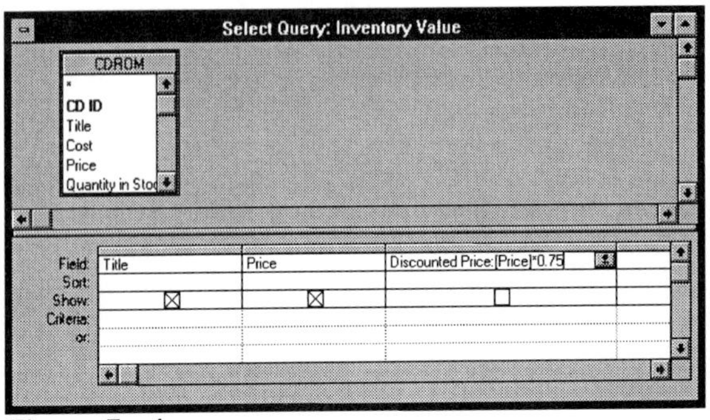

Figure 7 - 4

7. Click the **Datasheet View** button on the toolbar to see the resulting dynaset (see Figure 7 - 5).

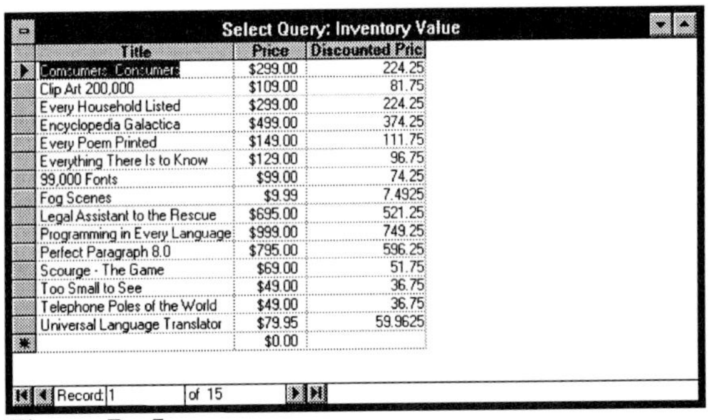

Figure 7 - 5

Each product will be listed together with its regular price and the discounted price, but the calculated results are not formatted to look like prices.

8. Return to the query design by clicking the **Design View** button on the toolbar.
9. With the cursor anywhere in the **Discounted Price** column, click the **Properties** button on the toolbar (see Figure 7 - 6).

   The Properties List for this field in the query opens. Although our previous exposure to Properties was on a report design, almost everything in Access has a Properties List that controls its details and options.

10. Click on the **Format** line in the Properties List, click the drop-down arrow to open the list of formats, and pick **Currency**.

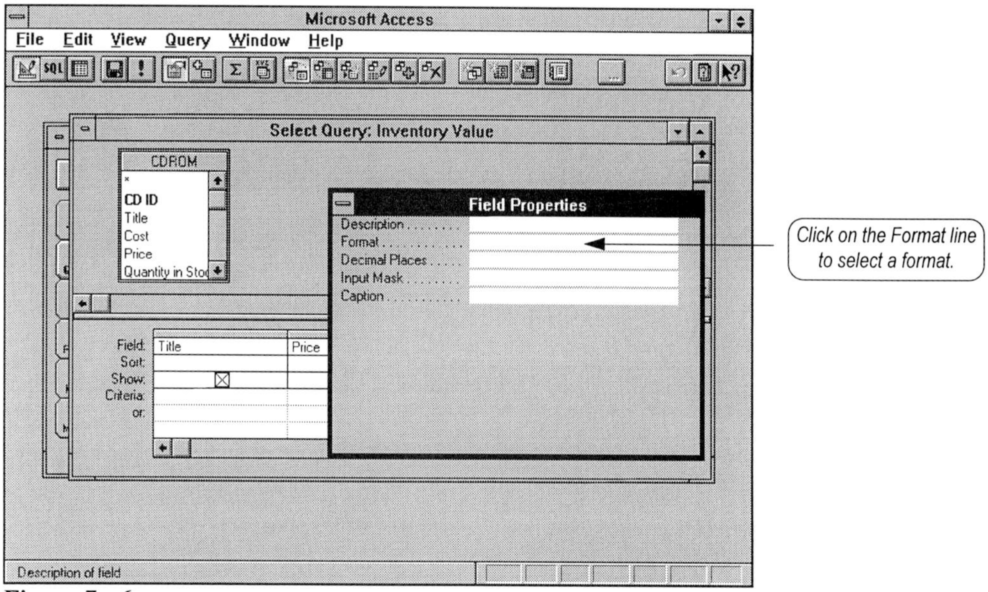

Figure 7 - 6

11. Close the Property List by clicking the **Properties** button again.
12. Click the **Datasheet View** button on the toolbar to see the result (see Figure 7 - 7).

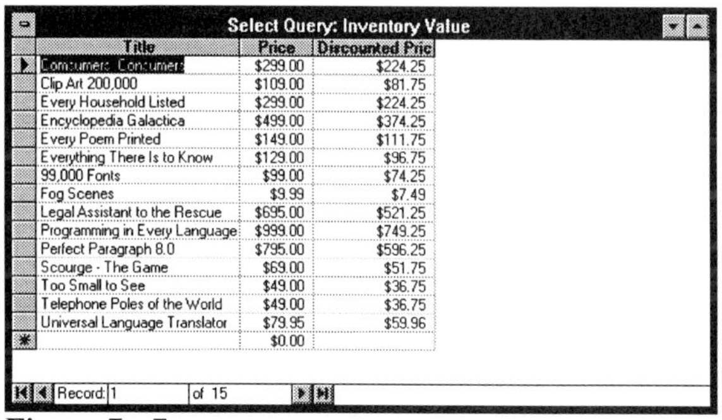

Select Query: Inventory Value

Title	Price	Discounted Pric
Consumers Consumers	$299.00	$224.25
Clip Art 200,000	$109.00	$81.75
Every Household Listed	$299.00	$224.25
Encyclopedia Galactica	$499.00	$374.25
Every Poem Printed	$149.00	$111.75
Everything There Is to Know	$129.00	$96.75
99,000 Fonts	$99.00	$74.25
Fog Scenes	$9.99	$7.49
Legal Assistant to the Rescue	$695.00	$521.25
Programming in Every Language	$999.00	$749.25
Perfect Paragraph 8.0	$795.00	$596.25
Scourge - The Game	$69.00	$51.75
Too Small to See	$49.00	$36.75
Telephone Poles of the World	$49.00	$36.75
Universal Language Translator	$79.95	$59.96
	$0.00	

Record: 1 of 15

Figure 7 - 7

13. Click the **Print** button on the toolbar to print the dynaset and click **OK** in the Print dialog box.
14. Choose **FILE/Close** to close the query.

    As this is a one-time sale, we do not need to save this query.
15. Click the **No** button in answer to **Save changes to Query**.

SUMMARY CALCULATIONS IN QUERIES

Rather than producing a calculated result for each listing as in the previous section, a *summary calculation* produces an overall result. Examples would include the count of how many products are in the CDROM table, the average price of all products, or the total inventory value of the entire CDROM table.

To perform a Summary Calculation Query:

- Click the **Query** tab on the left edge of the **Database** window.
- Click the **New** button at the top of the **Database** window.
- Choose the **New Query** button.
- Add the desired table (or tables) from the **Add Table** dialog box.
- Select the field(s) you want summarized.
- Switch the query into a summary query by clicking the **Totals** button Σ on the toolbar or choosing **VIEW/Totals** in the menu. This will add a **Total**: line to the QBE Grid (see Figure 7 - 8), where you select the desired summary calculation.
- Open the drop-down list on the new **Total:** line, and pick the summary operation.
- View the resulting dynaset.

Activity 7.3: A Summary Calculation Query for Average Price

We want to know the average price of a CDROM. We will not save this query.

1. The **SALES** database should be open.
2. Click on the **Query** tab.
3. Click the **New** button at the top of the **Database** window.
4. In the **New Query** dialog box, click on the **New Query** button.
5. Since we are interested in the CDROM table, pick **CDROM** and click the **Add** button.
6. CDROM is the only table we need to calculate Average Price, so click the **Close** button to close the **Add Table** dialog box.
7. Double-click on the **Price** field in the list of fields to include it in the QBE Grid.
8. Click the **Totals** button Σ on the toolbar to include the **Total**: line in the QBE Grid (see Figure 7 - 8).

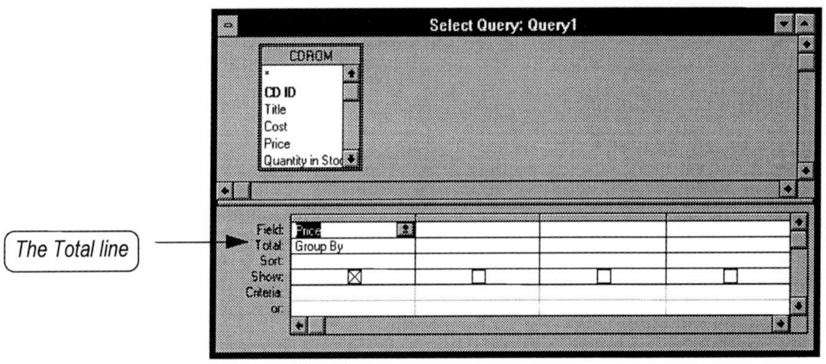

Figure 7 - 8

*The **Group By** operator will appear on the **Totals**: line. We will discuss its meaning in the section on Grouping two sections ahead.*

9. Click on the **Total**: line in the **Price** column and click the drop-down arrow that appears in order to open the list of operations.
10. Choose **Avg** by clicking on it (see Figure 7 - 9).

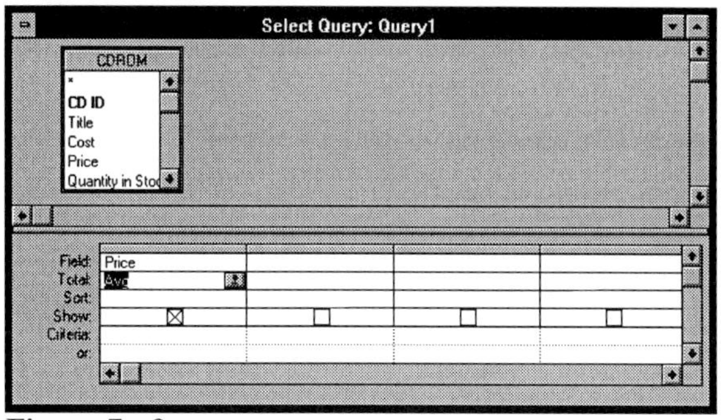

Figure 7 - 9

11. Click the **Datasheet View** button on the toolbar to see the result.

    The answer for the average price should be $288.60.

12. Choose **FILE/Close** to close the query.
13. Click the **No** button in answer to **Save changes to Query...**.

QUERYING A QUERY

Just as a table can be the basis for a query, so can another query. Instead of selecting a table name from the list in the **Add Table** dialog box, click on the **Queries** option and select from the queries that are listed. In all other ways the operation is identical to a query based on a table.

To perform a Query based on a Query:

- Open the **Select Query** window.
- Click on the **Queries** option (see Figure 7 - 10) in the **View** section of the **Add Table** dialog box.

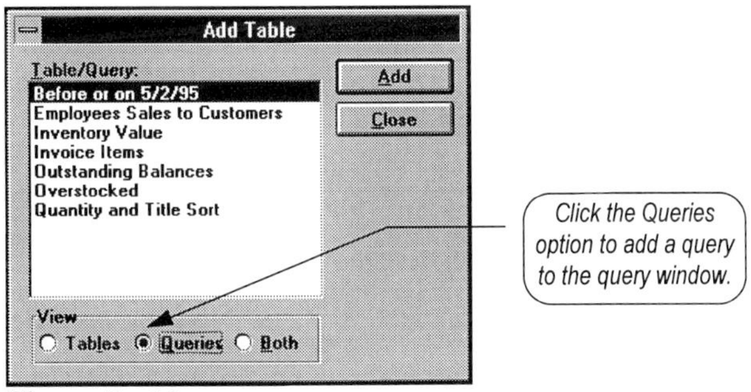

Figure 7 - 10

- Add the desired query and close the **Add Table** dialog box.
- Add any desired field(s) and set up any calculations.
- View the resulting dynaset.

Activity 7.4: A Summary Calculation for Total Inventory Value

From the Inventory Value query we did earlier, we want to know the total inventory value of all the products combined. We will save this query.

1. The **Sales** database should be open.
2. Click on the **Query** tab.
3. Click the **New** button at the top of the **Database** window.
4. In the **New Query** dialog box, click on the **New Query** button.
5. Since we are interested in the results from the Inventory Value query we performed earlier, click the **Queries** option under View in the bottom of the **Add Table** dialog box (see Figure 7 - 10).
6. Pick **Inventory Value** and click the **Add** button.
7. Close the **Add Table** dialog box.
8. Double-click on the **Inventory Value** field in the list of fields to include it in the QBE Grid.
9. Click the **Totals** button Σ on the toolbar to include the **Total**: line in the QBE Grid.
10. Click on the **Total**: line in the **Inventory Value** column and click the drop-down arrow that appears in the column to open the list of operations.
11. Choose **Sum** (see Figure 7 - 11).

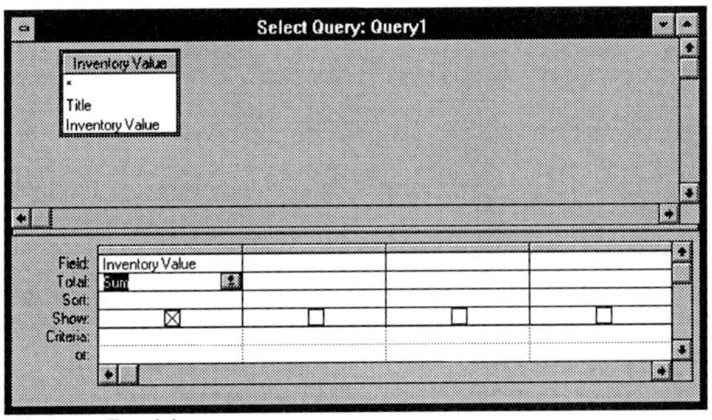

Figure 7 - 11

12. Click the **Datasheet View** button on the toolbar to see the result.

    The total inventory value should be $102,778.18.
13. Save the query by picking **FILE/Save Query As**, entering the name: **Total Inventory Value**, and clicking the **OK** button.
14. Choose **FILE/Close** to close the query.

GROUPING IN CALCULATIONS

The CDROM table has classifications for the types of CDROMs in the **Notes** field. We need to know the maximum and minimum price for each category.

This last phrase, for each category, means we do not want the one maximum and minimum for all the items in the table; we want the CDROMs grouped by type and then the maximum and minimum within each category. The *Group By* operator that appears automatically when you switch a query to a Totals query does exactly that. It makes groups based on the values in each field that contains the Group By operator, and summarizes the groups. Our grouping field will be **Notes**.

Since the Group By operator appears automatically on the Totals: line, you must be careful not to include in the QBE Grid any fields that contain different values within a single group. If you do, *Access* will group more finely than you intended. For example, if we included the titles for the CDROMs in the QBE Grid, the maximum and minimum would be grouped by each different title instead of by the type. There is no way to remove the Group By operator; thus you may not include the field.

To use the Group By operator in summary queries:

- Set up the query.
- Switch the query into a summary query by clicking the **Totals** button [Σ] on the toolbar or choose **VIEW/Totals** in the menu.
- In the field that is to be summarized, open the drop-down list on the **Total:** line, and pick the summary operation.
- In all other fields leave the Group By operator.
- View the resulting dynaset.

Activity 7.5: Grouping in Summary Calculations

We need the maximum and minimum price for each type of CDROM. To calculate those results, we need to perform a summary calculation using the **Notes** and **Price** fields from the CDROM table. We will save this query.

1. The **Sales** database should be open.
2. Click on the **Query** tab.
3. Click the **New** button at the top of the **Database** window.
4. In the **New Query** dialog box, click on the **New Query** button.
5. Pick **CDROM** and click the **Add** button.
6. Close the **Add Table** dialog box.
7. Double-click on the **Notes** field in the list of fields.
8. Double-click on the **Price** field.
9. Click the **Totals** button [Σ] on the toolbar to include the **Total**: line in the QBE Grid.
10. Click on the **Total**: line in the **Price** column and click the drop-down arrow that appears in order to open the list of operations.
11. Choose **Min** (see Figure 7 - 12).
12. Leave **Group By** in the **Notes** column (see Figure 7 - 12).

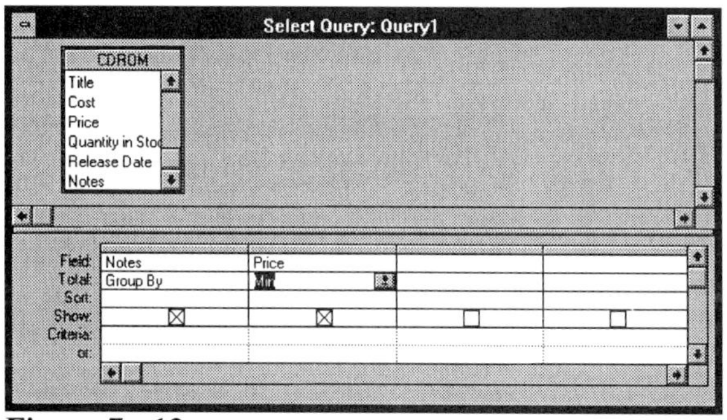

Figure 7 - 12

13. Click the **Datasheet View** button on the toolbar to see the result (see Figure 7 - 13).

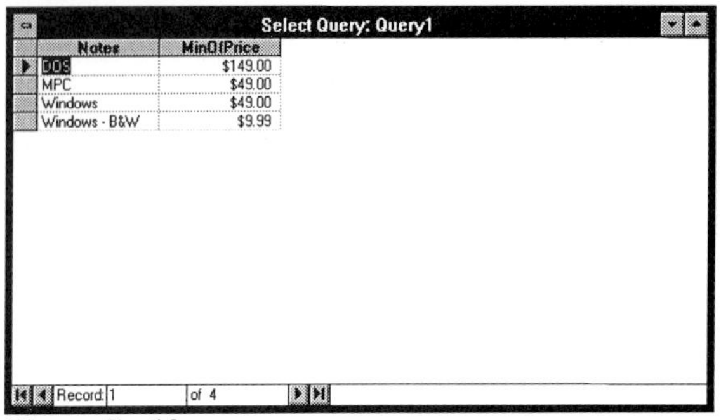

Figure 7 - 13

*Each type from the **Notes** field should have one line with a minimum Price. But we also need the Maximum Price.*

14. Click the **Design View** button to return to the design.
15. Double-click on the **Price** field again to include a second copy of that field in the QBE Grid (see Figure 7 - 14).
16. Click on the **Totals**: line in this second **Price** column and click the drop-down arrow that appears in order to open the list of operations.
17. Choose **Max** (see Figure 7 - 14).

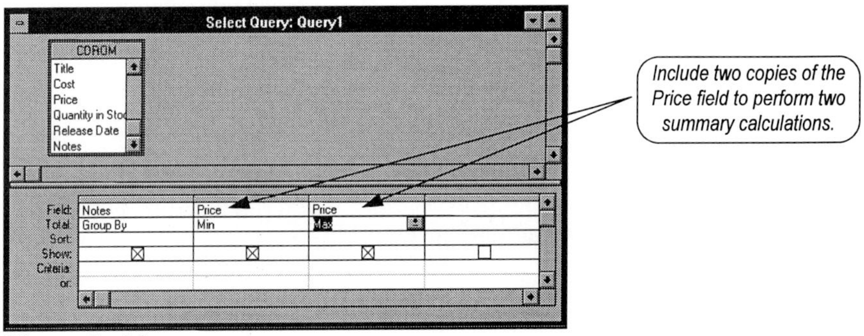

Figure 7 - 14

18. Click the **Datasheet View** button on the toolbar to see the result (see Figure 7 - 15).

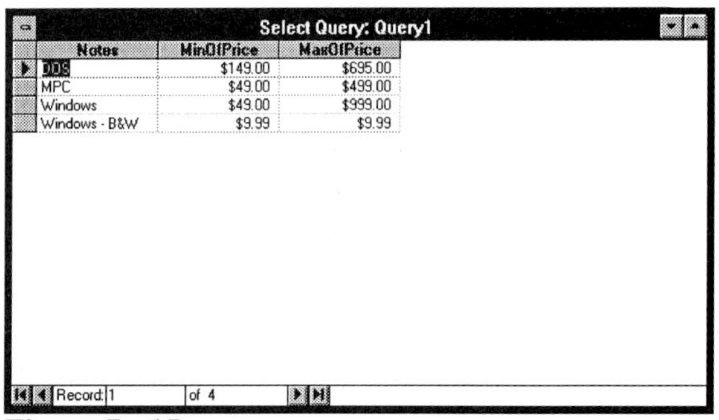

Figure 7 - 15

For each type of CDROM, both the Minimum and the Maximum Price should be listed.

19. Save the query by picking **FILE/Save Query As**, entering the name: **Min & Max Price by CDROM Type**, and clicking the **OK** button.
20. Click the **Print** button on the toolbar and click **OK**.
21. Choose **FILE/Close** to close the query.

THE UPDATE QUERY

Just as we often need to edit the data in various records to keep it up to date, there are occasions when many or all of the records need the same change to one or more fields. For example, when an area code changes, dozens of customers may need their records updated. Perhaps the manager decides to lower all prices of CDROMs by 7%. Such mass changes would be tedious and prone to error if edited one record at a time. The solution is the Update Query.

An Update Query will alter the values in one or more fields in selected records or every record throughout an entire table in one operation. You set up a regular query, then convert it to an Update Query with the toolbar button or the menu choice **QUERY/Update**. This adds a new line to the QBE Grid named **Update To:** and removes the **Sort**: and **Show**: lines (Figure 7 - 16). The **Update To**: line is where you specify the new value or calculated value for the field.

To perform an Update Query:

- Open the **Select Query** window.
- Click the **Update Query** button  on the toolbar or pick **QUERY/Update** in the menu.
- Add the field(s) that will be updated.
- Add the fields and enter any criteria to restrict which records will be updated.
- To perform the update, click the **Run** button  on the toolbar or choose **QUERY/Run** in the menu.

Activity 7.6: An Update Query

Because of increased competition, we need to lower our prices. The decision is made to lower them 7%. We will save this query.

1. The **Sales** database should be open.
2. Click on the **Query** tab.
3. Click the **New** button at the top of the **Database** window.
4. In the **New Query** dialog box, click on the **New Query** button.
5. Since we need to change prices in the CDROM table, pick **CDROM** and click the **Add** button.
6. Close the **Add Table** dialog box.
7. Double-click on the **Price** field in the list of fields to include it as the first field in the QBE Grid.
8. Click the **Update Query** button  on the toolbar to switch the query type (Figure 7 - 16).

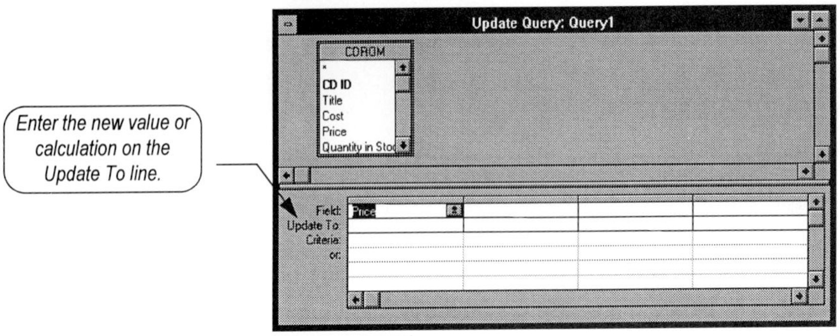

Figure 7 - 16

9. Click on the **Update To**: line in the **Price** column and enter **[Price]*0.93** (see Figure 7 - 17).

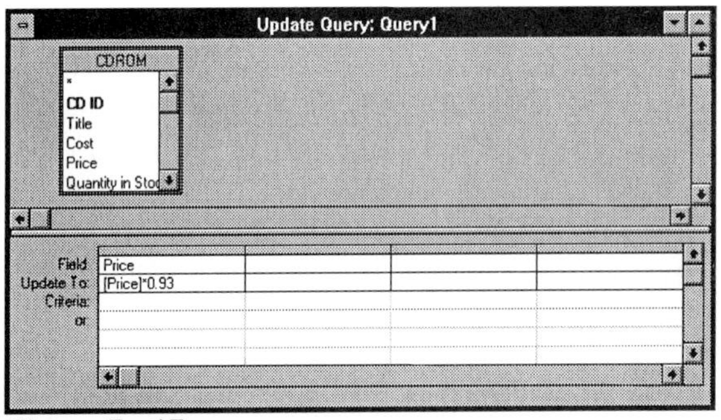

Figure 7 - 17

Since the original price was 100%, reducing the prices by 7% would leave 93%.

10. Before we make the changes, click the **Datasheet View** button on the toolbar to see the original prices as shown in Figure 7 - 18.

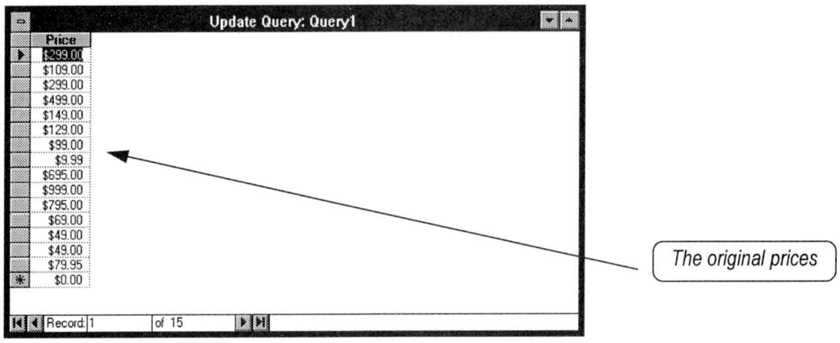

Figure 7 - 18

11. Write down the first price.
12. Return to the design by clicking the **Design View** button on the toolbar.
13. Click the **Run** button on the toolbar to initiate the changes.
14. Click the **OK** button in the **15 row(s) will be updated.** alert box (Figure 7 - 19).

When you click the OK button, Access changes the data in the original table. Thus, you must be sure you mean to update the records.

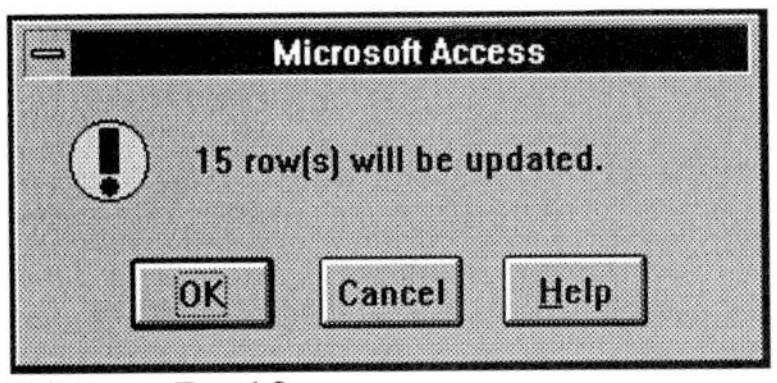

Figure 7 - 19

15. Click the **Datasheet View** button  on the toolbar to see the altered prices (Figure 7 - 20).

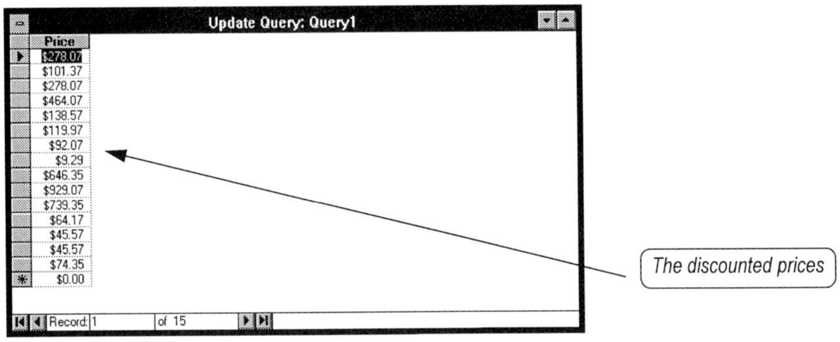

Figure 7 - 20

The new prices should be a bit lower than they were a minute ago. Compare the new first price with the original price you wrote down in step 11.

16. Save the query by picking **FILE/Save Query As**, entering the name: **Reduce Prices 7%**, and clicking the **OK** button.
17. Choose **FILE/Close** to close the query.

Notice the different icon in front of the name of an action query (see Figure 7 - 21). That is to warn you that this query alters the data in the table.

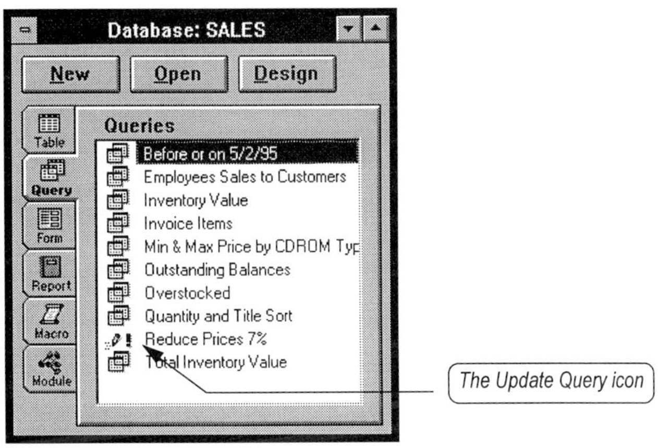

Figure 7 - 21

THE DELETE QUERY

Eventually a table contains outdated records and the owner may decide to delete those listings. In a previous lesson we deleted a single record by selecting it and pressing the **DELETE** key. While that method is fine for a few records, it would get tedious if there were dozens or hundreds of records to delete. For such an operation one would use a Delete Query.

When a Delete Query is run, the deletion of records is permanent. Therefore, it is common practice (and wise) to set up the same criteria in a Select Query first, and view the resulting listings to confirm that the desired records will be deleted. Once the criteria have been verified, convert the query to a Delete Query and run it.

The * (asterisk) symbol at the top of the field listings in the top section of the **query** window (see Figure 7 - 22) is required for a Delete Query. The * represents all of the fields as a single block. It can be used in Select Queries too, but does not allow access to individual fields, so is rarely used that way. For Delete Queries, however, it is always placed in the first column of the QBE Grid. The * will be preceded by the table name and a period. For our query using the CDROM table that will place **CDROM.*** on the **Field**: line of the first column (see Figure 7 - 23). The fields for the criteria are then placed in the following columns and the criteria entered.

When the query is converted to a Delete Query, a **Delete**: line will be added as the second line of the QBE Grid (see Figure 7 - 26). The **Sort**: and **Show**: lines disappear. The **CDROM.*** column will show the word **From**, and all other columns will get **Where**. The word **From** marks the table from which the records will be deleted. The word **Where** designates the criteria.

To perform a Delete Query:

- Open the **Select Query** window with the table that contains the records to be deleted.
- Add the * (asterisk) from the list of fields in the table in the upper panel of the window (see Figure 7 - 22).

Add the asterisk to the QBE Grid to represent all fields for a Delete Query.

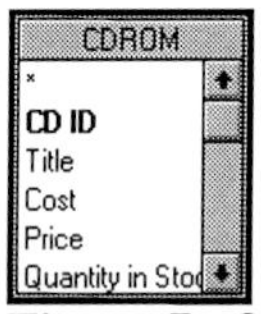

Figure 7 - 22

- Add the single field or combination of fields that hold the criteria as to which records should be deleted.
- Enter the criteria.
- View the resulting dynaset to confirm that the correct records have been selected.
- Switch the query into a delete query by clicking the **Delete Query** button on the toolbar or choosing **QUERY/Delete** in the menu.
- Run the query.

Activity 7.7: A Delete Query

Since orders for DOS CDROMs have fallen substantially in the last sales period, the company has decided CDROMs for DOS are outdated and should be dropped from the inventory. Your job is to remove the DOS CDROM listings from the CDROM table. Since the **Notes** field contains the type DOS, that is the field where we will test for the criterion.

1. The **Sales** database should be open.
2. Click on the **Query** tab.

3. Click the **New** button at the top of the **Database** window.
4. In the **New Query** dialog box, click on the **New Query** button.
5. Since we will delete the outdated DOS CDROMs, click on **CDROM**, click **Add**, and then close the **Add Table** dialog box.
6. Double-click the * at the top of the list of fields to install it in the first column of the QBE Grid (see Figure 7 - 23).

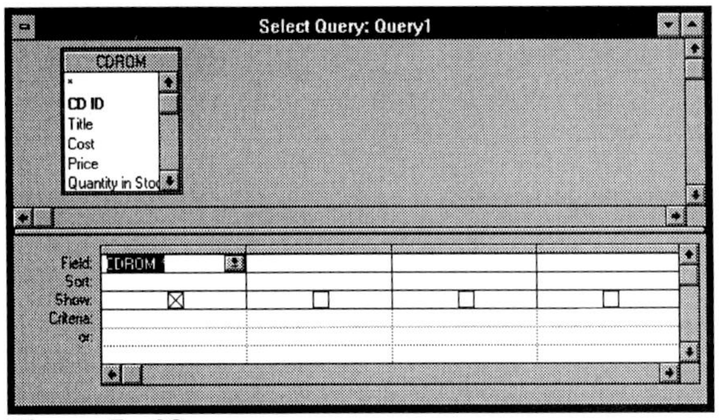

Figure 7 - 23

*The **Field**: line will show **CDROM.*** in the first column.*

7. Double-click the **Notes** field to place it in the second column of the QBE Grid.
8. On the **Criteria**: line in the **Notes** column of the QBE Grid, enter: **like "*DOS*"** (see Figure 7 - 24).

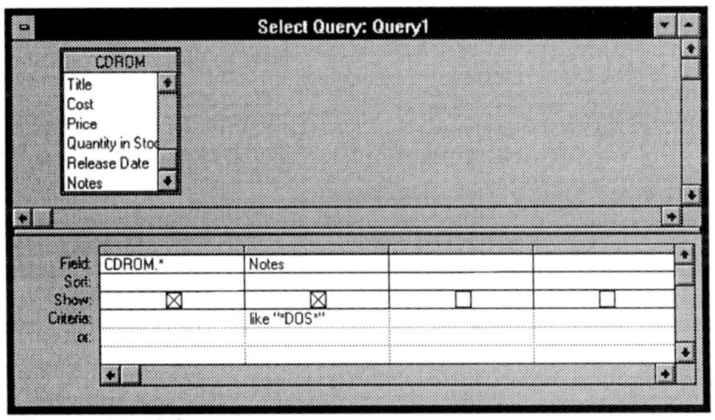

Figure 7 - 24

*The wild cards at the beginning and end of DOS will guarantee we find all records that contain DOS anywhere within the **Notes** field.*

9. Click the **Datasheet View** button on the toolbar to examine the results (Figure 7 - 25).

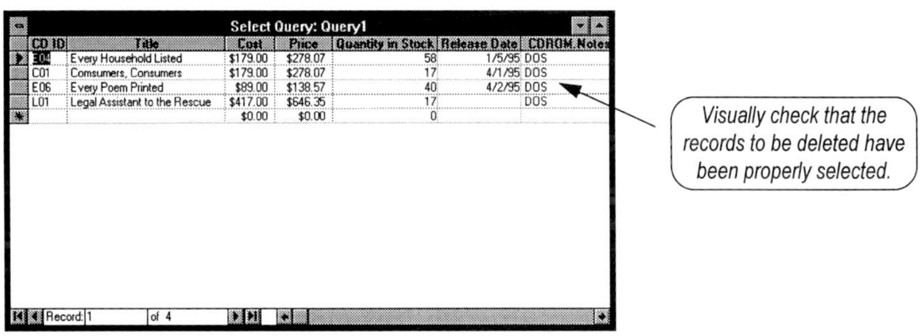

CD ID	Title	Cost	Price	Quantity in Stock	Release Date	CDROM.Notes
E04	Every Household Listed	$179.00	$278.07	58	1/5/95	DOS
C01	Comsumers, Consumers	$179.00	$278.07	17	4/1/95	DOS
E06	Every Poem Printed	$89.00	$138.57	40	4/2/95	DOS
L01	Legal Assistant to the Rescue	$417.00	$646.35	17		DOS
		$0.00	$0.00	0		

Record: 1 of 4

Figure 7 - 25

The four records should all have DOS as their entry in the ***Notes*** *field. These are the records we want to delete.*

10. Return to the design by clicking the **Design View** button on the toolbar.
11. Click the **Delete Query** button on the toolbar to switch the query to a Delete Query (Figure 7 - 26).

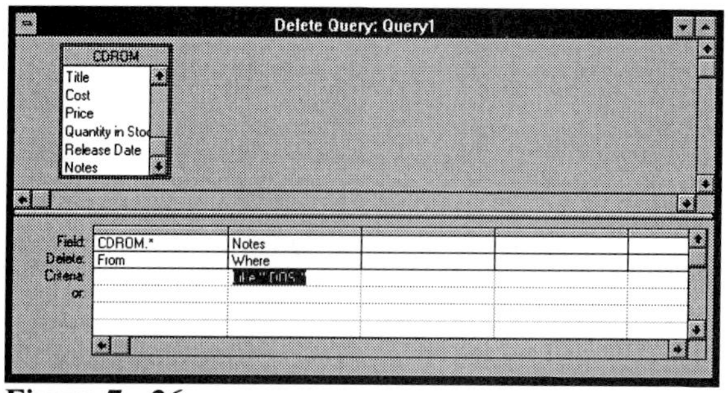

Figure 7 - 26

The ***Delete:*** *line appears in the QBE Grid.* ***From*** *is entered in the first column and* ***Where*** *in all other columns. Read this setup as* ***Delete From CDROM.* Where Notes is Like "*DOS*"****.*

12. Click the **Run** button on the toolbar.

The message ***4 row(s) will be deleted.*** *appears in an alert box (see Figure 7 - 27). You must be certain the correct records are about to be deleted, for, once you click the* ***OK*** *button, there is no way to get the deleted records back. If you are not sure, click the* ***Cancel*** *button and check the criteria again.*

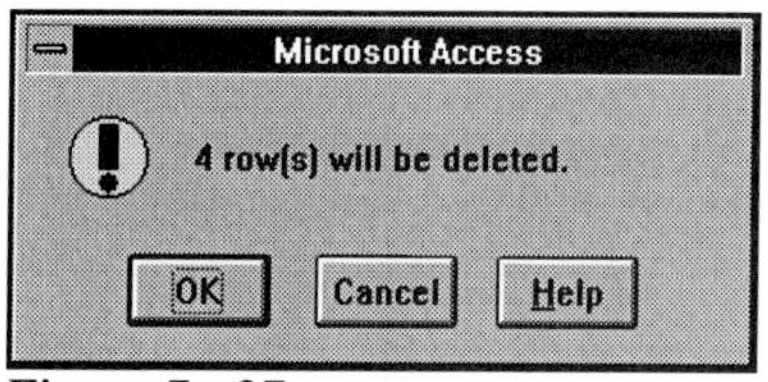

Figure 7 - 27

13. Click **OK** and the records are deleted.
14. Click the **Select Query** button on the toolbar to switch back so we can check the results.
15. Click the **Datasheet View** button on the toolbar to examine the results.

There should be no records listed, as the DOS CDROMs have been deleted.

16. Choose **FILE/Close** to close the query. Click the **No** button when *Access* asks about saving, as the query is no longer of any use and we do not need to save it.

SUMMARY

In this final project you have calculated several results from the CDROM table and updated its data. You calculated the individual inventory values, and later summed those results to calculate the total inventory value for the entire table. You calculated temporarily discounted holiday prices, then permanently discounted the prices 7% by updating the prices in the CDROM table. You calculated average, maximum, and minimum prices, including grouping the CDROMs by type. Finally, you deleted the outdated listings from the CDROM table.

KEY TERMS

Action Query	Delete Query	Grouping
Update Query	Summary Calculation	

INDEPENDENT PROJECTS

Independent Project 7.1: The School Newspaper

This Independent Project continues working with the Newspaper Ad database from Independent Project 6.1. The newspaper's business manager needs the following calculated results:

- The sum of all ads (see Figure 7 - 28). Only the sum of the Prices from the Ads table is needed.
- The sum of the ads grouped by size (see Figure 7 - 29). This needs the Price field and the Size field from the Ads table.
- The average price of an ad sold by each salesperson with their name included rather than their ID number (see Figure 7 - 30). This will require the names from the Sales Force table in addition to the Price from the Ads table.

Additionally, the issue date has been moved up one day to beat the start of exams. Therefore, every entry in the Issue Date field needs to be changed from 5/20/95 to 5/19/95.

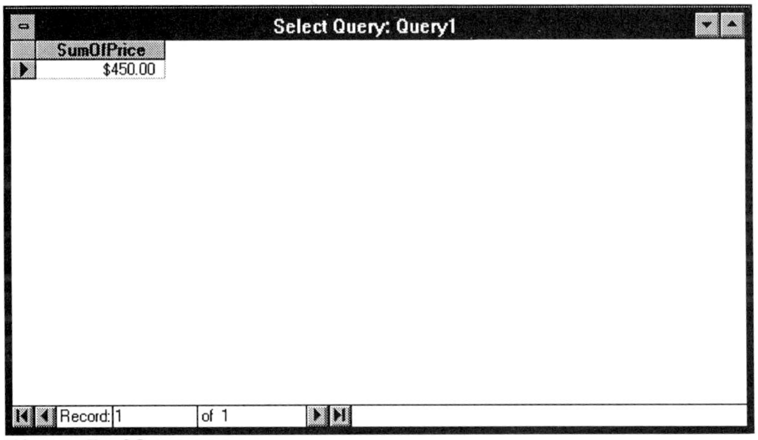

Figure 7 - 28

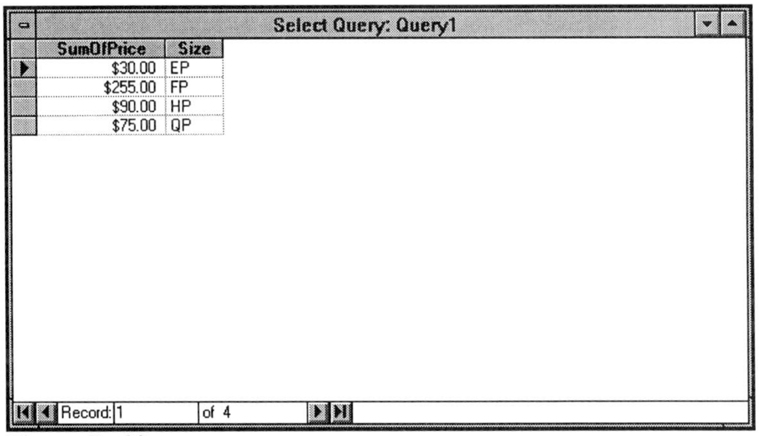

Figure 7 - 29

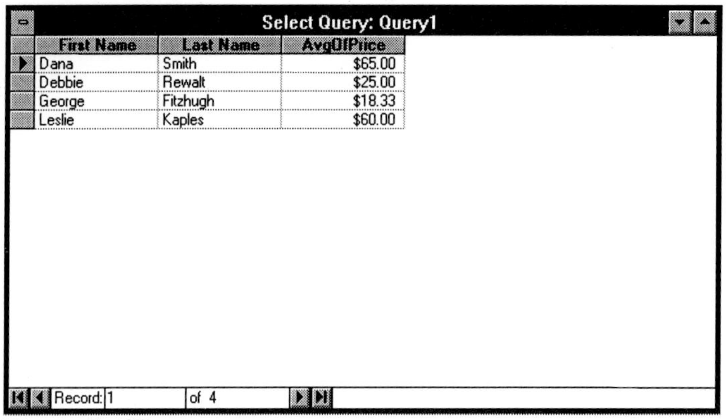

Figure 7 - 30

1. Run *Access* and maximize its window.
2. Open the **xercise1.mdb** database with **FILE/Open Database** or by clicking the **Open Database** tool on the toolbar, then clicking on the name **xercise1.mdb** and clicking the **OK** button.
3. Click on the **Query** button at the left edge of the database window.
4. Click the **New** button to start a new query.
5. Click the **New Query** button in the **New Query** dialog box.
6. Click on the name **Ads** in the list of tables and queries in the **Add Table** dialog box and click the **Add** button.
7. Click **Close** to close the **Add Table** dialog box.
8. Double-click on the name **Price** to place it in the first column of the QBE Grid.
9. Click the **Totals** button on the toolbar to install the **Total**: line.
10. Click on the **Total:** line in the Price column to move to that line.
11. Click the **drop-down arrow** to open the list of summary calculations.
12. Click on **Sum**.
13. Click the **Datasheet View** button on the toolbar to see the resulting sum (see Figure 7 - 28).
14. Print the result by clicking the **Print** button and clicking **OK** in the Print dialog box.
15. Click the **Design View** button to return to the query design.
16. For the second calculation you need only include the **Size** as a grouping field. Therefore, double-click on **Size** in the list of fields to place it in the second column of the QBE Grid. Leave the **Group By** operator alone.
17. Click the **Datasheet View** button on the toolbar to see the resulting sums (see Figure 7 - 29).
18. Print the result by clicking the **Print** button and clicking **OK** in the Print dialog box.
19. Click the **Design View** button to return to the query design.
20. The query for the average price of an ad sold by each salesperson needs the Sales Force table for the names in addition to the Ads table. Click the **Add Table** button on the toolbar or pick **QUERY/Add Table**.
21. Click on **Sales Force** and click the **Add** button to include its field list in the upper section of the query window. Access will link the two tables on Salesperson ID automatically.

22. Click the **Close** button in the **Add Table** dialog box.
23. Pick **EDIT/Clear Grid** to clear the QBE Grid.
24. Double-click on **First Name** in the Sales Force table to install it in the first column of the QBE Grid. Leave **Group By** on the **Total**: line.
25. Double-click on **Last Name** in the Sales Force table to install it in the second column of the QBE Grid. Leave **Group By** on the **Total**: line.
26. Double-click on **Price** in the Ads table to install it in the third column.
27. Click on the **Total:** line in the **Price** column, click the **drop-down arrow** to open the list of summary operators, and pick **Avg**.
28. Click the **Datasheet View** button on the toolbar to see the resulting averages (Figure 7 - 30).
29. Print the result by clicking the **Print** button and clicking **OK** in the Print dialog box.
30. Click the **Design View** button to return to the query design.
31. To prepare for updating the Issue Date, pick **EDIT/Clear Grid** to clear the QBE Grid.
32. Double-click on **Issue Date** in the Ads table to install it in the first column of the QBE Grid.
33. Click the **Totals** button on the toolbar to remove the **Total**: line from the QBE Grid.
34. Click the **Update Query** button on the toolbar or pick **QUERY/Update** to switch the query design to an update query.
35. On the **UpdateTo:** line in the Issue Date column of the QBE Grid type: **5/19/95**
36. Click the **Run** button on the toolbar or pick **QUERY/Run**.
37. In the **10 row(s) will be updated** alert box, click **OK**.
38. Close the query with **FILE/Close**. Click **No** in the **Save changes** alert box.
39. In the database window, click on the **Table** tab, click on **Ads**, and click the **Open** button to open the table.
40. Examine the Issue Date field. It should contain 5/19/95 in every record.
41. Close the table with **FILE/Close**.
42. Close the database with **FILE/Close Database**.
43. If you need to exit from *Access* and/or Windows, do so properly.

Independent Project 7.2: The Book Store

This Independent Project continues working with the Books database from the earlier lessons. The owner needs the following calculated results:

- The profit margin of each book. The Profit Margin is calculated as (Price - Cost)/Cost. The Title, Cost, and Price fields should be included as well (see Figure 7 - 31).
- The total inventory value (the Sum of Cost * Quantity in Stock) of all of the books (see Figure 7 - 32).
- The average price of the books from each publisher (see Figure 7 - 33). This needs the Name field from the Publishers table and the Price field from the Books table.

Additionally, the owner has decided not to deal with Atlantic Works (AW30) any further, so any of their books should be deleted from the Books table.

	Title	Cost	Price	Profit Margin
▶	Art Through Life	$13.50	$22.95	70.00%
	Calculus	$25.40	$42.95	69.09%
	Chemical Compendium	$34.50	$49.95	44.78%
	Economically Correct	$19.95	$32.95	65.16%
	Even More Poems	$12.60	$21.00	66.67%
	Look Up In The Sky	$17.00	$28.95	70.29%
	Modern Russian	$17.00	$28.50	67.65%
	Music Composition	$19.50	$32.95	68.97%
	Music Harmony	$19.50	$32.95	68.97%
	The Physics of Glass	$4.75	$7.95	67.37%
	Philosophize With Me	$18.50	$30.95	67.30%
	World of History	$20.95	$34.95	66.83%
*		$0.00	$0.00	

Figure 7 - 31

	Inventory Value
▶	$15,222.00

Figure 7 - 32

	Name	AvgOfPrice
▶	Atlantic Works	$32.95
	Books Plus	$14.48
	Bulky Books	$49.95
	College Editions	$32.13
	Texts and Tomes	$31.45

Figure 7 - 33

1. Run *Access* and maximize its window.
2. Open the **xercise2.mdb** database with **FILE/Open Database** or by clicking the **Open Database** tool on the toolbar, then clicking on the name **xercise2.mdb** and clicking the **OK** button.
3. Click on the **Query** button at the left edge of the database window.
4. Click the **New** button to start a new query.
5. Click the **New Query** button in the **New Query** dialog box.
6. Click on the name **Books** in the list of tables and queries in the Add Table dialog box and click the **Add** button.
7. Click **Close** to close the Add Table dialog box.
8. Double-click on the name **Title** to place it in the first column of the QBE Grid.
9. Similarly, double-click on **Cost** and **Price**.
10. Click on the **Field:** line in the fourth column and type: **Profit Margin:([Price]-[Cost])/[Cost]**
11. Press the **down arrow**, then double-click on the right edge of the **selector** to get a Best Fit for the column so you can see the entire calculation.
12. Click the **Datasheet View** button on the toolbar to see the results.
13. While the calculations were successful, the resulting values are a jumble of decimal places. To begin formatting the results, click the **Design View** button to return to the query design.
14. Click anywhere within the calculation on the Field: line in the fourth column.
15. Click the **Properties** button on the toolbar.
16. Click on the **Format** line in the properties list and click the **drop-down arrow** that appears.

17. Click on **Percent**, then close the Field Properties list by clicking the **Properties** button on the toolbar again.
18. Click the **Datasheet View** button on the toolbar to see the results (see Figure 7 - 31).
19. Print the result by clicking the **Print** button and clicking **OK** in the Print dialog box.
20. Click the **Design View** button to return to the query design.
21. Save this query by picking **FILE/Save As** and typing the name **Profit Margin**. Click the **OK** button.
22. Clear the QBE Grid with **EDIT/Clear Grid**.
23. For the inventory value calculation you need only to enter the calculation and switch to a Totals query. To begin, press **HOME**.
24. Enter: **Inventory Value:[Cost] * [Quantity in Stock]**
25. Press the **down arrow**, then double-click on the right edge of the **selector** to get a Best Fit for the column so you can see the entire calculation.
26. Click the **Totals** button on the toolbar.
27. Click on the **Total:** line in the column with the calculation, click on the **drop-down arrow** to open the list of operators, and choose **Sum**.
28. Click the **Datasheet View** button on the toolbar to see the resulting sum (see Figure 7 - 32).
29. Print the result by clicking the **Print** button and clicking **OK** in the Print dialog box.
30. Click the **Design View** button to return to the query design.
31. Save this query by picking **FILE/Save As** and typing the name **Inventory Value**. Click the **OK** button.
32. Clear the QBE Grid with **EDIT/Clear Grid**.
33. To begin the third query for the average price of a book for each publisher, click the **Add Table** button on the toolbar or pick **QUERY/Add Table**.
34. Click on **Publishers** and click the **Add** button to include its field list in the upper section of the query window. Access will link the two tables on Publisher Code automatically.
35. Click the **Close** button in the Add Table dialog box.
36. Double-click on **Name** in the Publishers table to install it in the first column of the QBE Grid. Leave **Group By** on the Total: line.
37. Double-click on **Price** in the Books table to install it in the second column of the QBE Grid.
38. Click on the **Total:** line in the **Price** column, click the **drop-down arrow** to open the list of summary operators, and pick **Avg**.
39. Click the **Datasheet View** button on the toolbar to see the resulting averages (see Figure 7 - 33).
40. Print the result by clicking the **Print** button and clicking **OK** in the Print dialog box.
41. Click the **Design View** button to return to the query design. You do not need to save this query.
42. To prepare for deleting the books from Atlantic Works, pick **EDIT/Clear Grid** to clear the QBE Grid.
43. Click on the **Totals** button on the toolbar to remove the Total: line.
44. Press **HOME** to jump to the first column.

45. Scroll to the top of the list of fields in the Books list and double-click on the * to install it into the QBE Grid. The first column will contain the entry **Books.*** which is required for a delete query.
46. Double-click on **Publisher Code** and **Name** in the Publishers table to include those fields in the QBE Grid.
47. Click the **Datasheet View** button on the toolbar, then press the **END** key to see the names of the publishers and their code numbers. Notice that Atlantic Works is code AW30.
48. Click the **Design View** button to return to the query design.
49. Click on the **Criteria:** line in the **Publisher Code** column of the QBE Grid.
50. Type **"AW30"** making sure the final character is a zero.
51. Click the **Datasheet View** button on the toolbar to check that only Atlantic Works is being selected. Two books, Music Composition and Music Harmony, should be listed.
52. Click the **Design View** button to return to the query design.
53. Click the **Delete Query** button on the toolbar or pick **QUERY/Delete** from the menu to convert the query to a delete query. The Books.* line should say **From** on the Delete: line, and Publisher Code and Name should have **Where** on the Delete: line.
54. Click the **Run** button on the toolbar or pick **QUERY/Run**.
55. In the **2 row(s) will be deleted** alert box, click **OK**.
56. Click the **Select Query** button on the toolbar or pick **QUERY/Select** from the menu to switch the query back to a select query.
57. Delete the **"AW30"** from the Criteria: line in the Publisher Code column.
58. Click the **Datasheet View** button on the toolbar to review the remaining books. Press the **END** key and Atlantic Works should not be listed.
59. Close the query with **FILE/Close**. Click **No** in the **Save changes** alert box.
60. Close the database with **FILE/Close Database**.
61. If you need to exit from *Access* and/or Windows, do so properly.

Independent Project 7.3: The Real Estate Office

This Independent Project continues working with the Real Estate Office database from the earlier lessons. The manager needs the following calculated results:

- The price per square foot of each commercial listing that is for Rent. The Price per square foot is calculated as Price/Size. Code, Address, City, Size, Floor, and Purchase or Rent should be included as well (see Figure 7 - 34).
- The average price per square foot of the commercial listings grouped by whether they are for Purchase or Rent (see Figure 7 - 35).
- The earliest and latest dates available for the properties in Commercial Listings (Figure 7 - 36) grouped by agency name and whether they are for purchase or rent. This should include the Agency Name from the Agency table and the Purchase or Rent and date Available fields from the Commercial Listings table.

Additionally, all of the listings for Research Park, Stamford have been given to the Right Properties agency (RP12). The listings in Commercial Properties need to be updated.

Code	Address	City	Size	Floor	Purc	Price per Sq Ft
ES52	5 Elm St.	Greenwich	4800	1	R	$15.00
LW17	1 Lewis Way	Danbury	12000	2	R	$10.42
GP25	12 Gedney Place	Danbury	8900	3	R	$11.80
RR19	952 River Rd.	Stamford	3750	6	R	$13.07
FA28	18 Frost Ave.	Greenwich	3700	2	R	$14.05
*			0	0		

Figure 7 - 34

Purc	Price per Sq Ft
P	$212.70
R	$12.87

Figure 7 - 35

Agency Name	Purchase or Rent	MinOfAvailable	MaxOfAvailable
George Winkle	P	6/1/95	6/1/95
Priceless Properties	P	5/15/95	6/1/95
Profitable Properties	R	7/1/95	9/1/95
Regal Real Estate	R	8/1/95	8/1/95
Right Properties	P	8/1/95	10/1/95
Smith and Cross	R	6/1/95	7/15/95

Figure 7 - 36

1. Run *Access* and maximize its window.
2. Open the **xercise3.mdb** database.
3. Open a new query.
4. Add **Commercial Listings** and close the Add Table dialog box.
5. Install the **Code**, **Address**, **City**, **Size**, **Floor**, and **Purchase or Rent** fields into the QBE Grid.
6. On the Field: line in the seventh column type: **Price per Sq Ft:[Price]/[Size]**
7. Format this calculation for **Currency** in the Properties List.
8. Enter the criterion for Rent (**"R"**) in the Purchase or Rent column.
9. Click the **Datasheet View** button on the toolbar to see the results (see Figure 7 - 34).
10. Print the result.
11. Return to the query design.
12. Save this query as **Price per Sq Ft**.
13. To begin the grouping by Purchase or Rent, move to the first column of the QBE Grid.
14. Remove the **Code**, **Address**, **City**, **Size**, and **Floor** fields.
15. Remove the criterion in the Purchase or Rent column.
16. Switch the query to a **Totals** query.
17. Make the **Price per Sq Ft** field an Average.
18. View the resulting averages (see Figure 7 - 35).
19. Print the result.
20. Return to the query design.
21. Use **FILE/Save As** to save this query as **P or R Price per Sq Ft**.
22. Clear the QBE Grid to get ready for the third query.
23. Add the **Agencies** table to the top of the query window. *Access* should create the link on Agency Code automatically.
24. Add the **Agency Name**, **Purchase or Rent**, and **Available** fields to the QBE Grid.

25. On the Total: row open the drop-down list of operators and switch **Available** to **Min**. Leave **Group By** for the other two columns.
26. Double-click on **Available** again to install a second copy of that field in the next column of the QBE Grid, and from the list of operators on the Total: line pick **Max**.
27. View the result (see Figure 7 - 36).
28. Print the result.
29. Return to the query design.
30. Use **FILE/Save As** to save this query as **Agency First and Last Dates**.
31. To prepare for updating the agency for the Research Park properties, clear the QBE Grid.
32. Remove the **Agencies** table by clicking on the gray selector that names the table at the top of the list of fields in the top section of the query window and pressing the **DELETE** key. (This was not required, but keeps the workspace tidier.)
33. Remove the **Total:** line by clicking the **Totals** button on the toolbar.
34. Add **Address** to the QBE Grid.
35. Enter: **like "*Research Park*"** on the Criteria: line.
36. Add **Agency Code** to the QBE Grid.
37. View the result to check it for accuracy. There should be four listings.
38. Return to the query design.
39. Switch the query to an **Update Query**.
40. On the **UpdateTo:** line in the Agency Code column type: **RP12**
41. Run the query with the run button.
42. In the **4 row(s) will be updated** alert box, click **OK**.
43. Switch the query back to a Select Query.
44. View the result. All four listings should now have RP12 for the Agency Code.
45. Close the query without saving.
46. Close the database.
47. If you need to exit from *Access* and/or Windows, do so properly.

Independent Project 7.4: The Veterinarian

This Independent Project continues working with the veterinarian database from the earlier lessons. She needs the following calculated results. Create and save each query (except you should not save the delete query), then print each dynaset.

- The average weight of each type of animal.
- The age of the cats. Age is calculated as **(#today's date#-date of birth)/365**. Substitute the current date for the words "today's date". Note that you must type the pound signs around the current date. Also, the parentheses are mandatory. Include the pet name, type of animal, date of birth, and age.
- The count of how many of each type of pet belongs to each owner. This will need both tables.

Additionally, Paula Smith has moved to another region of the country. Her pet's listings should be deleted from the table with a delete query.

Appendix: Features Reference

The following table contains a summary of the main features presented in the lessons. As you know, most features in *Access* can be performed in a variety of ways. Many of the menu bar commands can also be selected from The Quick Menus. Listed mouse shortcuts involve the use of the buttons on the Standard and Formatting Toolbars and other mouse techniques. Shortcut keys are keystrokes of function keys. Many features require that the text be selected prior to executing the command. If you need more detail on using these features, the table contains a reference to the lesson describing its use.

Features	Mouse Shortcut	Menu Bar Commands	Shortcut Keys	Lessons
Exit Access	Double-click Application Control Menu	FILE/Exit	ALT+F4	I
Run Access	Double-click Access icon		ENTER when name is highlighted	I
Open a database	Click Open Database toolbar button	FILE/Open Database	CTRL+O	I
Close a database	Double-click Document Control Menu	FILE/Close Database	CTRL+F4	I
Open a table	Double-click table name or click Opne button in database window when name is highlighted		ENTER when name is highlighted	I
Close a table	Double-click Document Control Menu	FILE/Close	CTRL+F4	I
Help	Click Help button on toolbar, then click on object	HELP/Contents or HELP/Search	F1 or SHIFT-F1	I
Create a new database	Click New Database toolbar button	FILE/New Database	CTRL-N	1
Create a new table	Click New button in database window while Table tab is active	FILE/New/Table		1
Switch panes	Click in the other pane		F6	1
Move to next field	Click in next field		TAB	1
Save a design	Click Save button on toolbar	FILE/Save	CTRL-S	1
Close a design window	Double-click Document Control Menu	FILE/Close	CTRL+F4	1
Move to previous field	Click in previous field		SHIFT+TAB	2
Print	Click Print button on toolbar	FILE/Print	CTRL+P	1

Features	Mouse Shortcut	Menu Bar Commands	Shortcut Keys	Lessons
Modify a table's structure	Click Design View button on toolbar when table is open	VIEW/Table Design		
Primary Key	Click Set Primary Key button on toolbar	EDIT/Set Primary Key		1
Move to next record	Click Next Record Navigation Button	RECORDS/Go To/ Next	DOWN ARROW	2
Move to previous record	Click Previous Record Navigation Button	RECORDS/Go To/ Previous	UP ARROW	2
Move to first record	Click Next Record Navigation Button	RECORDS/Go To/ First	CTRL+UP ARROW	
Move to last record	Click Next Record Navigation Button	RECORDS/Go To/ Last	CTRL+DOWN ARROW	
Move to first field	Use scroll bar, then click in field		HOME	2
Move to last field	Use scroll bar, then click in field		END	2
Size a field	Drag right edge of Field Selector box	FORMAT/Column Width		2
Best Fit a field	Double-click right edge of Field Selector box	FORMAT/Cclumn Width/Best Fit		2
Move a field	Click on Field Selector, then drag to new position			2
Edit Mode	Click mouse in field		F2	2
Replace Mode	Double-click mouse in field		F2	2
Search	Click Find button on toolbar	EDIT/Find	F7 or CTRL-F	2
Delete a record	Click Cut button on toolbar when record is selected	EDIT/Delete when record is selected	DELETE when record is selected	2
Select a record	Click on Record Selector box	EDIT/Select Record	SHIFT+SPACEBAR	2
Import a table	Click Import button on toolbar	FILE/Import		3
Attach a table	Click Attach Table button on toolbar	FILE/Attach Table		3
Rename a table		FILE/Rename when highlight is on table name		3
Create a form	Click New button in database window when Form tab is selected	FILE/New/Form		3
Create a query	Click New button in database window when Form tab is selected	FILE/New/Query		4
Include a field in QBE Grid	Double-click field name or click and drag name to QBE Grid		type name on Field: line	4